LITTLE-KNOWN STORIES

ABOUT THE

DOCTRINE & COVENANTS

DAN BARKER

CFI
AN IMPRINT OF CEDAR FORT, INC.
SPRINGVILLE, UTAH

ISBN 13: 978-1-4621-1054-4

Published by CFI, an imprint of Cedar Fort, Inc., 2373 W. 700 S., Springville, UT 84663
Distributed by Cedar Fort, Inc., www.cedarfort.com

LIBRARY OF CONGRESS CATALOGING-IN-PUBLICATION DATA

Barker, Dan, 1958- author.
 Little-known stories about The Doctrine and Covenants / Dan Barker.
   pages cm
 ISBN 978-1-4621-1054-4 (alk. paper)
 1. Doctrine and Covenants--History. 2. Church of Jesus Christ of Latter-day Saints--History--19th century. 3. Mormon Church--History--19th century. I. Title.

 BX8628.B39 2012
 289.3'2--dc23

                              2012033421

Cover design by Rebecca J. Greenwood
Cover design © 2012 by Lyle Mortimer
Edited and typeset by Melissa J. Caldwell

Printed in the United States of America

10 9 8 7 6 5 4 3 2 1

CONTENTS

PREFACE

John Whitmer

The book of scripture known to the general Church population as the Doctrine and Covenants is extremely vital in explaining who we are and why we do the things we do as members of the Church. It's the Lord's communication to his prophets outlining the role, functions, and procedures of priesthood and Church government.

Similar to the doctrines, its history is equally impelling. Essentially, it's the story of John Whitmer, the second Church historian, meticulously recording the revelations as received by the Prophet Joseph Smith from the Lord and collecting those revelations that predate his call as scribe to the Prophet (those revelations given prior to the fall of 1830) into the *Book of Commandments and Revelations,* known to most as *Revelation Book 1.* The story begins with the conference of elders held at Hiram, Ohio, at the John Johnson farm, on November 1–3, 1831. There the elders enthusiastically voted to publish ten thousand copies of the revelations into what was to become the Book of Commandments. It's a story of John Whitmer and Oliver Cowdery's journey of nine hundred miles, one month's travel on foot from Kirtland, Ohio, to Independence, Missouri, in 1832 to the Church printing establishment of W. W. Phelps, where they began the laborious, yet exciting, work of placing in book form the revelations of the Lord to the Church membership. The story takes a bizarre twist when mobs raged during July 1833, destroying both the home and the press of W. W. Phelps. Revelations were dumped into the street as if they were trash. Courageously, Mary and Caroline Rollins (fifteen and thirteen years old) saved what they could (essentially the first sixty-four sections of our current Doctrine and Covenants.

The Book of Commandments would live on into what would eventually become the Doctrine and Covenants. Fortunately, W. W. Phelps published some of the revelations from *Revelation Book 1* into the Church's first newspaper, *The Evening and Morning Star*. The culmination of the Book of Commandments, *The Evening and Morning Star, Revelation Book 1*, and *Revelation Book 2* formed the material included in the first edition (1835) of the Doctrine and Covenants. (While *Revelation Book 1* was in Missouri, a second book was purchased, and approximately fifty more revelations were recorded from early 1832 to late 1834. Frederick G. Williams was the main scribe, but Orson Hyde, Oliver Cowdery, and Joseph Smith also acted as recorders). This first edition isn't the Doctrine and Covenants as we know it today (the 1981 edition). Nonetheless, the 1835 edition of the Doctrine and Covenants did include 95 of the 103 sections published from what would have been the Book of Commandments (http://text.farmsresearch.com/publications /jbms/?vol=18&num=2&id=500).

Other editions of the Doctrine and Covenants are the 1833 Book of Commandments; 1835 Doctrine and Covenants; 1844 Nauvoo edition; 1845 Liverpool, England, edition; 1876; 1879; 1921; 1981. The first foreign language edition was the 1851 Welsh edition.

I want the reader to understand that this is not a commentary (trust me—I'm not that bright or enlightened to produce such a work). *Little Known Stories about the Doctrine and Covenants* is a compilation of the behind-the-scene stories. I realize that each section is made up of numerous stories that helped shaped the situation or the reason the Lord provided the inspired instruction. I will present a *very* abbreviated history of each section, a story which in most cases aids in explaining the situation surrounding the event, and, finally, a fact that has a wow factor to it. (Not unless, of course, you're a Church history buff, employed by the Church History Department, or a BYU Church history professor). As a twist, I've included a question in each section to test your knowledge and to have a little fun. (If you see me on the street and you punch me, I'll understand). The questions are answered at the end of the book and, in most cases, give additional information in relation to the section.

Authorship is not mine alone to claim, I had plenty of help along the way. I want to thank the people at Cedar Fort for their hard work. (My grades in English class pretty much say it all. Trust me, there was plenty of room for improvement.) To Jennifer Fielding, the acquisitions editor at Cedar Fort, for encouraging me to submit an idea for the Doctrine and Covenants gospel study year in 2013. This book is the fruition of that idea. This book and, for that matter, the previous two books I've compiled, never would have materialized without the fact that "I was born of goodly parents." I have my parents and siblings to thank for keeping me "on the straight and narrow path." Finally, I'd like to thank Kate. She accepted responsibility thirty-one years ago in the Canada Alberta Temple to make sure I continued to behave. I appreciate her for this and her genealogical skills, plus volunteering with some of the research for this book. I came to a dead end while working on section 47—I have Kate to thank that there is even a section 47 included in this book.

THANK YOU ALL!

SECTION 1

BRIEF HISTORICAL BACKGROUND: At a break in the conference of elders held in Hiram, Ohio, on November 1, 1831, Joseph Smith received this revelation. The elders voted to combine the revelations into a Book of Commandments

THE STORY: John Hancock, the president of the Second Continental Congress, will be remembered into the eternities for his flamboyant signature on the Declaration of Independence. Why was it so large and obvious? It's been said that Hancock wanted King George to be able to read the signature without spectacles.

Mr. Hancock can insinuate all he wants about the king's eyesight; however, I think the size of his signature runs far deeper than the possibility of the King of England misplacing his glasses and overlooking Hancock's surname. I seriously believe the reason John Hancock signed the way he did was due to his passion and conviction to the truth of the Declaration of Independence.

Little did John Hancock foresee when he signed the Declaration that in a little more than fifty years, one of his descendants would also be attaching his name to the truthfulness and validity on another inspired document: the Book of Commandments.

As the conference convened at Hiram, Ohio, the ten elders present determined that the revelations the Prophet Joseph had received should be published into a book titled the Book of Commandments. And the Lord commanded it to be so as he revealed to the Prophet during a recess in the conference these words as stated in verse 6, "Behold, this is mine authority, and the authority of my servants,

1

and my preface unto the book of my commandments, which I have given them to publish unto you, O inhabitants of the earth."

Joseph required volunteers to step forward and bind their names to a statement he drafted concerning the legitimacy and truthfulness of the revelations. Five of the elders signed; however, four other elders in attendance—Oliver Cowdery, David Whitmer, John Whitmer, and Peter Whitmer Jr.—had already linked their names to the Book of Mormon as witnesses, and therefore they did not sign the Book of Commandment statement.

The revelations were compiled and circulated so additional names could be gathered as witnesses in the Kirtland, Ohio, and Jackson County, Missouri, areas. One elder who affixed his signature to the truth of the Book of Commandments was Levi Hancock. Levi didn't go overboard like his ancestor, John Hancock; nevertheless, there's something compelling about Levi's signature. He's the only one of the eighteen witnesses who autographed his name in pencil. Realizing this, he jotted the following after his name, "Never to be erased." Although Levi's signature blended with the other seventeen signatures, these four simple words highlighted his, creating a bolding effect similar to his ancestor, John Hancock.

http://www.deseretnews.com/article/705379193/
Lost-Book-of-Commandments-witnesses-found.html

THE FACT: The following is the testimony and the signatures of those witnesses who placed their names in the Book of Commandments:

> We, the undersigners, feel willing to bear testimony to all the world of mankind, to every creature upon the face of all the Earth and upon the islands of the sea, that God hath borne record to our souls, through the Holy Ghost shed forth upon us, that these commandments are given by inspiration of God and are profitable for all men and are verily true.
>
> We give this testimony unto the world, the Lord being our helper;
>
> And it is through the grace of God, the Father, and his son, Jesus Christ, that we are permitted to have this privilege of bearing this testimony unto the world, in the which we rejoice exceedingly,

praying the Lord always, that the children of men may be profited thereby. Amen."

Sidney Rigdon, Orson Hyde, Wm. E. McLellin, Luke Johnson, Lyman Johnson, Reynolds Cahoon, John Corrill, Parley Pratt, Harvey Whitlock, Lyman Wight, John Murdock, Calvin Beebe, Zebedee Coltrin, Joshua Fairchild, Peter Dustin, Newel Knight, **Levi Hancock; never to be erased**, Thomas B. Marsh

http://www.deseretnews.com/article/705379193/
Lost-Book-of-Commandments-witnesses-found.html

QUESTION:

1.   Who is Levi Hancock?
     a. One of a number of bodyguards to the Prophet Joseph Smith (Mormon tough guy)
     b. General Authority
     c. Spiritual leader to the Mormon Battalion
     d. All of the above

SECTION 2

BRIEF HISTORICAL BACKGROUND: On the evening of September 21, 1823, in his family home at Manchester, New York, Joseph received an appearance and communication from the angel Moroni.

THE STORY: It's been stated "the best things come in small packages." If this really is the case, and I believe it is, then this section with all three of its verses provides us with a wealth of knowledge and understanding on the role of Elijah the prophet.

This revelation was received twelve years prior to the actual visitation of Elijah in the Kirtland Temple. Edersheim in his work *The Temple* says:

> To this day, in every Jewish home, at a certain part of the Paschal service [i.e., when they drink the "third cup"]—the door is opened to admit Elijah the prophet as forerunner of the Messiah, while appropriate passages are at the same time read which foretell the destruction of all heathen nations. It is a remarkable coincidence that, in instituting his own Supper, the Lord Jesus connected the symbol, not of judgment, but of his dying love, with his "third cup."
>
> http://books.google.com/books?id=LHT6a0E909QC&lpg=PA177&ots=0ux8b
> ScCSf&dq=edersheim-passover&pg=PA177#v=onepage&q&f=false

Some may refer to it as coincidence or sheer irony that Elijah appeared in the Kirtland Temple on April 3, 1836. April 3 of that year also coincided with the third day of the Paschal feast, the day that the Jews opened their homes to invite Elijah. Little did they realize that he did appear, not in their homes, but in the Kirtland Temple.

> http://byustudies.byu.edu/PDFLibrary/23.4RicksAppearance
> -0b45aa1d-d798-495f-a063-6afe95da6fdc.pdf

THE FACT: As interesting as the above story is, the significance of the situation is enhanced when one discovers the actual time of day that Elijah appeared to Joseph Smith and Oliver Cowdery was also the very hour of the day, in their time zone, that Jewish families were preparing to begin the feast of the Passover.

> http://byustudies.byu.edu/PDFLibrary/23.4RicksAppearance
> -0b45aa1d-d798-495f-a063-6afe95da6fdc.pdf

QUESTION:

2. In what year did section 2 first appear in the Doctrine and Covenants?

    a. The 1921 edition
    b. The 1835 edition
    c. In 1876
    d. In the 1833 Book of Commandments

SECTION 3

BRIEF HISTORICAL BACKGROUND: During July 1828, Joseph received revelation at Harmony, Pennsylvania, in connection to the lost 116 pages of manuscript translated from the Book of Mormon.

THE STORY: As members we're well versed with the story of Martin Harris losing the 116 pages of the Book of Mormon translation. It's common knowledge that Martin was instructed by the Prophet to show the manuscript to only a select few individuals, two of which were Martin's wife, Lucy, and her sister, Polly Cobbs. Many believe Lucy Harris is responsible for the theft of the manuscript due to the antagonism she felt toward Joseph Smith and his wanting to "defraud" her husband out of his money to pay for the publishing cost of the Book of Mormon. Because of these feelings, Lucy hauled Joseph before a magistrate in Lyons, New York. A number of witnesses were called to the stand to prove Lucy's certainty that young Joseph Smith was only interested in her husband's money, nothing more. One witness stated that Joseph Smith really didn't have gold plates, but rather the box he housed them in was empty. Others stated the box was filled with sand or lead and was part of his demented ploy to fool Mr. Harris. It was Martin's testimony that relieved Joseph Smith of the false claims laid against him. Martin states the following:

> I can swear that Joseph Smith has never got one dollar from me by persuasion. . . . I have never seen in Joseph Smith, a disposition to take any man's money without giving him a reasonable compensation in return.

At the conclusion of Martin's testimony, the Judge instructed those in attendance to keep such ridiculous matters out of his court room and then closed court, allowing Joseph to walk free.

Lucy Harris's feelings toward the Prophet and the work was

actually positive early in the translation of the Book of Mormon, showing a complete interest in the project.

The question might be asked, who was the first monetary donor toward the cause of the Book of Mormon translation? Most would answer Martin Harris; however, another came forward with money before Martin did. While Lucy Mack Smith visited with both Lucy Harris and Polly Cobbs, she shared the story of the gold plates and how it was that her young Joseph had them in his possession. Enthralled by the story, and obviously believing the mother of the prophet, both Lucy Harris and Polly offer money to help in the translation of the record. When Lucy Mack turned down the offer, Lucy Harris visited Joseph Smith, again with the offer of a money donation. Joseph only succeeded in gaining Lucy Harris's displeasure when he stated: "I always prefer dealing with men rather than their wives." With such a statement, most would turn and walk away; nevertheless, after claiming to see a dream of the gold plates, Lucy Harris returned to Joseph and again offered him money. This time, not refusing, Joseph accepted her gift of twenty-eight dollars, money that had been given to her as an inheritance at the passing of her mother.

http://maxwellinstitute.byu.edu/publications/jbms/?vol=14&num=2&id=373

THE FACT: After the loss of the 116 pages, finger-pointing ensued. Lucy Mack Smith placed the blame on not only Lucy Harris but also on Martin. Lucy Harris vehemently denied the accusations. What's fascinating is Joseph Smith's attitude during this black time in his life. He could have been caught up in the same spirit of allegation and accusation, but rather, if there was to be finger-pointing, he pointed the finger at himself, realizing that the loss was a direct "consequence of my having wearied the Lord in asking for the privilege of letting Martin Harris take the writings." The Lord solidified Joseph's grief when he stated: "And when thou deliveredst up that which God had given thee sight and power to translate, thou deliveredst up that which was sacred into the hands of a wicked man" (Doctrine and Covenants 3:12; 10:1, 7). Martin had "set at naught the counsels of God, and [had] broken the most sacred promises which were made before God, and [had] depended upon his own judgment and boasted in his own wisdom" (D&C 3:13).

http://maxwellinstitute.byu.edu/publications/jbms/?vol=14&num=2&id=373

QUESTION:

3.   While in the Grandin printing shop, when the first sixteen pages of the Book of Mormon were pulled off the press, which future original member of the Quorum of the Twelve Apostles did Martin Harris meet?

   a. Sidney Rigdon
   b. Brigham Young
   c. Thomas B. Marsh
   d. George A. Smith

SECTION 4

BRIEF HISTORICAL BACKGROUND: Joseph Smith received the following revelation for his father, while his father visited him at Harmony, Pennsylvania, in February of 1829.

THE STORY: The father of the Prophet, Joseph Smith Sr., was anxious to know what the Lord would have him do to help the cause of the kingdom. Many members approached the prophet with this same request. The Lord didn't disappoint the senior Smith making clear to him that he was to open his mouth and share the gospel. The following story illustrates how seriously Joseph Smith Sr. obeyed the Lord's counsel.

   In the fall of 1830 a man came to the Smith home in Manchester,

New York, and demanded payment on a fourteen-dollar debt. The man was quick to point out that he would forgive the debt if Joseph Smith Sr. would renounce his religion and burn all the copies of the Book of Mormon in their home. Joseph Sr. refused, leading to his arrest and confinement in the Canandaigua jail. While in jail he recorded these feelings:

> I shuddered when I first heard these heavy doors creaking upon their hinges; but then I thought to myself, I was not the first man who had been imprisoned for the truth's sake; and when I should meet Paul in the paradise of God, I could tell him that I, too, had been in bonds for the Gospel which he had preached. And this has been my only consolation.

Lucy Mack Smith, History of Joseph Smith by His Mother
(Salt Lake City: Bookcraft, 1979), 185

Joseph Sr. was imprisoned for thirty days. Remembering the Lord's instructions, he taught the gospel to his fellow prisoners and, upon his release, baptized them into the Church.

Kelly, Brian and Petrea, Illustrated History of The Church
(American Fork, Utah: Covenant Communications, 2008), 68

THE FACT: As a young missionary called to serve in the Massachusetts Boston Mission, I can recall well standing in the old mission home across the street from the Church Office Building in Salt Lake City with two to three hundred other elders reciting in unison section 4 of the Doctrine and Covenants. It was powerful and left a lasting impression that has never diminished over the years. If the field is truly "white for the harvest," as the Lord stated, then it would seem reasonable to expect that Church growth since 1830 would reflect this.

From the Church's initial inception of six members in 1830, it took 117 years (until 1947) to reach the one million mark. The two million member mark was surpassed in 1963, in a short span of sixteen years. Then in 1971, eight years after the two million mark, Church membership had grown to three million Latter-day Saints. Currently, Church growth adds an additional million members every three years. The present population of the Church stands at about 14 million.

http://newsroom.lds.org/topic/church-growth

QUESTION:

4. In what year was the greatest percent growth in Church membership?

    a. 1830
    b. 1996
    c. 2010
    d. 1857

SECTION 5

BRIEF HISTORICAL BACKGROUND: Martin Harris had humbly repented for losing the 116 pages of manuscript and desired to physically see the plates. Joseph Smith received revelation from the Lord in March 1829, at Harmony, Pennsylvania, informing Martin, that if humble and faithful, his desire would be realized.

THE STORY: Martin did see the plates and remained true to his testimony as first recorded in the back of the original copies of the Book of Mormon. It's true that Martin did leave the Church for a time. Nevertheless, he was never forgotten by the leaders of the Church as the following story depicts.

In 1869, an Elder Stephenson was called on a mission to the Eastern States. On his way, he stopped in Kirtland to visit with Martin Harris. It was on this visit that he gave Martin Harris the idea to migrate to Salt Lake City and surround himself with the Saints. At first opposed to the suggestion, Martin Harris eventually wrote Brigham Young in 1870 in favor of the move west. Elder Stephenson accompanied Martin Harris on the train trip west and then relates a time when he, Martin Harris, President George A. Smith, and John Henry Smith were riding in a carriage to enjoy a bath at the warm springs in the vicinity of Salt Lake City. As the group came to a rise in the landscape, they stopped and looked down on the city spreading out below them. It was here that Martin could get a view of the temple lot with the temple still under construction and the immense Tabernacle. After enjoying the vista for a moment, Martin exclaimed, "Who would have thought that the Book of Mormon would have done all this?"

On occasion, while attending baptisms and noting the number of individuals in attendance, Martin Harris, with an uplifted heart, would cry out, "Just see how the Book of Mormon is spreading!"

Martin Harris passed away July 10, 1875, in Clarkston, Cache County, Utah. Previous to his passing that July afternoon, he held a Book of Mormon in his hands and bore testimony to those present surrounding his bed. He had seen the angel, he had seen the plates turned leaf by leaf before his eyes, and he knew what he had seen and never denied it to his dying breath. A story tells that just a few hours before his passing, Bishop Simon Smith entered his room and broke the news to Martin, "It's just been announced, the Book of Mormon will be translated into Spanish!" Martin was so energized by the news that the bishop noted Martin's voice had strength and a vigor not seen since prior to Martin's decline. Bishop Smith noted just the mere mention of the Book of Mormon infused new life into Martin. Brother Harris spoke for two additional hours prior to his passing.

http://www.gapages.com/harrim1.htm

THE FACT: Not only was Martin Harris instrumental in the coming forth of the Book of Mormon, but little did he know, as a result of his missionary efforts, one of his posterity would one day serve in the leading councils of the Church. The following is from Elder Dallin H. Oaks April 1999 conference address titled, "The Witness: Martin Harris":

> In 1832 Martin Harris's older brother, Emer, who is my great-great-grandfather, was called on a mission from Ohio (see D&C 75:30). Emer spent a year preaching the gospel near his former home in

northeastern Pennsylvania. During most of this time Emer's companion was his brother Martin, whose zeal in preaching even caused him to be jailed for a few days. The Harris brothers baptized about 100 persons. Among those baptized was a family named Oaks, which included my great-great-grandfather. Thus, my middle name and my last name come from the grandfathers who met in that missionary encounter in Susquehanna County in 1832–33.

http://www.lightplanet.com/mormons/conferences/99_apr/oaks_martin.htm

QUESTION:

5. While still living in Kirtland, Ohio, in 1860, Martin Harris told a census taker that his occupation was what?

    a. A farmer
    b. A witness
    c. A Mormon preacher
    d. The caretaker of the Kirtland Temple

SECTION 6

BRIEF HISTORICAL BACKGROUND: The Prophet Joseph Smith received revelation for Oliver Cowdery at Harmony, Pennsylvania, during April 1829.

THE STORY: Oliver was anxious and desired a witness from the Lord concerning the inspired work that Joseph Smith is involved in. The Lord reminded Oliver in verses 22–24 that he had already received a witness of the truth of the work and if he desired a further witness he must "cast your mind upon the night that you cried unto me in your heart, that you might know concerning the truth of these things." What manifestation did Oliver Cowdery receive?

Joseph Smith records that while in conversation with Oliver Cowdery, Oliver shared with the Prophet how it was confirmed to him that this work was true. Oliver stated that while boarding at the Smith home in Manchester, New York, and after hearing the account from the Smith family of Joseph Smith and the gold plates (Joseph and Emma were living in Harmony, Pennsylvania, at this time) that Oliver approached the Lord in prayer and the Lord answered his prayer, although he kept this manifestation secret. Oliver's secret? The Lord showed to him a vision of the plates and a confirmation of its truthfulness. Lucy Mack Smith describes Oliver Cowdery's enthusiasm for the work after he received his affirmation from the Lord. She states:

> From this time, Oliver was so entirely absorbed in the subject of the record that it seemed impossible for him to think or converse about anything else.
>
> Alexander L. Baugh, *Days Never to be Forgotten*
> (Salt Lake City: Deseret Book, 2009), 27

THE FACT: In verse 14 of section 6, the Lord tells Oliver, "Verily, verily, I say unto thee, blessed art thou for what thou hast done; for thou hast inquired of me, and behold, as often as thou hast inquired thou hast received instruction of my Spirit. If it had not been so, thou wouldst not have come to the place where thou are at this time."

What drove Oliver to journey to Harmony to be with the Prophet Joseph? According to Lucy Mack Smith, Joseph's mother, one afternoon it had rained incessantly. Because of rain and condition of the roads, Lucy honestly thought there would be little chance that Oliver would be coming home that night from school, and most likely he would stay with friends much closer to the schoolhouse. Regardless of the rain, Oliver was determined to reach the Smith home. After entering the home, Oliver announced, "I have now resolved what I will do[,] for the thing which I told you seems working in my very bones insomuch that I cannot for a moment get rid of it." Lucy wrote that after hearing Joseph Sr. explain the marvelous circumstances surrounding the unearthing of the gold plates, Oliver pondered continually on the subject and became convinced that he was the person who was to act as scribe for the Prophet. Once Oliver had established this course of action, I imagine he had a difficult time keeping his mind on teaching the children he had a responsibility to educate. As the Lord stated, "Thou hast received instructions of my Spirit," and it's obvious that because of the Spirit, Oliver's mind was consumed with what he should do. Oliver then revealed his intention to travel to Harmony with Samuel and there speak with Joseph Smith. Oliver added, "I have made it a subject of prayer, and I firmly believe that it is the will of the Lord that I should go. If there is a work for me to do in this thing, I am determined to attend to it."

Oliver did become the scribe for Joseph. In light of his experience with the Spirit and the answer to his prayers, it is not surprising that Oliver would pen the following statement:

> These were days never to be forgotten—to sit under the sound of a voice dictated by the inspiration of heaven, awakened the utmost gratitude of this bosom!

Alexander L. Baugh, <i>Days Never to be Forgotten</i>
(Salt Lake City: Deseret Book, 2009), 26, 38

QUESTION:

6. Surprisingly, it wasn't Oliver Cowdery who originally contracted to teach school in Manchester, New York. If it wasn't Oliver, then who was it?

    a. Porter Rockwell
    b. Samuel Smith
    c. Lucy Mack Smith
    d. Lyman Cowdery

SECTION 7

BRIEF HISTORICAL BACKGROUND: A revelation given to both Joseph and Oliver during April 1829 at Harmony, Pennsylvania, in answer to whether John the Beloved still tarried on the earth or had died as other men.

THE STORY: This subject has been debated for centuries by Christians the world over. The argument stems from John 21:20–23 when the Lord speaking to Peter, but referring to John, states, "But if I will that he should tarry till I come, what is that to thee?" So did John die or didn't he? Obviously it was a question that for the moment created some discussion between Joseph and Oliver. History fails to reveal who was taking what side on the issue; we only have what little knowledge can be gleaned from *History of the Church:*

> During the month of April I continued to translate, and he [Oliver Cowdery] to write, with little cessation, during which time we received several revelations. A difference of opinion arising between us about the account of John the Apostle, mentioned in the New Testament, as to whether he died or continued to live, we mutu[a]lly agreed to settle it by the Urim and Thummim and the following is the word which we received.
>
> Joseph Smith, in *History of the Church*
> (Salt Lake City: Deseret Book, 1950), 1:35–36

Joseph and Oliver then received their answer, proving once again that the windows of heaven are open and a loving Heavenly Father understands the necessity to communicate to man today.

THE FACT: Section 7 teaches that the Apostle John will prophesy and minister to the heirs of salvation. The following are a few facts about the Apostle John's whereabouts:

The Apostle John ministered to the Prophet Joseph Smith and Oliver Cowdery in 1829 when he assisted Peter and James in the restoration of the Melchizedek Priesthood (see D&C 27:12).

In a conference of the Church on 3 June 1831, the Prophet Joseph Smith taught concerning John's ministry: "John the Revelator was then among the Ten Tribes of Israel who had been led away by Shalmaneser, king of Assyria, to prepare them for their return from their long dispersion."

Joseph Smith, in History of the Church, 1:176

Elder Heber C. Kimball recorded an appearance of John in the Kirtland Temple:

When the Prophet Joseph had finished the endowments of the First Presidency, the Twelve and the Presiding Bishops, the First Presidency proceeded to lay hands upon each one of them to seal and confirm the anointing; and at the close of each blessing the whole of the quorums responded to it with a loud shout of Hosanna! Hosanna! etc.

While these things were being attended to the beloved disciple John was seen in our midst by the Prophet Joseph, Oliver Cowdery, and others.

Orson F. Whitney, Life of Heber C. Kimball
(Salt Lake City: Bookcraft, 1992), 91–92

QUESTION:

7. It's common knowledge that John wrote the Gospel of John, the book of Revelation, and three epistles. Part of John's prophecy and ministry to the world is the number of people who have read the Bible since 1815. What's this number, and in how many languages has portions of the Bible been translated?

    a. 500 million and into 1,544 languages
    b. 3.88 billion and 2,233 languages
    c. 1.2 billion and 549 languages
    d. 2.1 billion and 377 languages

SECTION 8

BRIEF HISTORICAL BACKGROUND: A revelation directed to Oliver Cowdery through Joseph Smith at Harmony, Pennsylvania, during April 1829, in response to Oliver's desire to translate.

THE STORY: The Liahona, the Urim and Thummim, and seer stones are objects with which the Lord has used to communicate to man. Most Church members are familiar with and understand their place in Book of Mormon and Church history. Interestingly, the Lord, in reference to Oliver Cowdery, instructs in verse 6, "Now this is not all thy gift; for you have another gift, which is the gift of Aaron; behold, it has told you many things." Joseph Fielding Smith explains:

> There was another gift bestowed upon Oliver Cowdery, and that was the gift of Aaron. Like Aaron with his rod in his hand going before Moses as a spokesman, so Oliver Cowdery was to go before Joseph Smith. Whatever he should ask the Lord by power of this gift should be granted if asked in faith and in wisdom. Oliver was blessed with the great honor of holding the keys of this dispensation with Joseph Smith, and like Aaron [Exodus 4:10–17], did become a spokesman on numerous occasions. It was Oliver who delivered the first public discourse in this dispensation.
>
> Roy W. Doxey, comp., *Latter-day Prophets and the Doctrine and Covenants* (Salt Lake City: Deseret Book, 1978), 1:82

Verse 8 reads, "Therefore, doubt not, for it is the gift of God; and you shall hold it in your hands, and do marvelous works; and no power shall be able to take it away out of your hands, for it is the work of God." Is this verse of scripture referring to the gift of Aaron or is it an item that Oliver Cowdery would hold in his hands to translate? To clarify the meaning, it's necessary to turn to the original edition of the Book of Commandments. In the original, the preceding verse reads as follows:

Now this is not all, for you have another gift, which is the gift of *working with the rod*: behold it has told you things: behold there is no other power save God, that can cause this *rod of nature*, to work in your hands, for it is the work of God.

In Melvin J. Petersen, "Preparing Early Revelations for Publication," *Ensign*, Feb. 1985, 20

It's evident that Oliver Cowdery had in his possession a rod—possibly a divining rod that would act as the Urim and Thummin and assist in the translation of the gold plates. Hyrum Andrus writes the following:

It seems evident that the Lord entrusted Oliver with a sacred instrument through which he could translate by the Spirit of revelation. . . . Having received instructions on the use of the sacred instrument which he possessed, Oliver Cowdery sought to translate from the Plates of Mormon, probably through the instrument which had been entrusted into his care. But he failed.

Hyrum L. Andrus, *Doctrinal Commentary on the Pearl of Great Price* (Salt Lake City: Deseret Book, 1967), 6

Some individuals may wonder why the revelation in the Book of Commandments reads differently than our current edition of the Doctrine and Covenants. Melvin J. Petersen states the following:

The meaning of this revelation as recorded in the Book of Commandments and in the Doctrine and Covenants is not clear. History does not record that Oliver Cowdery or anyone else living at the time it was given had a problem understanding it, but today some of the revelation (as given in the original) is unclear to us.

Melvin J. Petersen, "Preparing Early Revelations for Publication," *Ensign*, Feb. 1985, 20

Accordingly, when the text of the revelation was prepared for review in 1835, it was altered. But who changed it? Both Joseph Smith and Oliver Cowdery were part of the committee to revise the Book of Commandments when the wording of this 1829 revelation was changed.

Richard Lloyd Anderson, "The Mature Joseph Smith and Treasure Searching," *BYU Studies* 24, no. 4 (Fall 1984)

THE FACT: A further study will indicate that it was Sidney Rigdon who initially changed the original, as found in Revelation Book 1, and reads as follows:

> . . . remember this is thy gift now this is not all for thou hast another gift which is the gift of working with the sprout Behold it hath told you things Behold there is no other power save God that can cause this thing of Nature to work in your hands.

To read like this:

> . . . remember this is your gift now this is not all for you have another gift which is the gift of working with the rod Behold it has told you things Behold there is no other power save God that can cause this rod to work in your hands.

Shortly, an additional revision was made by the publication committee (Joseph Smith, Oliver Cowdery, and Frederick G. Williams) in the Book of Commandments (Chapter 7:3), which stated:

> Now this is not all, for you have another gift, which is the gift of working with the rod: behold it has told you things: behold there is no other power save God, that can cause this rod of nature, to work in your hands, for it is the work of God.

In the 1835 Doctrine and Covenants (Doctrine and Covenants 8:6–8), this was revised to read:

> Now this is not all thy gift; for you have another gift, which is the gift of Aaron; behold, it has told you many things; Behold, there is no other power, save the power of God, that can cause this gift of Aaron to be with you. Therefore, doubt not, for it is the gift of God; and you shall hold it in your hands, and do marvelous works; and no power shall be able to take it away out of your hands, for it is the work of God.

According to the FAIR website:

> We know based upon the text of the revelation that Oliver possessed a gift of working with something alternately referred to as a "sprout," "thing of nature," or "rod of nature." We also know that the Lord approved of Oliver's use of this gift. The reference was later changed to the "gift of Aaron," but we can only speculate as to the exact reason why. We do not know if the "rod" referred to by Sidney Rigdon when

he edited the revelation was referring to a divining rod, since there is no other record beyond the revelation itself that indicates this.

We do know that Oliver's gift had to do with receiving revelation, and that Oliver attempted to employ it during the period in which the Book of Mormon was being translated. We also know that Oliver's experience in attempting to translate produced one of the lasting lessons which continues to be taught in Church even today—the knowledge that one must study things out in their mind in order to know the truth of something.

http://en.fairmormon.org/Doctrine_and_Covenants/
Oliver_Cowdery_and_the_%22rod_of_nature%22

QUESTION:

8. Which person listed below was **not** a scribe for Joseph while translating the Book of Mormon?

   a. Joseph Knight Sr.
   b. Rueben Hale
   c. Emma Smith
   d. Martin Harris

SECTION 9

BRIEF HISTORICAL BACKGROUND: Oliver Cowdery received instructions from the Lord through the Prophet Joseph Smith at Harmony, Pennsylvania, in April 1829.

THE STORY: The Lord commanded Oliver through Joseph Smith to satisfy himself for the time being to write for the prophet. In verse 2, the Lord instructs Oliver that there are other records he will give Oliver the power to translate. What other records could the Lord be referring to? We understand that a portion of the Book of Mormon is sealed. Could it be that the Lord had this in mind? Also, it wasn't too many years after this when Joseph Smith purchased the Egyptian mummies that also included the Book of Abraham. So why didn't Oliver translate even "other records?"

President Joseph F. Smith alluded to this when he commented that maybe we as a Church would have these other scriptures at our disposal, but since the general Church membership failed to follow the commandments as outlined in the Book of Mormon and the Doctrine and Covenants, these additional scriptures have been withheld. History has repeated itself on a number of occasions in Church history. Why is it that President Brigham Young and other General Authorities traveled extensively throughout Utah Territory to call the Saints to repentance in what became known as "the reformation"? Those willing to repent and follow the commandments were rebaptized into the Church. Similar situations point to the softening of gospel principles in Jackson County, Missouri, Zion's Camp, and the Saints attitude toward the united order. President Joseph F. Smith goes on to say that it was because of Oliver's disobedience, by falling away from the Church for a time, that this ability to translate other scripture was taken away. Joseph Smith also experienced this at the time of Martin Harris's negligence in losing the 116 translated pages of the Book of Mormon. The difference between Joseph and Oliver is Joseph humbled himself and had his ability restored, whereas Oliver failed in his attempt to shed himself of pride. President Joseph F. Smith continues:

> Oliver Cowdery was a party to this failure by turning away from the Church for a number of years when it needed his service. He therefore lost his privilege to translate through his own disobedience, and the people have lost the privilege of receiving the "greater things" spoken of by the Lord to Mormon (3 Nephi 26:8–11) until the day shall come when they are willing to be obedient in all things and will exercise faith such as was had by the brother of Jared. It should be remembered that such faith has rarely been seen on the earth. It appears, therefore, that we must wait until the reign of unrighteousness is at an end before the Lord will give to the people these

writings, containing "a revelation from God, from the beginning of the world to the ending thereof." (2 Nephi 27:7)

Joseph Fielding Smith, *Church History and Modern Revelation* (Salt Lake City: Deseret Book, 1949), 1:52–53

THE FACT: It's possible the Lord had other scriptures in mind for Oliver to help translate, scriptures that were hidden deep in the heart of the Hill Cumorah:

Heber C. Kimball, *Journal of Discourses,* 28 September 1856

In response to a Brother Mills's statement about the handcart pioneers, Heber C. Kimball said: "How does it compare with the vision that Joseph and others had, when they went into a cave in the hill Cumorah, and saw more records than ten men could carry? There were books piled up on tables, book upon book. Those records this people will yet have, if they accept of the Book of Mormon and observe its precepts, and keep the commandments."

Manuscript History of Brigham Young, 5 May 1867

President [Heber C.] Kimball talked familiarly to the brethren about Father Smith, [Oliver] Cowdery, and others walking into the hill Cumorah and seeing records upon records piled upon table[s,] they walked from cell to cell and saw the records that were piled up.

Elizabeth Kane Journal, 15 January 1873

Although not a member of the Church, Elizabeth Kane lived in St. George, Utah, and entertained the company of Brigham Young. She recorded the following discussion:

"I asked where the plates were now, and saw in a moment from the expression of the countenances around that I had blundered. But I was answered that they were in a cave; that Oliver Cowdery though now an apostate would not deny that he had seen them. He had been to the cave. . . . Brigham Young's tone was so solemn that I listened bewildered like a child to the evening witch stories of its nurse. . .

"Brigham Young said that when Oliver Cowdery and Joseph Smith were in the cave this third time, they could see its contents more distinctly than before. . . . It was about fifteen feet high and round its sides were ranged boxes of treasure. In the centre was a large stone table empty before, but now piled with similar gold plates, some of which lay scattered on the floor beneath. Formerly the sword of Laban hung on the walls sheathed, but it was now unsheathed and lying across the plates on the table; and One that was with them said it was never to be sheathed until the reign of Righteousness upon the earth."

http://maxwellinstitute.byu.edu/publications/jbms/?vol=13&num=1&id=338

QUESTION:

9. William Dame Horne's journal entry of 14 January 1855 states that "Joseph, Hyrum, Cowdery, and Whitmer" entered the cave in Cumorah and saw a number of items. Which item did they not see?

    a. Laban's sword
    b. The Liahona
    c. Aaron's breastplate
    d. A Book of Mormon

SECTION 10

BRIEF HISTORICAL BACKGROUND: Joseph Smith received revelation during the summer of 1828 in relation to the lost 116 manuscript pages from the Book of Mormon translation. This revelation was received in Harmony, Pennsylvania.

THE STORY: The preface in the first edition of the Book of Mormon read as follows:

> To the Reader—As many false reports have been circulated respecting the following work, and also many unlawful measures taken by evil designing persons to destroy me, and also the work, I would

inform you that I translated, by the gift and power of God, and caused to be written, one hundred and sixteen pages, the which I took from the Book of Lehi, which was an account abridged from the plates of Lehi, by the hand of Mormon; which said account, some person or persons have stolen and kept from me, notwithstanding my utmost exertions to recover it again—and being commanded of the Lord that I should not translate the same over again, for Satan had put it into their hearts to tempt the Lord their God, by altering the words, that they did read contrary from that which I translated and caused to be written; and the same over again, they would publish that which they had stolen, and Satan would stir up the hearts of this generation, that they might not receive this work: but behold, the Lord said unto me, I will not suffer that Satan shall accomplish his evil design in this thing: therefore thou shalt translate from the plates of Nephi, until ye come to the record of Nephi; and thus I will confound those who have altered my words. I will not suffer that they shall destroy my work; yea, I will shew unto them that my wisdom is greater than the cunning of the Devil. Wherefore, to be obedient unto the commandments of God, I have, through his grace and mercy, accomplished that which he hath commanded me respecting this thing.

Scot Facer Proctor and Maurine Jensen Proctor, *The Revised and Enhanced History of Joseph Smith By His Mother* (Salt Lake City: Bookcraft, 1996), 172

THE FACT: In a January 1996 *Ensign* article, Elder Jeffrey R. Holland shared his interesting perspective in relation to the lost 116 manuscript pages of the Book of Mormon:

> At least six times in the Book of Mormon, the phrase "for a wise purpose" is used in reference to the making, writing, and preserving of the small plates of Nephi (see 1 Nephi 9:5; Words of Mormon 1:7; Alma 37:2, 12, 14, 18). We know one such wise purpose—the most obvious one—was to compensate for the future loss of 116 pages of manuscript translated by the Prophet Joseph Smith from the first part of the Book of Mormon (see D&C 3, 10).
>
> But it strikes me that there is a "wiser purpose" than that, or perhaps more accurately, a "wiser purpose" in that. The key to such a suggestion is in Doctrine and Covenants 10:45. As the Lord instructs Joseph Smith on the procedure for translating and inserting the material from the small plates into what had been begun as

the translation of the abridged large plates, he says, "Behold, there are many things engraven upon the [small] plates of Nephi which do throw *greater views* upon my gospel" (emphasis added).

So clearly this was not a *quid pro quo* in the development of the final Book of Mormon product. It was not tit for tat, this for that— 116 pages of manuscript for 142 pages of printed text. Not so. We got back more than we lost. And it was known from the beginning that it would be so. We do not know exactly what we have missed in the lost 116 pages, but we do know that what we received on the small plates was the personal declarations of three great witnesses, three of the great doctrinal voices of the Book of Mormon, testifying that Jesus is the Christ.

I am suggesting that Nephi, Jacob, and Isaiah are three early types and shadows of Oliver Cowdery, David Whitmer, and Martin Harris—witnesses positioned right at the front of the book where Oliver, David, and Martin (who in spite of their later difficulties remained true to their testimony) would later be positioned. But Nephi, Jacob, and Isaiah bore a very special witness—they testified of the divinity of Jesus Christ, the Son of God, he who would be the central, commanding, presiding figure throughout the Book of Mormon.

Jeffrey R. Holland, "For a Wise Purpose," *Ensign,* Jan. 1996

QUESTION:

10. Chronologically, where does section 10 really belong in the Doctrine and Covenants?

    a. Exactly where it is, between sections 9 and 11

    b. It should be the preface to the Doctrine and Covenants

    c. Immediately after section 3

    d. It was mistakenly included in the 1981 edition

SECTION 11

BRIEF HISTORICAL BACKGROUND: Revelation directed to Hyrum Smith through Joseph Smith at Harmony, Pennsylvania, in May 1829.

THE STORY: The Lord states in section 124, "I, the Lord, love him [Hyrum] because of the integrity of his heart, and because he loveth that which is right before me." This commendation from the Lord could only be what he meant when he stated in verse 10 of section 11 that Hyrum "had a gift." He was quick to negotiate a dispute, forgive an enemy, or extend the hand of fellowship. The Prophet on occasion would say that "if Hyrum could not make peace between two who had fallen out, the angels themselves might not hope to accomplish the task." On one occasion, an elder spoke out against the Prophet Joseph. John Taylor, who was a witness to the incident, saw the need to reconcile with the man in hopes of not losing him from the Church. Brother Taylor soon discovered that Hyrum was one step ahead of him and had placed the arm of fellowship around one who was separating himself from his spiritual leaders. Realizing this, John Taylor stepped back from the situation, knowing that if Hyrum could not reconcile the individual, then he stood little chance to be successful himself.

http://lds.org/ensign/1995/11/hyrum-smith-firm-as
-the-pillars-of-heaven?lang=eng

See *Prophets And Patriarchs of The Church of Jesus Christ of Latter-Day Saints* by
Matthias F. Cowley at http//books.google.com

THE FACT: John Taylor shares the following scene at the Carthage Jail just moments after the martyrdom of the Prophet and Hyrum:

> These reflections and a thousand others flashed upon my mind. I thought, why must the good perish, and the virtuous be destroyed? Why must God's nobility, the salt of the earth, the most exalted of

the human family, the most perfect types of all excellence, fall victims to the cruel, fiendish hate of incarnate devils?

The poignancy of my grief, I presume, however, was somewhat allayed by the extreme suffering that I had endured from my wounds.

Soon after I was taken to the head of the stairs and laid there, where I had a full view of our beloved and now murdered brother, Hyrum. There he lay as I had left him; he had not moved a limb; he lay placid and calm, a monument of greatness even in death; but his noble spirit had left its tenement, and was gone to dwell in regions more congenial to its exalted nature. Poor Hyrum! He was a great and good man, and my soul was cemented to his. If ever there was an exemplary, honest, and virtuous man, an embodiment of all that is noble in the human form, Hyrum Smith was its representative.

See *Prophets And Patriarchs of The Church of Jesus Christ of Latter-Day Saints* by Matthias F. Cowley at http//books.google.com

QUESTION:

11. Which position did Hyrum Smith *not* hold?
    a. Assistant President of the Church
    b. Foreman of the stone quarry during the construction on the Kirtland temple
    c. Patriarch of the Church
    d. Presiding Bishop

SECTION 12

BRIEF HISTORICAL BACKGROUND: In May 1829 at Harmony, Pennsylvania, Joseph Smith received the following revelation for Joseph Knight Sr.

THE STORY: In verse 8, the Lord reveals, "And no one can assist in this work except he shall be humble and full of love, having faith, hope, and charity, being temperate in all things, whatsoever shall be entrusted to his care." Joseph Knight Sr. was this and more. Often referred to as the second family of the restoration, Joseph Knight and his family were true friends to the Prophet. It was Joseph Knight who loaned a horse and buggy to Joseph to transport the plates home from the Hill Cumorah. It was Joseph Knight who sent supplies to the Prophet and Oliver on occasion so that they wouldn't have to leave the all important work of translating the Book of Mormon. The Prophet would praise Joseph Knight Sr. years later, saying, "If it wasn't for this timely help, the world would not have received the Book of Mormon as fast as it did." The first miracle in this dispensation was performed on the Joseph Knight farm when Joseph Smith cast an evil spirit out of Newell Knight, son of Joseph Knight. It was Joseph Knight, who, when Joseph Smith was unlawfully arrested, hired two local farmer friends, a James Davidson and John Reid (possibly Reed), who were both well versed in the law to defend the Prophet.

Years later, Joseph Smith would record the name of Joseph Knight Sr. in "The Book of the Law of the Lord," a book where Joseph Smith recorded the names of his closest and most loyal friends. It was also in Nauvoo that the Prophet noticed his aged friend Joseph Knight Sr. hobbling down a Nauvoo Street. Joseph ran out to the street and, putting his arm around the aged gentleman, gave him his cane, stating that Brother Knight needed it more than he did. Yes, Joseph Knight listened well to the Lord's counsel and gave unfailing love and charity.

http://www.lds.org/ensign/1989/01/the-knight-family-ever-faithful
-to-the-prophet?lang=eng

THE FACT: The following from the *Church News*, July 7, 2009:

> A walking cane given as a symbol of friendship from the Prophet Joseph Smith to Joseph Knight Sr. is now in the possession of the Church History Department, a donation from descendants of Brother Knight, a figure in early Church history.

The donation was made in a May 29 presentation at the Family History Library in Salt Lake City, at which Elder Marlin K. Jensen of the Seventy, Church Historian and Recorder, received the cane from Jim Knight, a spokesman for the Knight family descendants gathered for the presentation.

"This cane is a memorial of friendship, of mutual faith, that Joseph Smith and the Joseph Knight family share," Brother Knight said.

"Our family often talks about what transpired when Joseph Smith presented the cane to Joseph Knight Sr. Joseph Smith spotted his dear friend, Joseph Knight, hobbling down a Nauvoo street. Father Knight, in his 70s, had been the Prophet's friend for almost 20 years.

"Joseph stepped up to him, put his arm around him, pressed his elderly friend's gnarled fingers onto the top of the cane and said, 'Brother Knight, you need this cane more than I do.'

"The Prophet told Father Knight to keep the cane as long as he lived and to pass it on to Knight descendants with the first name of Joseph."

Brother Knight said the cane passed in turn to five succeeding generations of Joseph Knights. "Now, it's my generation's responsibility to ensure that the cane is safely preserved for the Knight family descendants and the Church members to enjoy," he said.

http://www.ldschurchnews.com/articles/57568/
Joseph-Knight-cane-presented-to-Church.html

QUESTION:

12. The day the Church was organized, how many of the sixty people in attendance were Knights or related to the Knights through marriage?

    a. 6
    b. 20
    c. 17
    d. 31

SECTION 13

BRIEF HISTORICAL BACKGROUND: On May 15, 1829, on the banks of the Susquehanna River, Joseph Smith and Oliver Cowdery were ordained to the Aaronic Priesthood under the hands of John the Baptist.

THE STORY: Joseph Smith records, "It was on the fifteenth day of May, 1829, that we were ordained under the hand of this messenger, and baptized" (Joseph Smith—History 1:72). In a state of religious zeal, Oliver Cowdery submits a far more detailed account— the first published account of the occasion. He states:

> The angel of God came down clothed with glory, and delivered the anxiously looked for message, and the keys of the gospel of repentance!—What joy! what wonder! what amazement!... Our eyes beheld—our ears heard. As in the 'blaze of day;' yes, more—above the glitter of the May Sun beam.... Then his voice, though mild, pierced to the center, and his words, "I am thy fellow-servant," dispelled every fear. We listened—we gazed—we admired! 'Twas the voice of the angel from glory—'twas a message from the Most High!... But, dear brother think, further think for a moment, what joy filled our hearts and with what surprise we must have bowed, ... when we received under his hand the holy priesthood, as he said, "upon you my fellow servants, ... I confer this priesthood and this authority."
>
> http://rsc.byu.edu/archived/days-never-be-forgotten-oliver-cowdery/4-oliver-cowdery-second-witness-priesthood-restorati

THE FACT: For almost six years Joseph Smith was well aware this day would come, although he might not have known that he was to be one of the worthy recipients of the blessing. On September 22, 1823, Moroni educated Joseph when he stated, "When they [the gold plates] are interpreted the Lord will give the holy priesthood to some, and they shall begin to proclaim this gospel and baptize by water, and after that they shall have power to give the Holy Ghost by the laying on of their hands."

http://www.lds.org/ensign/1996/12/the-restoration-of-the-aaronic-and
-melchizedek-priesthoods?lang=eng

QUESTION:

13. What passage of scripture prompted Joseph Smith and Oliver Cowdery to retire to the woods near Harmony, Pennsylvania, on the banks of the Susquehanna River and inquire about baptism?

    a. Mosiah 18:14–16
    b. Matthew 3:16
    c. Moses 6:52
    d. 3 Nephi 11:22–26

SECTION 14

BRIEF HISTORICAL BACKGROUND: Revelation given to David Whitmer at his father's home in Fayette, New York, through Joseph Smith. This revelation was received June 1829.

THE STORY: Oliver Cowdery wasn't the only individual whose interest was piqued by reports of a "golden bible" found buried in a hill south of Palmyra. This reported discovery spread like wildfire throughout the surrounding countryside. Some were motivated by greed, developing schemes to rid Joseph of the unearthed treasure, whereas others, such as Oliver Cowdery and David Whitmer, only wanted to know if in fact the gold plates purported to be what they were—strictly from God. It was in Palmyra where Oliver Cowdery met David Whitmer for the first time. Why was David Whitmer in Palmyra, thirty-six miles northeast of his father's farm in Fayette, New York? It was to quench his curiosity, to satisfy his inquisitiveness as to the reality of the plates. History is silent on how the two men met. Is it possible they accidentally bumped shoulders on a Palmyra sidewalk or possibly ate lunch in the same tavern? None of this is important. The Lord had a purpose and this purpose was now fulfilled as a third witness was found who would attach his name to the new scripture. I'm certain David was all ears when Oliver stated he lived under the same roof with the Smith family. I can imagine David's excitement when Oliver shared with him what information he had learned from the Smith family as they explained the visions, the angel, and the yearly visits, culminating in the reception of the ancient record.

Oliver explained his forthcoming trip to see the Prophet in Harmony, Pennsylvania, to Whitmer, and the two men agreed that Oliver, once he reached his destination, would write David and inform him if the rumors buzzing around the country were true. Oliver kept his promise. Shortly after Cowdery's arrival in Harmony, he wrote David announcing that he was Joseph's scribe and was "convinced that Smith had the records." It wasn't long when a second letter arrived complete with direct quotes from the gold plates translation and a confirmation to the truth of the work. Finally, David opened a third letter with a request that Oliver, Joseph, and his young wife, Emma, be permitted to travel to Fayette and stay at the Whitmer farm to complete the translation.

As much as David wanted to extend the invitation, he couldn't; it wasn't his to give since it wasn't his home. He would have to receive permission from his parents. I can imagine the young David Whitmer approaching his parents explaining the situation. It helped that the Whitmers and the Smiths knew each other even though their farms were many miles apart. I imagine Peter Sr. and his wife, Mary, gave the situation serious reflection. The house was already full with four of the younger children still at home. Could they make room for three more individuals? Then there was the work around the farm.

If David went on his journey to Harmony to bring Joseph, Emma, and the scribe to their house, how much time would be lost on the farm? Peter Sr. finally approached David with the following proposition, "Why, David [you] know you have sowed as much wheat as you can harrow in tomorrow and next day, and then you have a quantity of plaster to spread." It was decided that David should not go to Harmony unless he got "a witness from God that it is very necessary." David prayed that he would be able to accomplish the required work much faster than expected. To everyone's astonishment, two days of work was completed in one day, prompting Peter Sr. to tell David to go to Harmony to "bring up the man and his scribe," believing that "there must be some overruling power in this thing."

Richard Lloyd Anderson, "The Whitmers:
A Family that Nourished the Church," Ensign, Aug. 1979.

THE FACT: David records the following miracle:

> I did not know what to do. I was pressed with my work. I had some twenty acres to plow, so I concluded I would finish plowing and then go. I got up on the morning to go to work as usual, and on going to the field, found between 5 and 7 acres of my ground had been plowed during the night. I do not know who did it, but it was done just as I would have done myself, and the plow was left standing in the furrow.

> Hyrum M. Smith, and Jane M. Sjodahl, Doctrine and Covenant Commentary
(Salt Lake City: Deseret Book Company, 1923), 73

At the emergence of the last gospel dispensation, farmers added plaster to the soil to cut down on the soils acidity. David Whitmer was required to spread the plaster before moving Joseph and Emma. As David went out to the fields, he noticed the work had already been done. He hunted down his sister and asked her if she knew who had spread the plaster. The following conversation took place:

> Surprised, she said, "Why do you ask me? Was it not all sown yesterday?"
>
> "Not to my knowledge," answered David.
>
> "I'm astonished at that," replied his sister, "for the children came to me in the forenoon, and begged of me to go out and see the men

sow plaster in the field, saying that they never saw anybody sow plaster so fast in their lives. I accordingly went, and saw three men at work in the field, as the children had said, but, supposing that you had hired some help, on account of your hurry, I went immediately into the house, and gave the subject no further attention."

Lucy Mack Smith, *History of Joseph Smith*
(Salt Lake City: Bookcraft, 1979), 136–37

QUESTION:

14. Which individual(s) saw the gold plates?

    a. Martin Harris
    b. Hiram Page
    c. Mary Whitmer
    d. All of the above

SECTION 15

BRIEF HISTORICAL BACKGROUND: A revelation given through Joseph Smith to John Whitmer. The Lord told John Whitmer things that only John was familiar with. This revelation was received in June 1829 at Fayette, New York.

THE STORY: John first met Joseph when his brother David brought the Prophet, his wife, and scribe to the family home in Fayette, New York. It's while Joseph was translating the Book of Mormon that John was asked to record some of the revelations, which Joseph Smith had received. Not only does John record revelations for the Prophet, but he begins recording the day to day history of the Church, the first such history. He would eventually become the first Church historian serving in this position from 1831 to 1838. John was also chosen to be one of the eight witnesses to the Book of Mormon. He followed the Church to Kirtland and then on to Missouri, where he was called to act as the Assistant President of the Church. Unfortunately, pride and the riches of the world took control of his heart. Using his position to gain control of land with Church funds and operating independent of the high council in Missouri led to his eventual excommunication. After the Church's expulsion from Missouri, John moved to Far West and established a successful farm and ranch.

http://www.moroni10.com/witnesses/John_Whitmer.html

THE FACT: Like the Three Witnesses who left the Church but defended their testimonies of the Book of Mormon, so likewise John Whitmer defended his testimony of seeing the gold plates even though he too had separated himself from the Church. The most notable occasion took place on April 5, 1835, when he rode with at least fifty men bound and determined not to eat or drink until they had killed "Joe" Smith. Eight men in this group approached Church member Theodore Turley and presented him with a revelation given to the Prophet, a revelation they were certain would never see its fulfillment. The group expressed their feeling that this was proof that Joseph Smith was a false prophet and tried to get Elder Turley to swear that if the revelation did not take place that he would denounce Mormonism and leave the Church. Brother Turley defended the Prophet and the revelation and then, turning to John Whitmer, said:

> "There are many things published that they say are true, and again turn around and say they are false?" Whitmer asked, "Do you hint at me?" Elder Turley said, "If the cap fits you, wear it; all I know is that you have published to the world that an angel did present those plates to Joseph Smith." John replied: "I now say, I handled those plates; there were fine engravings on both sides. I handled them." Then he described in the presence of these bitter enemies how the plates were fastened and he said, "They were shown to me by a supernatural power."

http://www.moroni10.com/witnesses/John_Whitmer.html

QUESTION:

15. What significant document did John Whitmer carry from Kirtland, Ohio, to Independence, Missouri, as he traveled with Oliver Cowdery during November 1831?

   a. The Book of Commandments
   b. Hymn books
   c. The Doctrine and Covenants
   d. *The History of the Church*

SECTION 16

BRIEF HISTORICAL BACKGROUND: Like his brothers David and John, Peter Whitmer Jr. received revelation through the Prophet Joseph Smith at his father's home in Fayette, New York, during June 1829.

THE STORY: The Lord's mandate that Peter Whitmer Jr. open his mouth and cry repentance (verse 6) to the people caused Peter to desire repentance and be baptized. In fact, nine individuals were baptized into the Church prior to its official organization on April 6, 1830. Joseph Smith and Oliver Cowdery were the first two individuals baptized on May 15, 1829, with Samuel Smith ten days later. It was in June 1829 that Joseph and Oliver baptized Hyrum Smith, David Whitmer, and Peter Whitmer Jr. (There is uncertainty who the other three individuals are).

http://www.lds.org/ensign/1980/06/i-have-a-question?lang=eng

THE FACT: One year after his baptism, the minutes of the June 9, 1830, conference indicate that Peter Jr. was already an elder (most likely received on April 6, 1830, at the organization of the Church).

> Minutes of the first Conference held in the Township of Fayette, Senaca County, State of New York; By the Elders of the Church, June 9th 1830. According to the Church Articles and Covenants. Elders Present:
>
> Joseph Smith, junior, Oliver Cowdery, Peter Whitmer [Jr.], David Whitmer, John Whitmer, Ziba Peterson
>
> Ezekiel 14th. Read by br. Joseph Smith jr. and prayer by the same Articles and Covenants read by Joseph Smith jr. and received by unanimous voice of the whole congregation, which consisted of most of the male members of the Church. Samuel H. Smith was then ordained an Elder under the hand of Oliver Cowdery; & Joseph Smith seignior and Hyrum Smith were ordained Priests.
>
> The following persons were then seated respectively and received their licenses, Viz:
>
> Elders of this Church:
>
> David Whitmer, John Whitmer, Peter Whitmer[Jr.], Ziba Peterson, Samuel H. Smith
>
> Priests of this Church:
>
> Martin Harris, Hyrum Smith, Joseph Smith sen.
>
> Teachers of this Church:
>
> Hiram Page and Christian Whitmer.
>
> Exhortation by Joseph Smith jr. and Oliver Cowdery, Conference adjourned to the 26th. September 1830, to be held in the same place.
>
> Br. Oliver Cowdery appointed to keep the Church record and Conference minutes until the next conference. Prayer by all the Brethren present and dismissed by Br. Oliver Cowdery. The above minutes were taken at the time of this conference by Oliver Cowdery.
>
> http://josephsmithpapers.org/paperSummary/minutes-9-june-1830

16. In 1830, Peter Whitmer Jr.'s first call by the Prophet Joseph Smith was to do what?

   a. Serve a mission
   b. Proofread the Book of Mormon manuscript
   c. Serve as a bodyguard for Oliver Cowdery
   d. Cut firewood for the prophets family

SECTION 17

BRIEF HISTORICAL BACKGROUND: Prior to Oliver Cowdery, David Whitmer, and Martin Harris viewing the gold plates, Joseph Smith received this revelation at Fayette, New York, in June 1829.

THE STORY: "Wherefore by the words of three, God hath said, I will establish my word. Nevertheless, God sendeth more witnesses, and he proveth all his words" (2 Nephi 11:3). Also, Ether 5:3–4 says, "And unto three shall they be shown by the power of God; wherefore they shall know of a surety that these things are true. And in the mouth of three witnesses shall these things be established; and the testimony of three, and this work, in the which shall be shown forth the power of God and also his word, of which the Father and the Son, and the Holy Ghost bear record—and all this shall stand as a testimony against the world at the last day." This discovery was made while translating the Book of Mormon—that there were to be three witnesses to this inspired book of scripture! Joseph records that Martin Harris, Oliver Cowdery, and David Whitmer were persistent in their request; in fact, Joseph used the word "teased" in describing the appeal of the three men. Joseph inquired of the Lord and received section 17.

Joseph, with the Three Witnesses retired to a forest of trees proximate to the Whitmer Farm. While here their desire was fulfilled. Joseph records the following:

> We beheld a light above us in the air, of exceeding brightness; and behold, an angel stood before us. In his hands he held the plates which we had been praying for these to have a view of. He turned over the leaves one by one, so that we could see them, and discern the engravings thereon distinctly. He then addressed himself to David Whitmer, and said, "David, blessed is the Lord, and he that keeps His commandments;" when, immediately afterwards, we heard a voice from out of the bright light above us, saying, "These plates have been revealed by the power of God, and they have been translated by the power of God. The translation of them which you have seen is correct, and I command you to bear record of what you now see and hear."
>
> http://maxwellinstitute.byu.edu/publications/transcripts/?id=21

THE FACT: David Whitmer not only had an angel address him by name, heard a voice from the heavens, and viewed the gold plates as the leaves of the plates were turned before his and the others eyes, but also more was shown on this afternoon—much more. David Whitmer states:

> We not only saw the plates of the Book of Mormon but also the brass plates, the plates of the Book of Ether, the plates containing the records of the wickedness and secret combinations of the people of the world down to the time of their being engraved, and many other plates . . . there appeared as it were, a table with many records or plates upon it, besides the plates of the Book of Mormon, also the Sword of Laban, the Directors i.e., the ball which Lehi had—and the Interpreters [Urim and Thummim]. I saw them just as plain as I see this bed (striking the bed beside him with his hand), and I heard the voice of the Lord, as distinctly as I ever heard anything in my life declaring that the records of the plates of the Book of Mormon were translated by the gift and power of God.
>
> 1878 interview between Orson Pratt and David Whitmer, recorded in *Book of Mormon Compendium*, 55–56.

QUESTION:

17. The Three Witnesses monument located in Richmond, Missouri, is positioned over whose grave?

   a. Oliver Cowdery
   b. Parley P. Pratt
   c. Lyman Wight
   d. David Whitmer

SECTION 18

BRIEF HISTORICAL BACKGROUND: Revelation given to Joseph Smith, David Whitmer, and Oliver Cowdery regarding the Melchizedek Priesthood. This revelation was received in June 1829 at Fayette, New York.

THE STORY: During this revelation, the Lord commands David Whitmer and Oliver Cowdery that it's their responsibility to find and choose Twelve Apostles and also a charge to preach the gospel. The Lord states in verse 41, "And you must preach unto the world, saying: You must repent and be baptized, in the name of Jesus Christ."

Truth be known, it was Oliver Cowdery and not Joseph Smith who preached the first public discourse in this dispensation at the home of Peter Whitmer Sr. in Fayette, New York. William E. McLellin heard David Whitmer proselyte and eventually was chosen by David Whitmer and Oliver Cowdery to serve in the original Quorum of the Twelve. When David finds William McLellin in Paris, Illinois, William was teaching school. He shares the following with his relatives:

One of these [visitors] was a witness to the book and had seen an angel which declared its truth (his name was David Whitmer). They were in the neighborhood about a week. I talked much with them by way of enquiry and argument.

David's preaching had such an astonishing effect on William, that Brother McLellin shut down his school and traveled the 450 miles on horseback to Jackson County, Missouri, to converse more on the Church with the elders, one of whom was Hyrum Smith. It didn't take long for William to accept the gospel, be baptized, and ordained an elder.

http://lds.org/ensign/1979/08/the-whitmers-a-family
-that-nourished-the-church?lang=eng

THE FACT: There is an innumerable supply of stories of those who opened their mouths and then let the Lord work the miracle. I imagine anyone that has served a mission could attest to this. Samuel Smith, the first missionary of the Church, comes to mind. He opened his mouth, yet he felt very much a failure. I'm sure he's chuckling now, simply because I'm certain the Book of Mormon he left with a Methodist minister, John P. Greene, (who eventually passed it on to Brigham Young, who eventually shared it with Heber C. Kimball) is now responsible for tens of thousands of baptisms, possibly even in the hundreds of thousands.

One of my favorite stories of opening one's mouth and preaching the gospel is the story of Eli H. Pierce. Today when we watch general conference, we fully expect temples to be announced and excited when the prophet first takes the podium. Back in the mid-to-late 1800s, men entered the Tabernacle during conference time, not with the thought of what temples will be built, but rather whose name was going to be called over the pulpit to serve a mission. Many men were called on missions in this manner. At one particular conference, a number of men were called to serve missions for the Church. Eli H. Pierce was one of the names announced on October 5, 1875, except Eli was not in the congregation. He would be the first to admit the reason he wasn't at conference was because he had no desire to be there—he was less active, and that's the way he preferred it. He was a railroad man that bought cigars like they were going out of style and had never read more than a few pages of scripture in his lifetime. One of his fellow work associates heard the call and immediately went to the telegraph office to send Eli the message. When the telegraph arrived, Eli was smoking a pipe and reading a novel. He states that after reading the call, he threw the novel in the waste basket (and never picked up one since), got rid of the pipe, was rebaptized, ordained a Seventy, and in one month from the time of the call was serving his mission in the state of New York. Brother Pierce said, "Remarkable as it may seem . . . a thought of disregarding the call, or of refusing to comply with the requirement, never once entered my mind." In fact, Eli would go on and serve three more missions. Here's a rundown of the numbers he accumulated, only because he knew if he opened his mouth the Lord would bless:

Baptisms, 108; ordinations, 11; children blessed, 37; branches organized, 5; branches reorganized, 1; marriages, 1; meetings held, 249; miles traveled, 9,870; total cost, $1,320.

http://speeches.byu.edu/reader/reader.php?id=6763

QUESTION:

18. Which individual was *not* a member of the 1830–1831 mission to the Lamanites?

    a. Ziba Peterson
    b. Parley P. Pratt
    c. Oliver Cowdery
    d. Martin Harris

SECTION 19

BRIEF HISTORICAL BACKGROUND: Revelation received by the Prophet Joseph Smith for Martin Harris. The revelation was given in Manchester, New York, in March 1830.

THE STORY: In verse 26 the Lord offers the following instruction to Martin Harris: "And again, I command thee that thou shalt not covet thine own property, but impart it freely to the printing of the Book of Mormon, which contains the truth and the word of God." The following is a brief summary of events leading to the publication of the translation.

In early June 1829, Martin Harris inquires the possibility of E. B. Grandin, the publisher of the *Wayne Sentinel* in Palmyra, taking on the work of publishing the Book of Mormon (Grandin would refer to it as the Mormon Bible). Mr. Grandin was not interested, causing Martin Harris to approach him a second time on the subject. Martin told Grandin that if he did not publish the book that it would publish in Rochester, in hopes that by saying so he could sway Mr. Grandin's attitude toward the work. Unable to persuade Grandin, Joseph and Martin traveled to Rochester.

The editor of the *Anti-Masonic Enquirer,* Thurlow Weed, said Joseph Smith was the first to approach him about the subject, and he told Joseph that he had no interest in the project. Joseph came back a second time in company with Martin Harris, "a substantial farmer residing near Palmyra." It was at this meeting that Martin "offered to become security for the expense of printing." Again, Mr. Weed turned Joseph down. Interestingly, an Elihu F. Marshall, also of Rochester, agreed to publish the Book of Mormon, but at a ridiculous price. Joseph realized at this point it might be best to meet for a third time with Mr. Grandin and hope he would have second thoughts on the project.

Grandin finally relented, agreeing to publish only after he and one of his employees, a Pomeroy Tucker, unsuccessfully tried "to divert Harris from his persistent fanaticism in that losing speculation." It's incredible to me that although Mr. Grandin considered publishing the Book of Mormon as a "losing speculation," he still published the book. Nevertheless, Mr. Grandin was not entering the venture without a guarantee from Martin, and he secured a note on Martin's farmland as collateral. Finally, agreement was reached between Grandin and Harris on August 17, 1829.

The initial agreement stated that Martin would provide the funds for half of the project and Joseph and Hyrum would supply the other half. Joseph tried to secure a loan from a George Crane of Macedon, but his application was denied. Joseph considered preselling the Book of Mormon to friends and associates around and in the town of Palmyra, but again this idea failed. Joseph's final hope was in his friend Josiah Stowell. In October 1829, Joseph met with Oliver Cowdery and stated that Stowell had the ability to get five or six hundred dollars toward the cause, although this was never realized. By January 1830, Martin Harris realized the price tag for the publication of the Book of Mormon would fall squarely on his shoulders.

On January 26, 1830, the work on the publication came to a halt primarily because of two circumstances. First, E. B. Grandin was swayed by rumors that Martin could not sell his farmland as stated in their agreement, and second, a resolution was passed by the citizens of Palmyra to boycott the Book of Mormon entirely. It wasn't until Martin obtained permission from Joseph Smith to equal selling rights, until at least the cost of publication was covered, that Mr. Grandin resumed the work.

Even though the townspeople of Palmyra considered Martin to be affluent, it's interesting to note that he applied for a $1300 loan through Charles Butler of the New York Insurance and Trust Company located in Geneva, New York. Surprisingly, the loan was refused.

About this time, Martin's wife, Lucy Harris, pressured her husband to turn his back on his obligation. Hyrum Smith sensed some hesitancy from Martin Harris and convinced Joseph to send someone to Canada to sell the copyright on the Book of Mormon in hopes of raising the necessary funds. Oliver Cowdery, Hiram Page, Joseph Knight Sr., and Josiah Stowell were sent north during the winter of 1829–1830. It was hoped that the copyright would be purchased for eight thousand dollars, but it failed to raise a single penny even though the men tried to convince those they thought could help in Kingston and York (now known as Toronto).

The Lord's edict to Martin Harris to "not covet thine own property, but impart it freely to the printing of the Book of Mormon," seems, at least for the moment, to have been forgotten. Martin was considered wealthy, yet he felt it necessary to negotiate at every turn to save what he could in property.

On March 26, 1830, the Book of Mormon became available for public sale in Grandin's bookstore. However, coincidental to this time, Lucy separated herself and the children from her husband, Martin, and moved to an eighty-acre farm. To add to Martin's mounting dejection was the fact that he was unsuccessful at any attempt to presell the Book of Mormon. Martin said to Joseph Smith and Joseph Knight Sr., "The Books will not sell for no Body wants them." It was also said that "Martin Harris . . . gave up his entire time to advertising the Bible to his neighbors and the public generally in the vicinity of Palmyra. He would call public meetings and address them himself." Also, "Harris became very boisterous on the subject of the book and preached about the country in the endeavoring to make sale of it—Harris is by some considered a deluded man partially insane, and by others as a cunning speculator in publishing this book for the sake of gain."

On April 7, 1831, Martin Harris sold 151 acres of his land to a Thomas Lakely. An agreement was settled with terms of payments on the land extending to October 1832. Unfortunately, the money did not come as Martin had hoped. It was a John Graves that ultimately rescued the land deal. He and his wife, Jane, lived just north of Palmyra. They had a widowed daughter, Christina Grainger, who lived with them along with her four children. Christina wore a money belt around her waist with three thousand dollars in gold coins. Christina loaned this money to her father, who used it to pay off Thomas Lakely for 150 and a quarter acres on January 28, 1832.

Finally, this:

> Thomas Rogers, second assignee on the original mortgage agreement between Martin Harris and Grandin, certified before the commissioner of deeds for Wayne County, Truman Hemingway, on 28

January 1832 that "said mortgage is redeemed paid off, satisfied and discharged." The long-standing debt [on the Book of Mormon] was duly retired.

http://maxwellinstitute.byu.edu/publications/jbms/?vol=14&num=2&id=373

THE FACT: Again, in verse 33 the Lord warns Martin: "And misery thou shalt receive if thou wilt slight these counsels, yea, even the destruction of thyself and property." Lucy Mack Smith records the following:

> A dense fog spread itself over [Martin's] fields, and blighted his wheat while in the blow, so that he lost about two thirds of his crop; whilst those fields, which lay only on the opposite side of the road, received no injury whatever.

http://maxwellinstitute.byu.edu/publications/jbms/?vol=14&num=2&id=373

QUESTION:

19. What rank did Martin Harris hold during the War of 1812?
    a. First Sergeant
    b. Private First class
    c. Captain
    d. Brigadier General

SECTION 20

BRIEF HISTORICAL BACKGROUND: Revelation given to the Prophet Joseph Smith at Fayette, New York, in April 1830.

THE STORY: This revelation, in combination with section 22, is commonly referred to as the Articles and the Covenants of the Church. It was extremely important to the early Church as it set forth teachings on Church organization and government. Among other things, this section teaches us about the duties of the elders and Aaronic Priesthood holders, the blessing of children, the sacramental prayers, and the mode of baptism. Verses 73 and 74 instruct, "The person who is called of God and has authority from Jesus Christ to baptize, shall go down into the water with the person who has presented himself or herself for baptism, and shall say, calling him or her by name: Having been commissioned of Jesus Christ, I baptize you in the name of the Father, and of the Son, and of the Holy Ghost. Amen. Then shall he immerse him or her in the water, and come forth again out of the water."

As members we understand this. We have been baptized by immersion, the required way as set forth in the scriptures and revelations. Many are familiar with the practice of rebaptism in the early pioneer Church, which continued into the 1890s; however, what may be less known is the practice of baptism for the restoring of health.

Thomas Kane, nonmember friend to the Saints, heard of the Church's plight at Winter Quarters and desired to meet with Brigham Young to see what he could do to alleviate the suffering through political avenues. Like many of the Saints at Winter Quarters, Thomas Kane also became deathly sick. It was at this time that some members of the Church believe Kane was baptized into the Church. Even Thomas Kane's wife believed he had been baptized, as she wrote in a letter after her husband's death that the Mormons performed some kind of "dunking ritual" on him.

At the Thomas L. Kane Lecture Series at BYU, during the fall of 2008, David J. Whittaker said, "It is pretty clear that Kane never became a member (Cannon was baptized for him [baptism for the dead] a year after Kane's death)." Whittaker believes Kane's wife is referring to a baptism of health and not a baptism for the remission of sins.

THE FACT: The earliest reference to baptism for health was most likely in 1841, when William Clayton recorded Joseph Smith's instructions to Samuel Rolfe to wash in the baptismal font.

Brother Samuel Rolfe being present, and being seriously afflicted with a felon on one hand president Joseph instructed him to wash in the font, and told him he would be healed, although the doctors had told him it would not be well before spring, and advised him to have it cut. He washed his hands in the font and in one week afterwards his hand was perfectly healed.

From BYU Studies we learn the following:

Although some were baptized for health purposes in the Nauvoo Temple font, still others resorted to the Mississippi River for this ordinance. The most notable example occurred when Joseph Smith baptized his wife Emma twice in the Mississippi River on 5 October 1842 because of her serious ill health, and then went with her on 1 November 1842, "to the temple [the font being the only part completed] for the benefit of her health." The Prophet's anxiety for his wife to receive baptism for health was such that a non-Mormon businessman reported that Joseph Smith had interrupted a business interview because "Mrs Smith lay Dangerously ill at the time and they were about to administer the Rights of Baptism to her." Apostle Willard Richards also baptized his wife frequently for her health.

In fact, when Reverend George Moore visited Nauvoo and its unfinished Temple, he recounted that "in the basement is the baptismal font, supported by 12 oxen. In this I learned that persons are baptized for the dead, and for restoration to health."

In an April 1842 conference, Joseph Smith instructed:

Baptisms for the dead, and for the healing of the body must be in the font, those coming into the Church, and those re-baptized may be baptized in the river.

In 1873, Brigham Young taught the following in the Tabernacle:

We can, at the present time, go into the Endowment House and be baptized for the dead, receive our washings and anointing, etc., for there we have a font that has been erected, dedicated expressly for baptizing people for the remission of sins, for their health and for their dead friends.

J. Stapely states in his November 3, 2005, article, *Baptism for Healing*:

> This practice of multi-use Temple fonts continued into the 20th century. My mother and her siblings were all baptized in the Manti Temple at the age of eight. The continuance of healing baptism did, however, subside much earlier. In a 1922 letter to Temple Presidents, the office of the First Presidency wrote:
>
> "We feel constrained to call your attention to the custom prevailing to some extent in our temples of baptizing for health, and to remind you that baptism for health is no part of our temple work, and therefore to permit it to become a practice would be an innovation detrimental to temple work, and a departure as well from the provision instituted of the Lord for the care and healing of the sick of His Church."

http://www.splendidsun.com/wp/baptism-healing/

QUESTION:

20. What other group of people believed in the legitimacy of baptism for healing?

    a. Shakers
    b. Native Americans
    c. Quakers
    d. Baptists

SECTION 21

BRIEF HISTORICAL BACKGROUND: Joseph Smith received this revelation at the organization of the Church on April 6, 1830, in the home of Peter Whitmer Sr., at Fayette, New York.

THE STORY: In verse 1 the Lord instructs Joseph thus: "Behold, there shall be a record kept among you; and in it thou shalt be called a seer, a translator, a prophet, an apostle of Jesus Christ, an elder of the church through the will of God the Father, and the grace of your Lord Jesus Christ."

This revelation was received the day the Church was organized. The Lord gives clear instructions to the membership who Joseph is when he states that he is "a seer, a translator, a prophet, an apostle of Jesus Christ," and finally, "an elder of the church through the will of God the Father." Many were drawn to him, whether they held positions in this world as political and government leaders or were in the most humble circumstances. Even his most bitter and vile enemies shrunk in awe of the man Joseph Smith as the following story will attest.

At a speech given in the Tabernacle, May 24, 1874, President George A. Smith related the following:

> During the bitter Missouri years when Joseph Smith and other Church leaders were held prisoners by the state, General Moses Wilson made the following observation: "He was a remarkable man. I carried him into my house, a prisoner in chains, and in less than two hours my wife loved him better than she did me."

President George A. Smith further stated that a number of years later the Wilsons had relocated to Texas where Mrs. Wilson's admiration for the Prophet was manifested in a daring act. General Wilson decided he would gather a mob against the Mormon missionaries. Mrs. Wilson caught wind of her husband's evil design, and although an aged lady, she rode her horse thirty miles to warn the elders.

Dan Barker, *Unique Stories and Facts from LDS History*
(Springville, Utah: Cedar Fort, 2010), 52

THE FACT: Verse 7 states: "For thus saith the Lord God: Him have I inspired to move the cause of Zion in mighty power for good, and his diligence I know, and his prayers I have heard."

The Lord was cognizant of the Prophet's diligence, and those who followed him also recognized this attribute.

Understanding the threat to Far West, Lyman Wight gathered fifty-three volunteers from Adam-ondi-Ahman to assist Far West, which was surrounded by the State Militia (mob). On October 31, 1838, Colonel George M. Hinckle betrayed Joseph Smith, Lyman Wight, and others into the hands of General Moses Wilson. That night General Wilson took Lyman Wight out of the camp in hopes of swaying his mind against the Prophet Joseph Smith. The following conversation ensues:

> General Wilson said, "Colonel Wight, we have nothing against you, only that you are associated with Joseph Smith. He is our enemy and a damned rascal, and would take any plan he could to kill us. You are a damned fine fellow; and if you will come out and swear against him, we will spare your life, and give you any office you want; and if you don't do it, you will be shot tomorrow at 8 o'clock." Colonel Wight replied, "General Wilson, you are entirely mistaken in your man, both in regard to myself and Joseph Smith. Joseph Smith is not an enemy to mankind, he is not your enemy; but is as good a friend as you have got. Had it not been for him, you would have been in hell long ago, for I should have sent you there by cutting your throat, and no other man but Joseph Smith could have prevented me and you may thank him for your life. And, now, if you will give me the boys I brought from Adam-ondi-Ahman yesterday, I will whip your whole army." Wilson said, "Wight, you are a strange man; but if you will not accept my proposal, you will be shot tomorrow morning at 8." Colonel Wight replied, "Shoot and be damned."

> http://www.boap.org/LDS/Early-Saints/LWight.html

QUESTION:

21. On April 6, 1830, it was necessary for all who had been baptized previously into the Church to be rebaptized. What other ordinance had to be re-performed?

    a. The taking of the sacrament
    b. For Joseph and Oliver to be ordained to the office of elder in the Melchizedek Priesthood
    c. To receive the Holy Ghost
    d. To have their feet washed

SECTION 22

BRIEF HISTORICAL BACKGROUND: In Manchester, during April 1830, Joseph Smith received the following revelation. All must be baptized into the Church even though they may have been baptized previously in another religion.

THE STORY: Shortly after the organization of the Church, some individuals were confused as to whether being rebaptized into the LDS faith was actually a necessary requirement, since they had already been baptized into other denominations. Joseph Smith approached the Lord and the Savior answered with: "Wherefore, although a man should be baptized an hundred times it availeth him nothing, for you cannot enter in at the strait gate by the law of Moses, neither by your dead works."

The Lord did not disappoint—he more than clarified the need for baptism into the Church. It was shortly after this that missions began and the Church flourished with many accepting baptism as an outward show of faith in their newfound religion.

Not all of the approximately sixty people in attendance at the organization of the Church on Tuesday, April 6, 1830, were adults. History teaches us that one young boy, eleven-year-old David Lewis, was also present. He listened and viewed the proceedings and felt what others had felt on this historic day, and like others, also desired baptism. I don't know if he was a member of another faith, but I do know he understood that to belong to the Church of Christ it was necessary to be baptized. It's possible he watched as others were baptized in nearby Seneca Lake that day. As he watched the six men, who had been baptized prior to this day, be rebaptized and then watch six others—including Porter Rockwell, the Prophet's sister Katherine Smith, and two brothers, Don Carlos and William—the yearning only increased in David's heart. The Prophet explained to young David that he would be more than willing to perform the ordinance for him, but because of his young age, it was necessary that he obtain the consent of his parents.

David went home and expressed his desire to his mother. His mother, not completely understanding why he would want to attach himself to the Church, gave permission for him to be baptized when he turned twelve. Twenty-nine days later, after the organization of the Church, Joseph Smith baptized David Lewis a member of the Church.

Brian and Petrea Kelly, *Illustrated History of the Church*
(American Fork, Utah: Covenant Communications, 2008), 49–50

THE FACT: Young George Reynolds also understood the necessity of baptism. With time George would advance to become a member of the First Council of the Seventy and secretary to five presidents of the Church. While being raised in England, he became friends with a member of the Church. At age nine, George desired baptism, but because of his young age, it was necessary for him to have his parents' consent, which they refused to give. George continued to attend church for a few years but then became fearful that the Saviors' Second Coming would take place before he could obtain the necessary permission to be baptized. Therefore, at the age of fourteen (1856), he went to a branch where he was unknown and was baptized the following Sunday.

Dan Barker, *Mormon History 101* (Springville, Utah: Cedar Fort, 2011), 35;
Bruce A. Van Orden, *George Reynolds: Prisoner for Conscience'Sake*
(Salt Lake City: Deseret Book, 1992)

QUESTION:

22. Where was the largest gathering of spectators at an LDS baptism?

    a. The River Ribble in Preston, England
    b. The Jordan River in Salt Lake City
    c. City Creek in Salt Lake City
    d. Lake Erie at Fairport, Ohio

SECTION 23

BRIEF HISTORICAL BACKGROUND: Joseph Smith
inquired of the Lord in behalf of Oliver Cowdery, Hyrum Smith,
Samuel Smith, Joseph Smith Sr., and Joseph Knight. This revelation
was received at Manchester, New York, during April 1830.

THE STORY: The following are the Lord's words to Samuel
Smith in verse 4: "Behold, I speak a few words unto you, Samuel; for
thou also art under no condemnation, and thy calling is to exhortation, and to strengthen the church; and thou art not as yet called to
preach before the world. Amen"

Samuel Smith became the first ordained missionary for the
Church in this dispensation. As Latter-day Saints, we are familiar
with the details of Samuel's encounter with the Greenes and how the
Book of Mormon that was left at the Greenes found its way into the
hands of Mrs. Greene's brother, Brigham Young, and then eventually to the Heber C. Kimball family.

Samuel sold a second Book of Mormon while on this first mission. Ironically, it was sold to a Methodist minister named Phinehas
Young, brother to Brigham Young. History states that Phinehas was
on his way home from a preaching circuit and eating dinner with a
family when the young Samuel Smith knocked at the door. The following conversation took place:

> "There's a book, sir, I wish you to read," Samuel said.
>
> Phinehas asked, "Pray, sir, what book have you?"
>
> "The Book of Mormon, or, as it is called by some, the Golden
> Bible."
>
> "Ah, so then it purports to be a revelation?" Phinehas asked.
>
> Samuel opened the book to the testimonies of the Three and
> Eight Witnesses and said, "Here is the testimony of the witnesses to
> the truth of the book."
>
> Phinehas read their testimonies. When Phinehas looked up
> from his reading, the young man said, "If you will read this book

with a prayerful heart and ask God to give you a witness, you will know the truth of the work."

Phinehas promised to read the book. Then he asked the young man's name.

"My name is Samuel Smith."

Phinehas had seen that name! "Then you are one of the witnesses."

"Yes," Samuel said. "I know the book is a revelation from God, translated by the power of the Holy Ghost, and that my brother, Joseph Smith, Jr., is a Prophet, Seer, and Revelator."

After arriving home Phinehas told his wife, "I have got a book here called the Book of Mormon, and it is said to be a revelation, and I wish to read it and make myself acquainted with its errors, so I can expose them to the world."

True to his promise, he read the Book of Mormon—twice in two weeks. Rather than finding any errors, he became convinced the book was true. On Sunday, when his congregation asked for his opinion of the book, "he defended it for ten minutes, when suddenly the Spirit of God came on him with such force that in a marvelous manner he spoke at great length on the importance of it. . . . He closed by telling the people that he believed the book."

http://lds.org/new-era/2004/09/the-first-latter-day-missionary?lang=eng

THE FACT: Though Samuel was not always as eloquent as his brothers or his companions, his testimony was strong. He said, "How could I doubt anything that I knew to be true?" In a blessing given by his father, Samuel was promised that his testimony would be received by thousands. This blessing was fulfilled through Samuel's six missions.

1. Spring and summer 1830: Samuel served alone in the neighboring communities around Palmyra, New York. (See the above story for experience from this mission.)

2. January 31, 1831, to April 1831: Samuel Smith and Orson Hyde preached the gospel in the vicinity of Kirtland, Ohio. In April they baptized about fifty people, many previously of the Campbellite faith.

[1832: Feb. 1]

We [Samuel H. Smith and Orson Hyde] left Kirtland and went as far as Painesville . . .

[1832: Feb. 27]

Baptized two young men: Horace Spencer and his brother. We confirmed them and ordained Brother Simons to be an Elder of the Church [in Springfield Twp., Erie Co., PA] and we baptized five and went again to Mr. Barr's.

http://olivercowdery.com/hurlbut/1832hyde.htm

3. June 4, 1831, to mid-November 1831: Samuel, who had recently been ordained a high priest, was one of many elders called to Independence, Missouri. He and his missionary companion, Reynolds Cahoon, had powerful missionary experiences. They returned to Kirtland on September 28 but were immediately asked to serve briefly in southern Ohio.

William E. McLellin was born in the state of Tennessee, supposed in 1806. He heard the gospel preached by Elders Samuel H. Smith and Reynolds Cahoon, while they were on their mission to Jackson County, Missouri, in the summer of 1831. He wound up his business and followed them to Jackson County. While on the way he was baptized and ordained an elder. He visited Kirtland, Ohio, in the fall.

http://www.boap.org/LDS/Early-Saints/Mcllelin.html

The first missionaries known to have visited Kentucky were Samuel H. Smith and Reynolds Cahoon. They passed through the northern part of Kentucky in late June 1831 on their way to Missouri.

http://www.ldschurchnews.com/missions/153
/Kentucky-Louisville-Mission.html

4. November 16, 1831, to late December 1831: Samuel Smith and William McLellin served in eastern Ohio. William recorded that Samuel laid his hands upon a badly scalded child and the burn was healed "in so much that it did not even so much as blister." This mission ended abruptly after forty days because William had murmured in his heart.

While William McLellin's writings speak of Harvey Whitlock and David Whitmer as the missionaries who helped convert him, Samuel H. Smith apparently also took part in his conversion. From Lucy Mack Smith's history, we get the impression that her son, Samuel H. Smith, and his companion, Reynolds Cahoon, were the first missionaries to make contact with William McLellin. He asked them to preach and "went out, and in a short time he had a large congregation seated in a convenient room, well lit up at his expense. After the meeting was dismissed, Mr. McLellin urged them to stay in the place and preach again, but they refused, as their directions were to go forward without any further delay than to warn the people as they passed" (Lucy Mack Smith, *History of Joseph Smith, Revised and Enhanced,* edited by Scot Facer Proctor and Maurine Jensen Proctor [Salt Lake City: Bookcraft, 1996], chap. 39).

Subsequently, Elders Whitlock and Whitmer preached to William—staying in the area long enough for their message to stick. William would follow them to Zion where he was baptized. It is interesting to note that the relationship between Samuel Smith and William McLellin began as missionary and investigator only to blossom into a missionary companionship within only a few months.

http://www.gospeldoctrine.com/DoctrineandCovenants/DC%2066.htm

5. February 1, 1832, to December 22, 1832: Samuel Smith and Orson Hyde were called to serve in New England. Their efforts resulted in about sixty baptisms and the establishment of four branches.

Orson Hyde, a native of Connecticut, turned twenty-seven in January 1832, at the time of his missionary call. Samuel Smith, a younger brother of Joseph Smith, was twenty-three years old at the time of his mission call to the eastern states. Elders Hyde and Smith commenced their difficult mission on February 1, 1832, from Kirtland, Ohio, and returned to Kirtland on December 22, 1832— serving for almost eleven months. The efforts of Orson Hyde and Samuel H. Smith were confined to the area east of the Connecticut River, in a line from Providence, Rhode Island, to Boston and vicinity, including Bradford, and on to Saco and Farmington, Maine. Their two-thousand-mile mission took them to Ohio, New York, Pennsylvania, Connecticut, Rhode Island, Massachusetts, Vermont, and Maine. The following report of their mission was published in *The Evening and the Morning Star*: "BROTHERS Orson Hyde, and Samuel H. Smith, have just returned to this place [Kirtland, Ohio], in good health and spirits, saying, that they had built up four churches; one in the state of Maine; two in Massachusetts, and one in Pennsylvania—They have baptized sixty or more, disciples, who they say, are strong in the faith, rejoicing in the Holy One of Israel."

6.   April 1841 to November 1841: Scott County, Illinois.

Samuel's first wife, Mary Bailey, died in 1841. On May 30, 1841, while in Scott County, Samuel would marry his second wife, Levira Clark.

http://josephsmithpapers.org/person/samuel-harrison-smith

http://lds.org/ensign/2008/08/samuel-h-smith-faithful
-brother-of-joseph-and-hyrum?lang=eng

QUESTION:

23.   Section 23 is a conglomeration of a number of revelations rolled into one. This section is broken down into how many sections in the Book of Commandments?

a. 3
b. 6
c. 5
d. 4

SECTION 24

BRIEF HISTORICAL BACKGROUND: Revelation given to Joseph Smith and Oliver Cowdery in connection with the many persecutions they were receiving in Harmony and the surrounding area. This revelation was received in July 1830.

THE STORY: It was as if the Lord was foreshadowing Joseph Smith's life when he stated in verse 8, "Be patient in afflictions, for thou shalt have many; but endure them, for, lo, I am with thee, even unto the end of thy days."

One such example was the visit of Oliver Cowdery, David Whitmer, and Joseph and Emma Smith to the Knights in the Colesville, New York, area. On June 26, Oliver preached at the home of Joseph Knight Sr., after which a number of those in attendance desired baptism. Some of Joseph's persecutors were also at the meeting. The men dammed a stream for the baptisms, but the mob destroyed the dam. The next day the dam was reconstructed, and then on June 28, 1830, thirteen individuals joined the Church, one of which was Emma Smith. As the small group of Saints retired to the Joseph Knight home to confirm those who had just been baptized, Joseph Smith was arrested on a "disorderly person" charge.

It's interesting that this charge would be levied against the Prophet, when, in fact, he was anything but disorderly. Nonetheless, as the Lord said, this would be his "lot in life."

Prior to receiving the plates, history reveals that Joseph Smith was hired by Josiah Stowell to help him in his pursuit to search for a lost Spanish treasure. This activity led to the disorderly conduct charge. Ironically, Joseph Smith was the individual that convinced Josiah to give up his search for the treasure. The laws at the time (1826) defined actions by "persons pretending . . . to discover where lost goods may be found" as "disorderly."

James B. Allen and Glen M. Leonard, *The Story of the Latter-day Saints* (Salt Lake City: Deseret Book, 1992), 41–42

THE FACT: Verse 17 reads, "And whosoever shall go to law with thee shall be cursed by the law."

Immediately after the arrest of Joseph Smith (he would be arrested twice in the same night), Joseph Knight Sr. seeks out two friends, John Reid and James Davidson, to represent the Prophet at his trial. While neither men were lawyers (in fact, both were farmers), they were well versed in the law. John Reid relates the prosecutions attempt at trying to convict the Prophet:

Neither talents nor money were wanting to insure them success. They employed the best lawyer in that county, and introduced twenty or thirty witnesses before dark, but proved nothing. Then they sent out runners and ransacked the hills and vales, grog shops (bars) and ditches, and gathered together a company that looked as if they'd come from hell and had been whipped by the soot boy thereof; which they brought forward to testify one after another, but with no better success than before, although they wrung and twisted into every shape, in trying to tell something that would criminate the prisoner. Nothing was proven against him however.

Brian and Petrea Kelly, *Illustrated History of the Church*
(American Fork, Utah: Covenant Communications, 2008), 54

QUESTION:

24. Joseph and Emma moved back to Fayette after the two court cases, when, in August 1830, Joseph desired to return to Colesville to confirm those who had been baptized earlier. How were Joseph and Emma able to pass by their enemies when they met the members of the mob working on the road?

    a. Joseph threatened to shoot anyone that would not let them through
    b. Porter Rockwell scared the mob off
    c. The mob saw angels defending them
    d. The mob looked right at them but did not recognize them

SECTION 25

BRIEF HISTORICAL BACKGROUND: Joseph Smith received revelation for his wife, Emma. This revelation was given on July 1830 in Harmony, Pennsylvania.

THE STORY: Among other things, the Lord wanted Emma to understand in verses 11 and 12, "And it shall be given thee, also, to make a selection of sacred hymns, as it shall be given thee, which is pleasing unto me, to be had in my church. For my soul delighteth in the song of the heart; yea, the song of the righteous is a prayer unto me, and it shall be answered with a blessing upon their heads."

Emma answered the Lord's call. In August 1835, the first Church hymnal was published, titled "A Collection of Sacred Hymns for the Church of the Latter-day Saints." The hymnal was composed of ninety hymns and measured a very small 3 x 4½ inches. The hymns were strictly text, not having any music to the words (1857 was the first year that music was included with the lyrics). More than a third of the hymnal was composed of original songs written by LDS members such as William W. Phelps, Eliza R. Snow, and Parley P. Pratt, the remainder being popular Protestant hymns of the age. Since no music accompanied the text, the songs were sung to popular melodies of the time.

http://music.ldsblogs.com/1238/emma-smith-and-the-first-hymns-of-the-ch

THE FACT: You might ask how many hymns from the original hymnal are found in our current hymn book. The answer is twenty-five, including

Redeemer of Israel
How Firm a Foundation
The Spirit of God
Gently Raise the Sacred Strain

http://music.ldsblogs.com/1238/emma-smith-and-the-first-hymns-of-the-ch

QUESTION:

25. What was the most commonly sung hymn during pioneer meetings?

    a. Adam-ondi-Ahman
    b. We Thank Thee, O God, for a Prophet
    c. Ye Elders Of Israel
    d. Come, Come Ye Saints

SECTION 26

BRIEF HISTORICAL BACKGROUND: At Harmony, Pennsylvania, in July 1830, Joseph Smith received revelation for himself, Oliver Cowdery, and John Whitmer.

THE STORY: This is one of the shorter sections in the Doctrine and Covenants—two verses—yet it is an important section because the Lord speaks on the law of common consent and the continual study of the scriptures. At this point in the history of the Church, Joseph Smith and his scribes Oliver Cowdery and John Whitmer had begun the translation of the King James Version of the Bible. This project consumed much of the men's time from June 1830 to July 1833. This was detailed work as it produced nearly five hundred pages and thousands of passages that were either confusing or contradicted. Because of this, the Lord inspired the Prophet to bring new clarity to the Bible. Joseph referred to this work as the new translation, although once in printed form, it was named the inspired revision or the inspired translation.

Just how extensive was this work? There are 3,400 verses that Joseph Smith, through inspiration, clarified. Yet he never finished it because he suffered a premature, martyr's death.

Robert J. Matthews, "Joseph Smith's Inspired Translation of the Bible," *Ensign*, Dec. 1972

THE FACT: Joseph Smith declared the following:

I believe the Bible as it read when it came from the pen of the original writers. Ignorant translators, careless transcribers, or designing and corrupt priests have committed many errors.

Robert J. Matthews, "Joseph Smith's Inspired Translation of the Bible," *Ensign*, Dec. 1972

26. How many times has the Bible been translated?

    a. 11 times
    b. 190 times
    c. 99 times
    d. 39 times

SECTION 27

BRIEF HISTORICAL BACKGROUND: Revelation given to Joseph Smith in relation to the sacrament. This revelation was received at Harmony, Pennsylvania, during August 1830.

THE STORY: Joseph Smith requests to have a meeting with his wife, John Whitmer, and Newell Knight and his wife. It's at this meeting when Joseph wishes to confirm his wife, Emma, and also Sister Knight members of the Church. Prior to the confirmation, Joseph desires to bless and partake of the sacrament. The Prophet leaves to purchase wine for the meeting. While on this trip, Joseph is met by an angel who instructs him that it does not matter what he uses for the sacrament, so long as it is done "with an eye single to the glory of the Lord."

The August 1989 *Ensign* includes an interesting article about the New family, who moved from the Salt Lake City area to Brevig Mission, Alaska. There Brother New accepted a teaching position in a remote little town just eighty miles south of the North Pole. What he and his wife hadn't counted on was the lack of supplies on the stores' shelves in the village. Their first Sunday they held sacrament meeting with only their family and one other village girl, who happened to be the only other member of the Church. Brother and Sister New weren't able to buy bread to use for the sacrament; however, Sister New was able to cook pancakes that substituted for the bread.

Prior to blessing the sacrament, Brother New read Doctrine and Covenants 27:2, which reads, "For, behold, I say unto you, that it mattereth not what ye shall eat or what ye shall drink when ye partake of the sacrament, if it so be that ye do it with an eye single to my glory—remembering unto the Father my body which was laid down for you, and my blood which was shed for the remission of your sins."

This was a great teaching opportunity for Brother New, because he was able to explain to his family that bread is to be used for the sacrament, but if bread is not available, then it's acceptable to substitute with another available commodity. He went on to teach that they had used pancakes as an exception because of their great need to partake of this spiritual blessing.

http://www.lds.org/ensign/1989/08/at-home-on-the-tundra?lang=eng

It's interesting that the complete use of water during the sacrament actually didn't take place in all congregations until the end of Brigham Young's presidency.

THE FACT: A letter sent by the First Presidency on July 11, 1877 to all wards encouraged the passing of the sacrament to children during Sunday School so they could learn the importance of the ordinance.

In early Church history, it was the practice to either have someone speak or to sing hymns during the sacrament. The custom of speaking during the administration of the sacrament discontinued shortly after Brigham Young's presidency. On May 2, 1946, the First Presidency issued the following statement:

> The ideal condition is to have absolute quiet during the passing of the sacrament, and that we look with disfavor upon vocal solos, duets, group signing, or instrumental music during the administration of this sacred ordinance.

> http://lds.org/ensign/1988/04/remembering-the-saviors-atonement?lang=eng

QUESTION:

27. Verse 12 speaks of the Lord sending Peter, James, and John, who ordained Joseph and Oliver to the apostleship. Little is said about this situation, but what is the event that led up to it?

  a. Joseph and Oliver praying in the woods
  b. Joseph and Oliver working the fields near Joseph's home in Harmony
  c. Joseph and Oliver escaping court with the help of their lawyer
  d. Joseph and Oliver fishing on the Susquehanna River

SECTION 28

BRIEF HISTORICAL BACKGROUND: Revelation given through Joseph Smith to Oliver Cowdery in reference to Hiram Page's seer stone. This revelation was received at Fayette, New York, in September 1830.

THE STORY: Hiram Page claimed to have in his possession a seer stone that provided him with many revelations. Newell Knight records that when he arrived in Fayette for the second conference of the Church, "he [Hiram Page] had quite a roll of papers full of these revelations," which had led a number of the Whitmers, Oliver Cowdery, and others astray, regardless of the fact that the revelations were in opposition to the New Testament and to the revelations received by Joseph Smith. Newell Knight further adds that the Prophet was extremely concerned with the situation, so concerned in fact, "that the greater part of the night was spent in prayer and supplication" concerning what he should do to defuse the situation. It was then Joseph received section 28.

The next day at conference, the Prophet reasoned with those who had been swayed by Hiram Page's revelation. To the joy of all, the seer stone was renounced and peace prevailed for the remainder of the conference.

Journal History, 26 September 1830.

THE FACT: It's easy to fault Hiram Page and those that followed him momentarily; however, a study of their previous religious background will help give additional knowledge and explain why they were so easily swayed. Many of these converts were from a Congregationalist environment, and, as such, any member claiming inspiration had the right to proclaim whatever doctrine they wanted to the rest of the congregation provided those listening concurred.

http://institute.lds.org/manuals/doctrine-and-covenants
-institute-student-manual/dc-in-021-28.asp

I failed to understand this as a young missionary serving many years ago in the Massachusetts Boston Mission, but this helps explain Reverend Rust. He was a Congregationalist minister that my companion and I taught while serving in Dover-Foxcroft, Maine. He was an open-minded, humble man with a great love for his parishioners. He loved the idea of the home teaching program we have in the Church and could see the benefits this would provide for his congregation. Sadly though, when he presented the idea to his congregation, not only did they reject the idea, but they also "fired" him from his own church.

QUESTION:

28. How did Hiram Page receive revelation through his seer stone?

   a. Kept it in his pocket
   b. Wore it around his neck
   c. Held it in his left hand
   d. Placed it in the bottom of a hat

SECTION 29

BRIEF HISTORICAL BACKGROUND: Revelation given in the presence of six elders pertaining to millennial events and the Second Coming. This revelation was received at Fayette, New York, in September 1830.

THE STORY: The Doctrine and Covenants is silent on the identity of the six elders, but the answer can be found in the Book of Commandments.

> The headnote in the Book of Commandments states that section 29 is, "a Revelation to the church of Christ, given in the presence of six elders, in Fayette, New York 1830." The minutes of the second conference of the Church (26 September 1830), found in the 'Far West Record,' list six elders present in addition to Joseph Smith: Oliver Cowdery, David Whitmer, John Whitmer, Peter Whitmer, Samuel H. Smith, and Thomas B. Marsh. These six men are undoubtedly the same six referred to in the headnote.
>
> http://www.gospeldoctrine.com/DoctrineandCovenants/DC%2029.htm

Verse 6 states the following, "And, as it is written—Whatsoever ye shall ask in faith, being united in prayer according to my command, ye shall receive."

There is strength in united prayer, whether that's in the leading councils of the Church or a husband and wife in combined prayer fervently seeking assistance to raise their family.

President Benson tells of the time when persecution reached a fever pitch while he was a young missionary serving in Northern England during 1922. His mission president instructed the missionaries to discontinue street meetings for the moment. At about this time, Elder Benson and his companion received a letter from a congregation, inviting them to come to their town to speak. They promised the elders that the people in their town didn't share the same sentiments that others felt. In addition, they promised the two elders that it would be a good meeting. Elder Benson and his companion prayed and fasted, then with humbled hearts attended the meeting. President Benson states that he prepared a talk on the apostasy, but realized at the conclusion of his speech, that he spoke with freedom on the divine mission of Joseph Smith and the Book of Mormon. After the meeting a number of nonmembers came forward and said, "Tonight we received a witness that the gospel is true as you elders teach it. We are now ready for baptism."

President Benson in the same *Ensign* article shares another time when World War II was over and he was assigned to deliver much-needed clothes, medicine, and food to the suffering Saints in war-torn Europe. President Benson desired to meet with the commander in charge over the American forces in the European area. When meeting the appointment officer, President Benson was told that he could not meet the general for at least three days. President Benson said he couldn't wait that long, that it was imperative he meet with him that very day. Again he was turned down. President Benson and his companion left the building and went to their vehicle, where they offered a fervent prayer. After fifteen minutes, he went back in the building and noticed there was a different appointment officer. Within fifteen minutes they were given permission to meet with the general. President Benson then states:

> We explained the welfare program and how it operated. Finally, he said, "Well, gentlemen, you go ahead and collect your supplies; and by the time you get them collected, the policy may be changed."
> We said, "General, our supplies are already collected; they're always collected. Within twenty-four hours from the time we wire the First Presidency of the Church in Salt Lake City, carloads of supplies will be rolling toward Germany. We have many storehouses filled with basic commodities."
> He then said, "I've never heard of a people with such vision." His heart was touched as we had prayed it would be. Before we left his office, we had a written authorization to make our own distribution to our own people through our own channels.
>
> http://lds.org/ensign/1977/05/prayer?lang=eng

THE FACT: Throughout the restoration period, the Lord blessed the Saints with miracles that resulted from the efforts of combined prayer. For instance, the Three Witnesses' desire to view the gold plates was in direct relation to their ability to supplicate the Lord as a group. Oliver Cowdery and Joseph Smith's effort to pray behind drawn curtains in the Kirtland Temple on April 3, 1836, led to a visitation from the Savior, Moses, Elijah, and Elias. The same is true for the Saints as they crossed the plains to the Salt Lake Valley. It was common for them to sing and dance around the campfire at the end of an arduous day and then as a group pray for their successful journey to their desert home. Great things happen in group prayer as the following story illustrates.

Four young missionaries were giving a street meeting in Oklahoma. They had just finished singing "Come, Come, Ye Saints," and couldn't help but noticed they had piqued the attention of the old Indian chief. The chief watched in wonder as the missionaries sang their song. At the conclusion, the old chief invited the missionaries to come to his hogan.

As the missionaries sat in the hogan, the chief shared with them an incredible story. He told them how he remembered many years earlier when the Mormons were a persecuted people and had fled to the west to find religious freedom. He spoke of Brigham Young taking his people to the Salt Lake Valley and also spoke of many other white men coming to the West to start new lives. The old chief said how his people were angered by the white man trespassing on their land and how they killed all that they could so that others would not come. He told of one night when a group of pioneers had camped for the evening in a small valley. He said that after their dinner, they sang and danced and then just before bed sang, "Come, Come Ye Saints." The old chief mentioned he had one thousand Indian braves with him that evening hiding behind rocks and trees, waiting for his command to strike down every pioneer with their bows and arrows. The chief stated a miraculous event happened that night when he gave the command.

"I gave the signal," he said. "But our fingers were like stone. Not one arrow was shot. We mounted our horses and rode away because we knew the Great Spirit was watching over the pale faces."

The old chief took a violin from behind the door and started to play "Come, Come, Ye Saints." Then he stopped, looked intently at the missionaries, and finished his story. "This is your song, but it is my song too. I play it every night before I go to bed. It brings the Great Spirit here to me and makes me and my people calm and happy."

Lucile C. Reading, Shining Moments vol. 1
(Salt Lake City: Deseret Book, 1985), 136–37

QUESTION:

29. This section is cross-reference with what Book of Mormon passage concerning the redemption of little children?

   a. Moroni 8:12
   b. Alma 17:4
   c. 3 Nephi 18:4
   d. Words of Mormon 1:5

SECTION 30

BRIEF HISTORICAL BACKGROUND: The Lord calls Oliver Cowdery and Peter Whitmer Jr. on a mission to the Lamanites. Joseph Smith receives this revelation September 1830 at Fayette, New York.

THE STORY: It's a familiar fact that four elders, after visiting the friendly Cattaraugus (Seneca) tribe in the Buffalo, New York, area, and leaving them with two copies of the Book of Mormon, made their way to Mentor, Ohio, just a few miles north of present-day Kirtland. While in Mentor, Parley P. Pratt presented a

Book of Mormon to a hospitable Sidney Rigdon (Parley P. Pratt's former minister when Parley belonged to the Reformed Baptist Society) and his wife. Sidney promised the elders he would read the book. For the next two weeks, while the elders were laboring in nearby Kirtland, Sidney poured over the Book of Mormon, hardly putting it down, not even to eat or rest. Sidney knew the book was true but faced a dilemma (this is where the story gets interesting).

Sidney Rigdon was the minister to a large congregation. As a minister, Sidney refused to preach for money. To get around this issue, his congregation built him a new church, complete with home and farm. Sidney and his wife were just getting ready to move into the new home when the elders first arrived on his front door. Sidney understood the consequence of accepting the Book of Mormon and converting to the new faith. Both he and his wife were cognizant they would not realize the new church, home, and farm, and he would be asked to leave his congregation. Nevertheless, because of a revelation, Sidney and his wife desired baptism.

http://www.einarerickson.com/index2.php?option=com
_content&do_pdf=1&id=121

THE FACT: The four elders experienced great success in Kirtland, and soon the first baptism was scheduled. Parley P. Pratt invited Sidney Rigdon and his wife to the baptism. They did attend; however, prior to his own baptism, Sidney asked that he could speak to his congregation once more. Like only Sidney could, he spoke eloquently to his flock, extending forgiveness to all and asking for forgiveness in return. He had his parishioners reduced to tears. At the baptism of Sidney and his wife the next morning, many in his congregation were present. After being raised out of the water by Oliver Cowdery, and while still standing in the water, Sidney immediately preached to those who witnessed the event. This speech caused many of his congregation to enter the water and to be baptized with him. Sidney hadn't even dried off yet was responsible for the conversion of numerous individuals.

Other future Church leaders who joined due to this first mission in the Kirtland area were Orson Hyde, John Murdock, Frederick G. Williams, and Philo Dibble.

http://www.einarerickson.com/index2.php?option=com
_content&do_pdf=1&id=121

QUESTION:

30. While on their mission, Oliver Cowdery, Parley P. Pratt, Peter Whitmer Jr., and Ziba Petersen converted many people in the Kirtland, Ohio, region. One of their converts would join them in their mission to the Lamanites. Who was it?
   a. Phil Dibble
   b. Orson Hyde
   c. John Murdock
   d. Frederick G. Williams

SECTION 31

BRIEF HISTORICAL BACKGROUND: A revelation given to Thomas B. Marsh through Joseph Smith at Fayette, New York, in September 1830.

THE STORY: Thomas B. Marsh spent much of his early life in the Albany to New York City area. After marrying his wife, his career path swung from the restaurant and hotel industry to the grocery business. After an unsuccessful one and a half years, he left the grocery business, moved to Boston, engaged in a foundry, and joined the Methodist church. Thomas Marsh then records this about the Methodists:

While engaged in this business I joined the Methodist Church and tried for two years to be a genuine Methodist, but did not succeed any better in getting Methodist religion than I did in the grocery business. I compared Methodism with the Bible, but could not make it correspond.

http://saintswithouthalos.com/b/marsh_tbh.phtml

THE FACT: Thomas records he felt inspired by the Spirit to take a trip west. He, along with his friend Benjamin Hall, traveled to Lima, Livingstone County, New York. After a three-month stay, Thomas and Benjamin decided to travel to the Boston area. Their first night on the journey home, they stayed with a family from Lyonstown. The next morning, while preparing for their day's trip, the lady of the house asked Thomas Marsh if he had heard about a "golden bible" found by a young man named Joseph Smith. Thomas replied that he had never heard of such news but was anxious to learn more, realizing that this might be why he had the urge to go west. The lady informed Thomas that he could learn more from a Martin Harris who lived in Palmyra. Thomas eventually found Martin in the Grandin printing shop in Palmyra just as the first sixteen pages of proof were struck off the press. Realizing Thomas's intent, Martin Harris guides him to the home of Joseph Smith Sr., where he met Oliver Cowdery. Oliver answered Thomas's numerous questions.

Thomas stayed in the area for two days and then journeyed back to Boston. He records the following:

> After arriving home and finding my family all well, I showed my wife the sixteen pages of the Book of Mormon which I had obtained, with which she was well pleased, believing it to be the work of God. From this time for about one year I corresponded with Oliver Cowdery and Joseph Smith, Jun., and prepared myself to move west.
>
> Learning by letter that the Church of Jesus Christ had been organized on the 6th day of April, 1830, I moved to Palmyra, Ontario County, in September following, and landed at the house of Joseph Smith, Sen., with my whole family.

http://saintswithouthalos.com/b/marsh_tbh.phtml

QUESTION:

31. After Thomas B. Marsh left the Methodist church, he found others with his same spiritual inclinations as himself. People would refer to this group as what?

    a. Dry Mormons
    b. Rebels
    c. Reformers
    d. Quietist

SECTION 32

BRIEF HISTORICAL BACKGROUND: In October 1830, at Fayette, New York, Joseph Smith received the following revelation calling Parley P. Pratt and Ziba Peterson to preach the gospel to the Lamanites along with Oliver Cowdery and Peter Whitmer Jr.

THE STORY: Verse 3 reads, "And Ziba Peterson also shall go with them; and I myself will go with them and be in their midst; and I am their advocate with the Father, and nothing shall prevail against them."

Parley and Ziba not only received their mission calls simultaneously, but they also experienced court time together. This next story is the fulfillment of the Lord's promise in verse 3. About fifty miles west of Kirtland, the five missionaries (remember, they now have Frederick G. Williams accompanying them) are invited into the home of Simeon Carter. It's while the missionaries are teaching the Carter family that Parley P. Pratt is arrested. Ziba tags along with him to the courtroom. In the courtroom Parley asked Ziba to sing the hymn "O How Happy Are They," to the judge. Why Parley and Ziba did this, history does not explain. This only served to exasperate the judge, partly due to the late hour (close to midnight), who let Ziba go but jailed Parley. Realizing that the charges against Elder Pratt were trumped up, the judge soon released him to join his missionary companions.

http://www.einarerickson.com/index2.php?option=com _content&do_pdf=1&id=121

THE FACT: Ziba Peterson's life takes an interesting turn shortly after the missionary group broke up. Ziba and Peter Whitmer were the only two missionaries that did not have the chance to preach to the American Indians. The two of them took jobs as tailors in Independence to support the five missionaries while the other three spent time preaching to the American Indians before they were ordered out by the government. To compensate for their missed opportunity, Ziba and Peter crossed the Missouri River on April 8, 1831. Ziba, in company with Oliver Cowdery, then traveled to Lafayette County to preach. Here Elder Peterson met and converted his future wife, Rebecca Hopper. Later that summer Ziba Peterson shared the gospel in the town of Lone Jack in southern Missouri. By May 1833, Ziba had been excommunicated from the Church and was teaching school in Lone Jack. In 1848, the Peterson family moved to Dry Diggins, California, where Ziba was elected sheriff. Other than his mission, he may be best noted for supervising the hanging of three desperadoes, which were the first legal hangings in the state of California. The town was renamed Hangtown. By the next year (1849), Ziba died of unknown causes in Placerville, California. His widow moved to the Napa Valley, purchasing land in the Sonoma area.

QUESTION:

32. Who sold the land to Rebecca Peterson in Sonoma?
    a. Levi Hancock, spiritual leader to the Mormon Battalion
    b. Samuel Brannan, leader of a group of Saints from New York City to San Francisco on the ship *Brooklyn* and the first California millionaire
    c. Lt. Col. Philip St. George Cooke, commanding officer of the Mormon Battalion
    d. Lilburn W. Boggs, former governor of the State of Missouri who issued the infamous extermination order

SECTION 33

BRIEF HISTORICAL BACKGROUND: Revelation given through Joseph Smith to Ezra Thayre and Northrop Sweet at Fayette, New York, during October 1830.

THE STORY: The Lord declares in verse 1, "Behold, I say unto you, my servants Ezra and Northrop, open ye your ears and hearken to the voice of the Lord your God, whose word is quick and powerful, sharper than a two-edged sword, to the dividing asunder of the joints and marrow, soul and spirit; and is a discerner of the thoughts and intents of the heart."

The following is Ezra's conversion story:

> When Hyrum [Smith] began to speak, every word touched me to the inmost soul. I thought every word was pointed to me. God punished me and riveted me to the spot. I could not help myself. The tears rolled down my cheeks, I was very proud and stubborn. There were many there who knew me, I dare not look up. I sat until I recovered

myself before I dare look up. They sung some hymns and that filled me with the Spirit. When Hyrum got through, he picked up a book and said, "here is the Book of Mormon." I said, let me see it. I then opened the book, and I received a shock with such exquisite joy that no pen can write and no tongue can express. I shut the book and said, what is the price of it? "Fourteen shillings" was the reply. I said, I'll take the book. I opened it again, and I felt a double portion of the Spirit, that I did not know whether I was in the world or not. I felt as though I was truly in heaven. Martin Harris rushed to me to tell me that the book was true. I told him that he need not tell me that, for I knew that it is true as well as he.

http://www.sugardoodle.net/Stories_Thoughts_Poems
/Doctrine%20n%20Covenants/D_C33.htm

THE FACT: Even though both Northrop Sweet and Ezra Thayre had direct communication from the Lord through the prophet, it still wasn't enough to keep them faithful in the Church. After the death of Joseph Smith in 1844, Ezra faltered and left, in spite of the fact that he was chosen to be a Seventy. Northrop only lasted a few months after his conversion before he chose to separate himself from the Church. Elder George A. Smith relates the following situation leading to Brother Sweet's departure:

Joseph Smith came to Kirtland, and taught that people in relation to their error. He showed them that the Spirit of God did not bind men nor make them insane, and that the power of the adversary which had been manifested in many instances was visible even from that cause, for persons under its influence became helpless, and were bound hand and foot as in chains, being as immovable as a stick of timber. When Joseph came to instruct these Saints in relation to the true Spirit, and the manner of determining the one from the other, in a short time a number of those who had been influenced by those foul manifestations, apostatized. Among the number was Wycom Clark; he got a revelation that he was to be the prophet—that he was the true revelator; and himself, Northrop Sweet and four other individuals retired from the Church, and organized the "Pure Church of Christ," as they called it, composed of six members, and commenced having meetings, and preaching, but that was the extent of the growth of his early schism.

http://www.sugardoodle.net/Stories_Thoughts_Poems
/Doctrine%20n%20Covenants/D_C33.htm

Unfortunately, Ezra or Northrop forgot the Lord's admonition and failed to pay attention to the Lord's counsel. People that do follow the Lord's will in their lives or the voice of the prophet cannot go astray.

QUESTION:

33. The Pure Church of Christ was what number of church to break from the LDS church?
    a. First
    b. Second
    c. Third
    d. Fourth

SECTION 34

BRIEF HISTORICAL BACKGROUND: Revelation given through Joseph Smith to nineteen-year-old Orson Pratt at Fayette, New York, on November 4, 1830.

THE STORY: None of us could fathom letting a ten-and-a-half-year-old child leave home and venture into the world, yet this is what Orson did and it became great preparation for the many missions he served for the Church. The Lord states in verse 10, "Wherefore, lift up your voice and spare not, for the Lord God hath spoken; therefore prophesy, and it shall be given by the power of the Holy Ghost." He understood the command, serving missions until no other person could match his record. Orson writes the following:

> From the age of 10 to 19 I saw much of the world and was tossed about without any permanent abiding place, but through the grace

of God, I was kept from many of the evils to which young people are exposed. The early impressions of morality and religion, instilled into my mind by my parents, always remained with me; and I often felt a great anxiety to be prepared for a future state, but never commenced in real earnest, to seek after the Lord until the autumn of 1829. I then began to pray very fervently, repenting of every sin. In the silent shades of night, while others were slumbering upon their pillows, I often retired to some secret place in the lonely fields or solitary wilderness, and bowed before the Lord and prayed for hours with a broken heart and contrite spirit; this was my comfort and delight. The greatest desire of my heart was for the Lord to manifest His will concerning me. I continued to pray in this fervent manner until September 1830, at which time two Elders of the Church of Jesus Christ of Latter-day Saints came into the neighborhood, one of which was my brother, Parley. They held several meetings which I attended.

Orson Pratt's Works (Salt Lake City: Deseret News Press, 1945), xi–xii

THE FACT: Parley's side of the story:

I addressed crowded audiences almost every day, and the people, who had known me from a child, seemed astonished—knowing that I had had but little opportunity of acquiring knowledge by study; and while many were interested in the truth, some began to be filled with envy, and with a lying, persecuting spirit. My father, mother, aunt Van Cott, and many others, believed the truth in part; but my brother Orson, a youth of nineteen years, received it with all his heart, and was baptized at that time, and has ever since spent his days in the ministry.

Autobiography of Parley P. Pratt, (Salt Lake City: Deseret Book, 1980), 43

Orson's side of the story:

Two Elders of this Church came into the neighborhood (one of which was his brother Parley). I heard their doctrine, and believed it to be the ancient Gospel; and as soon as the sound penetrated my ears, I knew that if the Bible was true, their doctrine was true. They taught not only the ordinances, but the gifts and blessings promised the believers, and the authority necessary in the Church in order to administer the ordinances. All these things I received with gladness. Instead of feeling, as many do, a hatred against the principles, hoping they were not true, fearing and trembling lest they were, I rejoiced with great joy, believing that the ancient principles of the Gospel were restored to the earth—that the authority to preach it was also restored. I rejoiced that my ears were saluted with these good tidings while I was yet a youth, and in the day, too, of the early rising of the kingdom of God. I went forward and was baptized. I was the only individual baptized in that country for many years afterward. I immediately arranged my business and started off on a journey of two hundred and thirty miles to see the Prophet. I found him in the house of old father Whitmer, in Fayette, Seneca County, State of New York,—the house where this Church was first organized, consisting of only six members. I also found David Whitmer, then one of the three witnesses who saw the angel and the plates. . . .

I called upon the Lord with more faith than before, for I had then received the first principles of the Gospel. The gift of the Holy Ghost was given to me; and when it was shed forth upon me, it gave me a testimony concerning the truth of this work that no man can ever take from me."

Roy W. Doxey, comp., *Latter-day Prophets and the Doctrine and Covenants* (Salt Lake City: Deseret Book, 1978), 1:363

QUESTION:

34. Orson Pratt holds the record for serving the most missions in the Church. How many did he serve?

    a. 14
    b. 17
    c. 19
    d. 11

SECTION 35

BRIEF HISTORICAL BACKGROUND: Revelation directing Joseph Smith to call Sidney Rigdon as his scribe during the Bible translation. This revelation was received in December 1830, at or near Fayette, New York.

THE STORY: The Lord, speaking to Sidney Rigdon through the Prophet Joseph Smith, states in verses 3–6, "Behold, verily, verily, I say unto my servant Sidney, I have looked upon thee and thy works. I have heard thy prayers, and prepared thee for a greater work. Thou art blessed, for thou shalt do great things. Behold thou wast sent forth, even as John, to prepare the way before me, and before Elijah which should come, and thou knewest it not. Thou didst baptize by water unto repentance, but they received not the Holy Ghost; But now I give unto thee a commandment, that thou shalt baptize by water, and they shall receive the Holy Ghost by the laying on of the hands, even as the apostles of old."

The Prophet had just called his two scribes Oliver Cowdery and John Whitmer on missions. This was a critical time for the Prophet Joseph since the project of translating the Bible was in full swing. Little did Joseph realize that Oliver would be instrumental in the conversion of Sidney Rigdon, the answer to Joseph's desire for a new scribe. And little did Sidney realize that the Lord was preparing him to fill this roll for the Prophet even prior to Brother Rigdon accepting the gospel. The Lord knew Sidney and understood his talents, and once Sidney had found the Prophet, through the spirit of inspiration, the Lord could put those talents to work assisting Joseph.

THE FACT: Joseph Fielding Smith explains the Lord's preparation of Sidney Rigdon, even prior to the missionaries coming to Ohio and finding him:

The Lord told Sidney that he had looked upon him and his works, having reference to his ministry as a Baptist and later as one of the founders of the "Disciples" with Alexander Campbell and Walter Scott. During those years the hand of the Lord was over him and directing him in the gathering of many earnest souls who could not accept the teachings of the sects of the day. His prayers in which he sought further light than the world was able to give, were now to be answered. The Lord informed him that he had been sent to prepare the way, and in the gathering of his colony and the building up of his congregation in and around Kirtland, the hand of the Lord was directing him, and the way for the reception of the fulness of truth was being prepared. It should be carefully noted that a great number of forceful, intelligent men who became leaders in the Church had been gathered by Sidney Rigdon, with the help of the Lord, in this part of the land. Without any question, the Spirit of the Lord had rested upon these men, as it did on Sidney Rigdon and Parley P. Pratt, to direct them to gather in Kirtland at that early day. When, therefore, Parley P. Pratt, Ziba Peterson and their companions came to Kirtland they found the way prepared for them through the preaching, very largely, of Sidney Rigdon, so that it was not a difficult matter for these missionaries to convince this group of the truth. While Sidney was preaching and baptizing by immersion without authority, which the Lord informed him in this revelation, yet it all resulted in good when the Gospel message reached them. These men were not only convinced and ready for baptism, but were in a condition by which the Priesthood could be given them, and this was done.

Joseph Fielding Smith, *Church History and Modern Revelation*
(Salt Lake City: Deseret Book, 1949), 1:160

QUESTION:

35. Oliver Cowdery is called on the Lamanite mission. Where was John Whitmer called to?

   a. To Canada
   b. To Kirtland, to watch over the branch
   c. To New York, to gather the New England Saints
   d. To Colesville, New York, to serve as branch president

SECTION 36

BRIEF HISTORICAL BACKGROUND: Revelation directed to Edward Partridge through Joseph Smith at Fayette, New York, during December 1830.

THE STORY: Edward Partridge was one of many who converted when Oliver, Parley, Ziba, and Peter preached the gospel in the Kirtland, Ohio, area. Even though he was converted to the faith, he refused baptism until he met the Prophet Joseph Smith. Shortly after Sidney Rigdon's baptism into the Church, Sidney and Edward journeyed eastward to meet the Prophet of God at Fayette, New York.

http://www.einarerickson.com/index2.php?option=com
_content&do_pdf=1&id=121

THE FACT: Why didn't Brother Partridge baptize into the Church in Kirtland like his counterpart Sidney? According to the following story, as related by Lucy Mack Smith, it's possible Edward had doubt that still clouded his mind as to Joseph's character.

In December of the same year [1830], Joseph appointed a meeting at our house. While he was preaching, Sidney Rigdon and Edward Partridge came in and seated themselves in the congregation. When Joseph had finished his discourse, he gave all who had any remarks to make, the privilege of speaking. Upon this, Mr. Partridge arose, and stated that he had been to Manchester, with the view of obtaining further information respecting the doctrine which we preached; but, not finding us, he had made some inquiry of our neighbors concerning our characters, which they stated had been unimpeachable, until Joseph deceived us relative to the Book of Mormon. He also said that he had walked over our farm, and observed the good order and industry which it exhibited; and, having seen what we had sacrificed for the sake of our faith, and having heard that our veracity was not questioned upon any other point than that of our religion, he believed our testimony, and was ready to be baptized, "if," said he, "Brother Joseph will baptize me."

"You are now," replied Joseph, "much fatigued, brother Partridge, and you had better rest to-day, and be baptized tomorrow."

"Just as Brother Joseph thinks best," replied Mr. Partridge, "I am ready at any time."

He was accordingly baptized the next day.

Scot Facer Proctor and Maurine Jensen Proctor, *The Revised and Enhanced History of Joseph Smith By His Mother* (Salt Lake City: Deseret Book, 1996), 249–50.

Question:

36. Immediately after being baptized by Joseph Smith in the Seneca River and then ordained an elder by Sidney Rigdon, where is Edward called to serve a mission?

   a. To his relatives in Massachusetts
   b. To catch up to Parley P. Pratt and help those elders teach the Lamanites
   c. To establish branches in the Kirtland area where he had just come from
   d. To prepare to go to England

Section 37

Brief Historical Background: The Lord commands Joseph Smith in December 1830 at Fayette, New York, that the Saints are to gather to the Ohio.

The Story: Because of the persecutions that the Saints were experiencing in the New York area, the Lord admonishes the Church to relocate to "the Ohio." The mission to the Lamanites helped produced 127 new converts to the Church in a three-week period. This number was considerably more than the total number of Saints throughout New York and Pennsylvania combined (approximately seventy). The environment in Kirtland was such that the Church could thrive for a time unmolested. In verse 1 of this section the Lord instructs, "Behold, I say unto you that it is not expedient in me that ye should translate any more until ye shall go to the Ohio, and this because of the enemy and for your sakes."

Joseph Smith had corrected the King James version of the Bible in Genesis 5:22. This is when Enoch and his people are first mentioned living in a condition "of one heart and mind, and dwelt in righteousness; and there were no poor among them" (Joseph Smith Translaton, Genesis 7:23.) I find it more than a coincidence that Joseph was working on this part of the Bible translation when he is told to move to Kirtland, Ohio. A review of the next twenty sections given in the Doctrine and Covenants will indicate the Lord revealing his "law" in connection with the consecration of properties, the building of a temple, the Sabbath, and establishing the economic order of the Church.

Robert J. Matthews, "Plain and Precious Things Restored," *Ensign*, July 1982

THE FACT: Not all were overjoyed at the influx of Mormon immigrants from the state of New York. This call to "the Ohio" definitely changed the landscape in the Kirtland area. What was a quaint community of 481 in 1820 would more than double to 1,018 by 1830. As a result of the Mormon immigration, the population of Kirtland would triple over the next seven years (http://eom.byu.edu/index.php/Kirtland,_Ohio). Needless to say, the persecution the Saints had escaped in New York found them again with the landing of steamships at Fairport Harbor. Eber D. Howe, editor of the anti-Mormon newspaper, the *Painesville Telegraph*, blindly penned the following article, titled "Mormon Emigration" on May 17, 1831:

> About two hundred men, women and children, of the deluded followers of Jo Smith's Bible speculation, have arrived on our coast during the last week, from the state of New York & are about seating

themselves down upon the 'promised land' in this county. It is surely a melancholy comment upon human nature to see so many people at this enlightened age of the world, truckling along at the ear of a miserable imposter, submitting themselves both soul and body, to his spiritual and temporal mandates, without a murmur, or presuming to question that it is all a command direct from Heaven.

http://www.mormonhistoricsitesfoundation.org/articles/InlandSeas.pdf

Regardless of what others publicly claimed, all that mattered was the Lord commanded, the Prophet instructed, and the Saints acted knowing there would be blessings in such an action. The small Church did not realize the heavenly manifestations waiting for them in Kirtland, such as increased revelations and a temple. The Lord would open the way for their safe arrival in the Kirtland area. For instance, Jared Cared (this is most likely a spelling mistake—Jared Carter is probably the individual quoted) in the article, "Mormon Migration on Lake Erie and Through Fairport Harbor," tells of what could very well be the first miracle performed on the waters in this dispensation. While sailing to Fairport Harbor, just north of Kirtland, Jared reports, their steamship hit dangerous winds. These winds were common on Lake Erie and many ships had sunk or broke up and people lost their lives. Brother Carter, who had just recently joined the Church on February 20, 1831 (baptized by Hyrum Smith), and although barely dry from baptism but high in faith, tells of calming the winds while traveling on the lake. He wrote:

> We had not gone far before we met with a stiff headwind which made us in considerable dangerous sailing. So that the Captain informed us of the danger, but at length we reached to Erie where the boat was tied by fonts, to wait for the wind. There was an influence as with a voice speaking with me. Go and command the winds in the name of Christ to cease. I immediately arose and went out of the hearing of the wicked crowd and said in the name of Jesus Christ, I command the winds to cease, and the wind from that moment began to cease and in about fifteen minutes it was stopped and the boat then soon started and we, in a few hours landed in Ohio, at Fairport.

http://www.mormonhistoricsitesfoundation.org/articles/InlandSeas.pdf

QUESTION:

37. The Prophet was not the only person to receive this revelation commanding the Saints to move to Ohio. Who else was instrumental in urging him?

    a. Emma Smith
    b. Joseph Smith Sr.
    c. Sidney Rigdon and Edward Partridge
    d. Oliver Cowdery and Parley P. Pratt

SECTION 38

BRIEF HISTORICAL BACKGROUND: On January 2, 1831, Joseph Smith received the following revelation at a conference of the Church in Fayette, New York.

THE STORY: There was some discussion at this conference regarding the Lord's request to move to Ohio. A number of the members had established farms, causing some to possess feelings that they really didn't want to let their property go and start over. Joseph Smith approached the Lord and received this revelation, wherein the Lord states in verse 37, "And they that have farms that cannot be sold, let them be left or rented as seemeth them good."

When the Lord speaks of leaving "farms that cannot be sold," it's obvious he was more than serious that the Saints make the move.

THE FACT: "Newel Knight said this entailed the sacrifice of their property. Newel sold 60 acres, Freeborn DeMille 61 acres, Aaron Culver 100 acres, and Father Knight 140 acres, with 'two

Dwelling Houses, a good barn, and a fine orchard.' Led by Newel, sixty-two Knight kin moved to Ohio as part of the first gathering."

William G. Hartley, "The Knight Family: Ever Faithful to the Prophet," *Ensign*, Jan. 1989, 46)

Newell Knight led the sixty-seven members of the Colesville Branch of the church, Martin Harris the fifty members of the Manchester Branch, and Thomas B. Marsh and Lucy Mack Smith the eighty members of the Fayette Branch. All Branches of the Church traveled separately, arriving in the Kirtland area between April and May of 1831.

http://eom.byu.edu/index.php/History_of_the_Church; http://www.mormonhistoricsitesfoundation.org/articles/InlandSeas.pdf

The following is a letter to the editor found in the *Palmyra Reflector* written January 26, 1831, from an individual in Waterloo, New York:

Elder S. Rigdon left this village on Monday morning last in the stage, for the "Holy Land," where all the "Gold Bible" converts, have recently received a *written* commandment from God, through Jo Smith, junior, to repair with all convenient speed after selling off the property. This command was at first resisted by such as had property, (the brethren from the neighboring counties being all assembled by special summons,) but after a night of fasting, prayer and trial, they all consented to obey the holy messenger.—Rigdon has for some time past been arranging matters with Smith for the final departure of the *faithful* for the "far west." The man of many CREEDS, (Rigdon) appears to possess colloquial powers to a considerable degree, and before leaving this vicinity left us his *blessing*. He delivered a discourse at the Court House immediately preceding his departure, wherein he depicted in strong language, the want of "charity and brotherly love" among the prevailing sects and denominations of professing christians, and sorry I am to admit, that he had too much truth on his side with regard to this particular. After denouncing dreadful vengeance on the whole state of New York, and this village in particular, and recommending to all such as wished to flee from "the wrath to come," to follow him beyond the "western waters," he took his leave.

https://ojs.lib.byu.edu/spc/index.php/RelEd/article/viewFile/2367/2204

QUESTION:

38. When the Fayette Saints arrived in Buffalo, New York, what did Thomas B. Marsh instruct Lucy Mack Smith not to do?
   a. Beg for food or housing
   b. Preach the gospel
   c. Override his priesthood authority
   d. Conduct group singing and prayers

SECTION 39 & 40

BRIEF HISTORICAL BACKGROUND: Revelation received January 5–6, 1831, at Fayette, New York, to Joseph Smith for nonmember James Covill.

THE STORY: James Covill had been a Baptist minister for over forty years when he approached Joseph Smith and, Nicodemus-like, indicated to the Prophet that he will do whatever the Lord asked of him. Similar to Nicodemus of old, once James understood that the Lord's will required him to be baptized and move to Ohio, it was more than he was willing to sacrifice. Such a move meant giving up the finer things of life afforded to him as a result of his ministerial career, moving to the western frontier of the United States, and carving out a new life—possibly a life of poverty. James Covill became an asterisk or an endnote because, after this occasion, he walked out of Church history . . . or did he?

In a listing of the branch membership of the Church at Ramus, Illinois (twenty miles southeast of Nauvoo), a sister by the name of Nancy Covill was found. She was born in 1810, and this branch's listing was taken in 1839, making her twenty-nine years old at the time. Is it possible, even though James did not join the Church as commanded by the Lord, that maybe a relative or one of his children eventually joined the Church due to their brief brush with the prophet in 1831? I realize there's danger in stating this because I don't have proof. My wife has researched Nancy Covill in hopes of making a connection, but as yet has come up empty-handed, and we recognize that there may be no connection at all between James and Nancy. In fact, by the 1840 census, no records of Nancy Covill can be found in Hancock County, Illinois. Obviously she moved or possibly married. The only reason I place my neck on the line and make this statement is to satisfy my desire that the situation among the Lord, James, and Joseph Smith might not have been a lost cause, but that something good did materialize by this heavenly manifestation to the minister. Again, I'm speculating, but could it be possible that Nancy was already a member and introduced James to the gospel and directed him to the Prophet? Wishful thinking.

THE FACT: In verse 19, the Lord instructs James, "Wherefore, go forth, crying with a loud voice, saying: The kingdom of heaven is at hand; crying: Hosanna! Blessed be the name of the Most High God." In this verse the Lord mentions of the Hosanna Shout, which is most notably engaged in during temple dedications. The Doctrine and Covenants makes reference to three occasions, Doctrine and Covenants 19:37, 36:3, and 39:19, in which the Lord encourages those so commanded to participate in the shout. The Lord commanded Martin Harris in Doctrine and Covenants 19 to preach the gospel, "even with a loud voice, with a sound of rejoicing, crying— Hosanna, hosanna, blessed be the name of the Lord God!" Related orders were given to Edward Partridge in December 1830 and finally to James Covill in January 1831. Steven Heath in his article "The Sacred Shout," in *Dialogue: A Journal of Mormon, Thought* shares the following:

> Perhaps the most unusual occurrence of this shout came in 1886 at the Utah State penitentiary in Salt Lake City. Many Mormon men were serving prison terms for unlawful cohabitation, including Lorenzo Snow, then president of the Quorum of the Twelve. At President Snow's funeral, Rudger Clawson, called just seven days

before as his second counselor, spoke of this unique experience:

He called the brethren together (there were some thirty-five or forty in all) and said in substance: "We have been sent to this place and are associated together in prison. It will be our privilege, if we so desire to express our feelings to the Lord by offering up unto Him the sacred shout." . . . The sacred shout was then offered up within those prison walls — a great and mighty shout to God and the Lamb. The foundation of the prison seemed to shake, and the shout ascended to heaven"

http://www.dialoguejournal.com/wp-content/uploads/sbi
/articles/Dialogue_V19N03_117.pdf

QUESTION:

39 & 40. How many times was the Hosanna Shout formally given in Joseph Smith's life time after the dedication of the Kirtland Temple?

    a. 12

    b. 5

    c. 1

    d. 9

SECTION 41

BRIEF HISTORICAL BACKGROUND: This is the first of many revelations Joseph Smith received in Kirtland, Ohio. Section 41 was given February 4, 1831.

THE STORY: As the Lord was preparing Sidney Rigdon to take over the task of serving as the Prophet Joseph Smith's scribe, even prior to his baptism, so too it appeared that Sidney's onetime parishioner Edward Partridge was also being groomed by the Lord to fulfill his call as bishop. The Lord required a man with a strong business background, one who had experience and understood land transactions, and one who excelled in leadership. Edward Partridge was all of this. He ran a successful hatter business, he owned multiple properties, and he was a respected civic leader in Painesville, Ohio. The Lord knew he would require a man who could administer to the demands of the "Law of Consecration" that the Lord was on the verge of revealing to the Prophet. Ironically, the Campbellites, which Edward Partridge was a member of at the time that Oliver Cowdery, Parley P. Pratt, Peter Whitmer Jr., and Ziba Peterson first appeared in the area, belonged to a religious society known as "Disciples," who believed that everyone in the society should have all things in common. Nevertheless, even after some of these people joined the Church, they still continued to practice what is known as "common stock." John Whitmer made an interesting observation that this practice didn't work because some thought it meant sharing everything including clothes, while others interpreted the rules differently. The Prophet Joseph Smith wrote:

> The branch of the Church in this part of the Lord's vineyard, which had increased to nearly one hundred members, were striving to do the will of God, so far as they knew it, though some strange notions and false spirits had crept in among them. With a little caution and some wisdom, I soon assisted the brethren and sisters to overcome them. The plan of "common stock," which had existed in what was called "the family," whose members generally had embraced the everlasting Gospel, was readily abandoned for the more perfect law of the Lord; and the false spirits were easily discerned and rejected by the light of revelation.

Edward Partridge had the experience the Lord required. Twice Edward posted advertisements in the local paper, once in January 1828 and again in September 1829 "to quit the hatting business and leave Painesville." His business never sold, making it possible for Oliver Cowdery to introduced him and his family to the gospel.

http://contentdm.lib.byu.edu/ETD/image/etd3238.pdf

THE FACT: Shortly after Joseph Smith baptized Edward Partridge in late December 1830, Edward traveled east to Pittsfield, Massachusetts, in hopes of sharing the gospel with his family. Arriving with high hopes, Edward soon realized his family, at least for the moment, did not desire the gospel. In her autobiography, Edward's daughter, Emily Dow Partridge, writes, "They pronounced him crazy," and one of his sisters ordered him out of her house and told him "never to come back again." Edward's parents were so concerned over his mental well-being that they sent their youngest son, James Harvey Partridge, to accompany Edward to Painesville, Ohio. Needless to say, Harvey was taught the gospel while in Ohio and joined the Church.

Emily tells of her father's trip to Fayette, New York. He was not yet a member but had been taught the gospel in the Kirtland area by the four elders to the Lamanites. Edward knew it was true and wanted to solidify his testimony by meeting the Prophet prior to being baptized. Emily writes of her father's homecoming after arriving in Kirtland with Joseph and Emma Smith and Sidney Rigdon:

> After his arrival home, his old and most intimate friends that had been so anxious for him to go and find out the truth of the reports about 'Mormonism' because of his honesty and superior judgment, pronounced him crazy when he declared the Book of Mormon true.
>
> http://www.boap.org/LDS/Early-Saints/EmPart.html

Edward Partridge's experience of informing his parents that he was a Latter-day Saint is a common story for many new members, even today. His story reminds me of my mother and her family's reaction when she announced she was going to unite with the Church. She was nineteen years old at the time and the consensus was she was doing a "crazy teenager thing." Yet she remained faithful to the Church and with time her mother (my dad was instrumental in her conversion) and one brother also joined. Her brother was a doctor, and so when he became a Latter-day Saint, "a man of science," much of the pressure was off my mom. President Monson, when he was a mission president in Ontario, was influential in the conversion of Dr. Koegler, my mom's brother. My grandfather never joined, and the remainder of my mom's siblings, one sister and two other brothers, also did not join. Nevertheless, since her "crazy teenage days," my mom has been loved and respected by her family.

QUESTION:

41. In this revelation, the Lord compares Edward Partridge to whom?
    a. Moses
    b. Nephi, son of Lehi
    c. Nathanael
    d. Paul

SECTION 42

BRIEF HISTORICAL BACKGROUND: On February 9, 1831, the Prophet Joseph Smith received the following revelation at Kirtland, Ohio. This revelation is known as "embracing the law of the Church."

THE STORY: In December 1830, Joseph Smith received section 38 of the Doctrine and Covenants when the Lord made the following promise in verse 32: "Wherefore, for this cause I gave unto you the commandment that ye should go to the Ohio; and there I will give unto you my law; and there you shall be endowed with power from on high."

In keeping with this stipulation, Joseph and Emma Smith, Sidney Rigdon, and Edward Partridge left Fayette, New York, for Kirtland, arriving in early February 1831. Shortly after their arrival, the Lord gave Joseph Smith section 41, in which the Lord made an additional stipulation by declaring in verses 2 and 3, "Hearken, O ye elders of my church whom I have called, behold I give unto you a commandment, that ye shall assemble yourselves together to agree upon my word; And by the prayer of your faith ye shall receive my law, that ye may know how to govern my church and have all things right before me."

On February 9, 1831, Joseph Smith assembled twelve elders and united in faith and prayers, and the Lord provided them with section 42, which became known as the "Law of the Church." It's interesting that this revelation was received on two separate days. On February 9, verses 1–73 were given to the Prophet. Two weeks later, on February 22, Joseph wrote to Martin Harris, "We have received the laws of the Kingdom since we came here and the Disciples in these parts have received them gladly." The following day, February 23, the Prophet and seven elders met to determine "how the Elders of the Church of Christ are to act upon the points of the Law." As a result, several additional paragraphs of instruction, comprising what is now Doctrine and Covenants 42:74–93, were recorded.

http://rsc.byu.edu/archived/doctrine-and-covenants-revelations-context/6-%E2%80%9C-laws-church-christ%E2%80%9D-dc-42-textual-and-histor

THE FACT: Not all members are familiar that section 42 was recorded in two subsequent visits from the Lord. What may be less understood is that verses 1–73 were received in answer to five questions that the Prophet inquired of the Lord:

1. "Shall the Church come together into one place or remain as they are in separate bodies?" (answered in verses 1–10);
2. "[What is] the Law regulating the Church in her present situation till the time of her gathering[?]" (answered in verses 11–69);
3. "How the Elders are to dispose of their families while they are proclaiming repentance or are otherwise engaged in the service of the Church?" (answered in verses 70–73);
4. "How far it is the will of the Lord that we Should have dealings with the wo[r]ld & how we Should conduct our dealings with them?" (answered in several sentences that were eliminated when the Doctrine and Covenants was published);

5. "What preparations we shall make for our Brethren from the East & when & how?" (also answered by text that was eliminated when the Doctrine and Covenants was published).

    http://rsc.byu.edu/archived/doctrine-and-covenants-revelations-context/6-
    %E2%80%9C-laws-church-christ%E2%80%9D-dc-42-textual-and-histor

QUESTION:

42. Which apostate's family donated to the Church a copy of the section 42 manuscript?

a. Symonds Ryder
b. John F. Boynton
c. Ezra Booth
d. John C. Bennett

SECTION 43

BRIEF HISTORICAL BACKGROUND: Revelation given to Joseph Smith at Kirtland, Ohio, in February 1831. This revelation was received regarding claims that some members were receiving revelations for the Church.

THE STORY: When the Church was organized on April 6, 1830, the Lord declared through his Prophet that the members of the Church are to "give heed unto all his words and command-ments. . .For his word ye shall receive, as if from mine own mouth, in all patience and faith" (D&C 21:4–5). In just a few short months, it was necessary for the Prophet to repeat this lesson again during the Hiram Page seer stone incident. Again, Joseph receives revelation in the form of section 28, in which the Lord states in verse 2, "no one shall be appointed to receive commandments and revelations in this church excepting my servant Joseph Smith, Jun." One and a half years later, it became imperative for the Lord to repeat a third time to the young Church the role of revelation from the Lord for the Church through his Prophet. This time, the Lord not only stated that Joseph is the only one that can receive revelation for the Church, but he also added, "Ye receive not the teachings of any that shall come before you as revelations or commandments. And this I give unto you that you may not be deceived, that you may know they are not of me" (D&C 43:5–6).

This third situation surfaced when a Mrs. Hubble claimed to have received revelations for the Church. John Whitmer wrote the following:

> She professed to be a prophetess of the Lord, and professed to have many revelations, and knew the Book of Mormon was true, and that she should become a teacher in the church of Christ. She appeared to be very sanctimonious and deceived some who were not able to detect her in her hypocrisy; others, however, had the spirit of discernment and her follies and abominations were manifest.
>
> *History of the Church*, 1:154

George A. Smith stated that in the early Church some elders had the notion that the Prophet was wrong on certain matters and took it into their own hands to spread deceiving reports, which only served to confuse some of the members. It was because of these actions the Prophet went to the Lord and was given revelation recorded as Doctrine and Covenants 43.

THE FACT: While some claimed to have revelation for the Church, others were acting strangely and causing confusion among the new converts. Problems arose with the manifestation of what was termed "strange notions and false spirits." There were some who had joined the Church and were living in the Kirtland area that entertained "wild enthusiastic notions." Early Ohio convert John Corrill shares the following insight in reference to the young people:

They conducted themselves in a strange manner, sometimes imitating Indians in their maneuvers, sometimes running out into the fields, getting on stumps of trees and there preaching as though surrounded by a congregation—all the while so completely absorbed in visions as to be apparently insensible to all that was passing around them.

Church History in the Fulness of Times, Church Educational System (Salt Lake City, Utah: The Church of Jesus Christ of Latter-day Saints, 1993), 92

QUESTION:

43. This revelation is often referred to as the Law of the Church. What else may it also be called?
    a. The Page/Hubble Law
    b. The Law of Revelation
    c. The Law of Christ
    d. The Law of the Prophet

SECTION 44

BRIEF HISTORICAL BACKGROUND: Revelation given to Joseph Smith and Sidney Rigdon at Kirtland, Ohio, February 1831. The Lord commanded the elders be called home from their missions for a conference in June.

THE STORY: Conferences have always been a source of spiritual uplift to the members of the Church. Joseph Smith understood this and felt the need to call the elders home. The following are a few conference oddities from the history of the Church:

- The general conference of 1833 was held on a ferryboat on the Big Blue River near Independence, Missouri.
- The first general conference held outside the United States was in Great Britain in 1840. This is also the same year that conferences switched from quarterly to semiannual events.
- Provo, Logan, St. George, and Coalville have all hosted general conferences.
- Due to a flu epidemic in 1919, April conference was postponed until June.
- The October 1957 conference was canceled due to another flu scare.
- During World War II, only Church leaders attended conference in the Assembly Hall because the Tabernacle was shut down during the war.

http://newsroom.lds.org/article/general-conference-history

THE FACT: I shared the story in section 18 of Eli H. Pierce, who was called to serve a mission over the pulpit at the October 1875 general conference. This was not unusual—in fact, it was quite normal. Men entered the tabernacle at conference time knowing they could possibly receive a mission call.

Although I've only mentioned men, we do know that women also serve missions in the Church and are valuable at what they do. In fact, I have a daughter who served in the Ohio Cleveland Mission and spent half of every day at the historical sites in Kirtland and proselyted the other half in east Cleveland suburbs. I understand that sister missionaries can get into doors that elders can only dream of. So, the question might be asked, who and when were the first sister missionaries called to serve in the Church? On April 1, 1898, Lucy Jane Brimhall and Amanda Inez Knight were called to serve as full-time missionaries to England.

Richard Neitzel Holzapfel et al, *On This Day in the Church* (Salt Lake City: Eagle Gate, 2000), 62

QUESTION:

44. In what year was general conference first viewed outside the intermountain region of Utah?

    a. 1949
    b. 1953
    c. 1923
    d. 1970

SECTION 45

BRIEF HISTORICAL BACKGROUND: Revelation given through Joseph Smith to the Church on March 7, 1831, at Kirtland, Ohio. Numerous false stories were circulating by word of mouth and press in hopes of stalling the successful growth of the Church.

THE STORY: The Church was growing by leaps and bounds in the Kirtland area. When Joseph first arrived in February 1831, there were approximately 100 individuals in the branch, with total Church membership around 300 members. At the close of 1831, Church membership had reached 680 members, followed by a 142 percent increase in growth from 1830, and then a 291 percent increase in 1832 with membership at 2,661. Is it any wonder that ministers began to worry about their flocks and circulate "false reports and foolish stories," that is mentioned in the heading of our current Doctrine and Covenants section 45? For example, Symonds Ryder, a Campbellite preacher joined the Church after reading a newspaper article elaborating on an earthquake in China. What caught his eye more than anything was the title of the article, "Mormonism in China." Why was it referred to as such when the Church's missionary efforts only extended to

Missouri, New England, and Canada? According to the story, "a young Mormon girl" had predicted the event six weeks earlier.

Church History in the Fulness of Times, Church Educational System (Salt Lake City: The Church of Jesus Christ of Latter-day Saints, 1993), 93

THE FACT: The following is a sampling of a comical (or sad— you be the judge) story that circulated in the early history of the Church. Mark Twain said:

> All men have heard of the Mormon Bible, but few except the "elect" have seen it, or, at least, taken the trouble to read it. I brought away a copy from Salt Lake. The book is a curiosity to me, it is such a pretentious affair, and yet so "slow," so sleepy; such an insipid mess of inspiration. It is chloroform in print. If Joseph Smith composed this book, the act was a miracle—keeping awake while he did it was, at any rate, if he, according to tradition, merely translated it from certain ancient and mysteriously engraved plates of copper, which he declares he found under a stone, in an out-of-the-way locality, the work of translating was equally a miracle, for the same reason. . . . Whenever he found his speech growing too modern—which was about every sentence or two—he ladled in a few such scriptural phrases as "exceeding sore," "and it came to pass," etc., and made things satisfactory again. "And it came to pass" was his pet. If he had left that out, his Bible would have been only a pamphlet."

Mark Twain (Samuel Clemens), *Roughing It* (Hartford, Connecticut: American Publishing Company, 1891), 128–29; Dan Barker, *Mormon History 101* (Springville, Utah: Cedar Fort, 2011), 131

QUESTION:

45. Not everything printed about the Church was false though. For instance, what did Leo Tolstoy (1828–1910), the great Russian novelist, say in regard to the Church?

   a. Like Nebuchadnezzar's dream, it would fill the entire earth
   b. It would become the greatest power the world has ever known
   c. It would settle in the shadows of the Wasatch Mountains
   d. It would be persecuted, but not die

SECTION 46

BRIEF HISTORICAL BACKGROUND: Revelation given at Kirtland, Ohio, March 8, 1831, to the Church. The Lord gives instructions on the manner of conducting Church meetings.

THE STORY: I have a son serving a mission in Uruguay, and my eldest son served in Chile. I rejoice along with them as I read their emails excitedly reporting their investigators that showed up to church. When I was a young missionary, I can recall well coming into many sacrament meetings late, just moments before the doors are closed to the chapel, eagerly anticipating the arrival of investigators. Yet it wasn't always like this. It seemed questionable to some, while the Church was in its infancy, that unbelievers would not be invited to Church meetings. I think when one studies the Church's past and realizes how many meetings were attended by those whose only intentions were to disrupt, it comes as no surprise that such practices were implemented. The following is the experience of John Murdock taken from his journal:

> And arrived at father Isaac Morley's about dark, and was soon introduced to those four men from New York, and presented with the Book of Mormon; I now said within myself, I have items placed before me that will prove to me whether it be of God or not viz: four men professing to be servants of the most high God, authorized to preach the gospel, and practice the ordinances thereof, and build up the Church after the ancient order; and having a book professing to have come forth by the power of God, containing the fullness of the gospel; I said if it be so their walk will agree with their profession, and the Holy Ghost will attend their ministration of the ordinances, and the Book of Mormon will contain the same plan of salvation as the Bible. I was sensible that such a work must come forth, but the question with me was, are these men that are to commence the work. I did not ask a sign of them by working a miracle, by healing a sick man, by raising a dead man, or, by casting out a devil; only I desired to know whether the Spirit would attend their ministration if the

Book of Mormon was not true, neither if they were not sent forth by God. Accordingly, that night was held the first confirmation meeting that was held in Ohio. And I said within myself it is a good time for me. For thought I, this night must prove it to be true, or false; I did not find out respecting the meeting till about ten o'clock at night. And at that time they had all left but three men; and I found they wanted to go to the meeting, and did not want those in, that had not been baptized. I said to them go, for if you wish to be alone, I do not blame you. The case is one of importance. They went and I stayed alone, and read the Book of Mormon.

http://www.boap.org/LDS/Early-Saints/JMurdock.html

THE FACT: The Lord gives the following instructions in verse 3, "Nevertheless ye are commanded never to cast any one out from your public meetings, which are held before the world."

Joseph Smith took this lesson to heart. By time the Church had located to Nauvoo, Illinois, not only were nonmembers encouraged to attend the Church's religious services, but also clergy from other denominations were invited to speak. The following from the *History of the Church*:

> At ten a.m., meeting at the stand. Willard Richards and Wilford Woodruff speak and then at half-past two p.m. Joseph Smith introduces Mr. de Wolf, a clergyman of the Episcopal Church, and requested the attention of the congregation in his behalf.

History of the Church, 5:427

QUESTION:

46. What Book of Mormon scripture caused some of the early Saints to question the practice of not inviting nonmembers to sacrament meeting?

   a. Helaman 11:21
   b. 4 Nephi 1:1
   c. Alma 1:19
   d. 3 Nephi 18:22

SECTION 47

BRIEF HISTORICAL BACKGROUND: Following this revelation, Joseph Smith designated John Whitmer as the Church historian. The Lord gave this revelation on March 8, 1831 at Kirtland, Ohio.

THE STORY: Not only did John Whitmer begin the history of the Church, but also about this time he collected the loose revelations that Joseph Smith has received and compiles them into *Revelation Book 1,* the forerunner to the Book of Commandments. John Whitmer acted as the Church Historian from 1831 to 1838, recording almost the entire Book of Commandments, with the exception of a few pages written by Oliver Cowdery. During this time he also recorded eighty-five pages of history. With all the exciting things that were happening in the young Church's history, it's safe to say that Brother Whitmer's eighty-five pages of history was sketchy at best. I suspect that John Whitmer's heart was never completely in it. In fact, when the Prophet Joseph extended the call, John told Joseph that the only way he would accept the position was if Joseph received revelation from the Lord stating that he was to fill the position. When John Whitmer left the Church in 1838, he also took this history with him. It wasn't until 1893, long after the death of John Whitmer (July 11, 1878) that the Church received this history.

http://josephsmithpapers.org/paperSummary/revelation-book-1; http://institute.lds.org/manuals/Doctrine-and-Covenants-institute-student-Manual/dc-in-041-47.asp

THE FACT: Joseph Smith states the following:

It is a fact, if I now had in my possession, every decision which had been had upon important items of doctrine and duties since the commencement of this work, I would not part with them for any sum of money; we have neglected to take minutes of such things, thinking, perhaps, that they would never benefit us afterwards; which, if we had them now, would decide almost every point of doctrine which might be agitated. But this has been neglected, and now we cannot bear record to the Church and to the world, of the great and glorious manifestations which have been made to us with that degree of power and authority we otherwise could, if we now had these things to publish abroad.

Since the Twelve are now chosen, I wish to tell them a course which they may pursue, and be benefited thereafter, in a point of light of which they are not now aware. If they will, every time they assemble, appoint a person to preside over them during the meeting, and one or more to keep a record of their proceedings, and on the decision of every question or item, be it what it may, let such decision be written, and such decision will forever remain upon record, and appear an item of covenant or doctrine. An item thus decided may appear, at the time, of little or no worth, but should it be published, and one of you lay hands on it after, you will find it of infinite worth, not only to your brethren, but it will be a feast to your own souls.

Here is another important item. If you assemble from time to time, and proceed to discuss important questions, and pass decisions upon the same, and fail to note them down, by and by you will be driven to straits from which you will not be able to extricate yourselves, because you may be in a situation not to bring your faith to bear with sufficient perfection or power to obtain the desired information; or, perhaps, for neglecting to write these things when God has revealed them, not esteeming them of sufficient worth, the Spirit may withdraw and God may be angry; and there is, or was, a vast knowledge, of infinite importance, which is now lost."

History of the Church, 2:198–99

Had the history and rise of the Church been recorded with equal seriousness, controversies and questions would have been less apt to surface. For instance, believe it or not, until a recent manuscript had been discovered in the Church Historian's Office, there were questions surrounding the place of the organization of the Church. We have been taught and accept the home of Peter Whitmer Sr. in Fayette, New York, as the confirmed site. However, because of an error in the Book of Commandments and other writings, many believe Manchester, New York, is the location of this event. This error in thinking originated with W. W. Phelps mistakenly inserting in a revelation heading in the Book of Commandments that

Manchester, New York, was the site of the organization of the Church. Even though Joseph Smith discovered this error and corrected it with the first edition of the Doctrine and Covenants in 1835, some still believed that Manchester, and not Fayette, was the site of the Church's organization. Of course it did little to help that the *Evening and the Morning Star* in an article titled, "Rise and Progress of the Church of Christ" (vol. 1 no. 10 March 1833), states, "It will be three years the sixth of April next, since the church of Christ was organized, in Manchester, New York, with six members. It has increased steadily in faith and works since; and the work has spread into several states." Another Church publication, the *Times and Seasons,* in a reprint of the Wentworth letter in March 1842 (vol. 3 no. 9 March 1, 1842, 708) confirms, "On the 6th of April, 1830, the 'Church of Jesus Christ of Latter-day Saints,' was first organized in the town of Manchester, Ontario co., state of New York." Is it any wonder Joseph Smith was prompted to say what he did in reference to keeping accurate records?

While laboring on the third volume of the *Joseph Smith Papers,* the editors discovered a manuscript in the vaults of the First Presidency that served to dispel the myth of Manchester, New York, being the site of the organization of the Church. Steven C. Harper states:

> The manuscript may have the effect of resolving a controversy that has arisen over whether the Church was organized at Fayette, N.Y., as has traditionally been understood, or at Manchester, N.Y. It does so by affirming that a revelation given on April 6, 1830, was given at Fayette, not at Manchester. "The 1833 Book of Commandments, heretofore the earliest source available, located this revelation in Manchester," he explained. Some authors thus argued that the traditional story of the Church's founding in Fayette lacked foundation in the historical record, "but we can now see that in this case, tradition and the historical record match up," he said.
>
> R. Scott Lloyd, " 'Major Discovery' Discussed at Mormon History Association Conference," *Church News*, 22 May 2009

47. What was the first history of the Church titled?
    a. History of the Church
    b. Mormon History
    c. Book of John Whitmer
    d. Comprehensive History of the Church

SECTION 48

BRIEF HISTORICAL BACKGROUND: Revelation given to Joseph Smith at Kirtland, Ohio, during March 1831. The Lord revealed his will concerning the purchasing of land to prepare for those Saints moving from the east.

THE STORY: The call was to "the Ohio," and for most, nothing less would satisfy their desire to follow the Lord's will and to unite themselves with the Prophet. Some were uncertain; nevertheless, most followed the command. A. G. Riddle records the following scene in Kirtland:

> They came, men, women, and children, in every conceivable manner, some with horses, oxen, and vehicles rough and rude, while others had walked all or part of the distance. The future 'City of the Saints' appeared like one besieged. Every available house, shop, hut, or barn was filled to its utmost capacity. Even boxes were roughly extemporized and used for shelter until something more permanent could be secured.
>
> http://eom.byu.edu/index.php/Kirtland,_Ohio

THE FACT: Looking back 182 years after the call to "the Ohio," we as Saints understand, even though the Saints at the time of the call might not have seen the larger picture, the purpose for the Lord's command. Let's consider for a moment how crucial the Kirtland years were to the Church. Half of the revelations in our current Doctrine and Covenants were received here. The Saints witnessed the miracle of the first temple in this dispensation and the resultant blessings that flowed from their sacrifice and diligence. The government of the Church evolved to include a First Presidency, a Quorum of the Twelve, and the Seventies. In addition, four future prophets of the Church were baptized during the Kirtland era: Brigham Young, John Taylor, Wilford Woodruff, and Lorenzo Snow. Truth be known, the leadership of the Church was influenced clear to 1951 from those who had contact with the Kirtland Saints.

The Church of Jesus Christ of Latter-day Saints, Our Heritage
(Salt Lake City: The Church of Jesus Christ of Latter-day Saints, 1996), 29

QUESTION:

48. When the Saints moved from New York to Ohio, where did they think the New Jerusalem was?
    a. Salt Lake City, Utah
    b. Jackson County, Missouri
    c. Kirtland, Ohio
    d. Nauvoo, Illinois

SECTION 49

BRIEF HISTORICAL BACKGROUND: Joseph Smith received revelation for Sidney Rigdon, Parley P. Pratt, and Leman Copley in March 1831, at Kirtland, Ohio. Leman was commanded of the Lord to go to the Shakers on a mission.

THE STORY: Leman Copley was a member of the Church in Thompson, sixteen miles northeast of Kirtland. He owned a 759-acre farm, which was critical at this time because approximately two hundred Saints were starting their trek from New York and would need a place to live. Unfortunately, even though Leman was LDS, he still clung to a few of his Quaker beliefs. Among other teachings, Quakers believed that Christ's Second Coming had already taken place and that Christ had made his appearance in the form of a woman, Ann Lee. They believed that a celibate life was regarded higher than marriage, that the eating of pork was forbidden, and that baptism by water was not essential (see heading to Doctrine and Covenants 49).

These brethren visited the Shaker community near present-day Cleveland, Ohio, and read section 49 to them.

THE FACT: On May 8, 1831, Sidney Rigdon, Parley P. Pratt, and Leman Copley visit Ashbel Kitchel, the presiding elder for the Quakers in this area. Ashbel asked that "neither [group] to force their doctrine on the other at this time, but let the time be spent in feeling of the spirit, as it was Rigdon's first visit . . . [and] he [Rigdon] said he would subject himself to the order of the place." Ashbel states that Parley P. Pratt instructs Sidney Rigdon and Leman Copley "to pay no attention to me [Ashbel] for they had come with the authority of the Lord Jesus Christ, and the people must hear it, etc."

Sidney Rigdon was then given permission to read section 49 of the Doctrine and Covenants, whereupon the congregation explained to the Brethren that they were satisfied with their religion and wanted nothing to do with Mormonism.

Unfortunately, this is where the meeting got messy. Ashbel continues:

> But Parley Pratt arose and commenced shaking his coat tail. He said he shook the dust from his garments as a testimony against us, that we had rejected the work of the Lord Jesus. Before the words were out of his mouth, I [Ashbel Kitchel] was to him and said, "You filthy beast, dare you presume to come in here and try to imitate a man of God by shaking your filthy [coat] tail." . . . I then turned to Leman [Copley], who had been crying while the message was reading, and said to him "you hypocrite, you knew better," . . . Sidney had been looking on all this time without saying a word. As he had done all he did only by liberty [with permission], nothing was said to him. . . . Parley's horse had not been put away, as he came too late, He mounted and started for home without waiting for anyone. Sidney [Rigdon] stayed for supper. . . . He was treated kindly and let go after supper, but Leman [Copley] tarried all night and started for home in the morning.
>
> Lawrence R. Flake, "A Shaker View of a Mormon Mission," *Brigham Young University Studies* 20, no. 1 (Autumn 1979): 94–99

QUESTION:

49. After the missionaries (Pratt, Copley, and Rigdon) leave the Shaker community, what does Ashbel Kitchel decide to do?

   a. Join the Church
   b. Return the favor by serving a mission himself to the Mormons
   c. Call the sheriff and complain
   d. Move further to the west where he will be left alone

SECTION 50

BRIEF HISTORICAL BACKGROUND: Because some members of the Church claimed spiritual phenomena, thinking they were receiving revelations, Joseph was given the following communication from the Lord at Kirtland, Ohio, during May 1831.

THE STORY: The Lord states in verses 2 and 3, "Behold, verily I say unto you, that there are many spirits which are false spirits, which have gone forth in the earth, deceiving the world. And also Satan hath sought to deceive you, that he might overthrow you."
John Whitmer records the following:

> Some had visions and could not tell what they saw. Some would fancy to themselves that they had the sword of Laban, and would wield it as expert as a light dragoon [soldier], some would act like an Indian in the act of scalping, some would slide or scoot on the floor, with the rapidity of a serpent, which they termed sailing in the boat to the Lamanites, preaching the gospel. And many other vain and foolish maneuvers, that are unseeming, and unprofitable to mention.
>
> Scot Facer Proctor and Maurine Jensen Proctor ed., *Autobiography of Parley P. Pratt* (Salt Lake City: Desert Book, 2000), n5 81

THE FACT: In verse 37, the Lord calls Parley P. Pratt and Joseph Wakefield to "go forth among the churches and strengthen them by the word of exhortation."

It's interesting that Joseph Wakefield would serve this mission and two more before falling away from the Church. He was instrumental in the conversion of George A. Smith, cousin to the Prophet Joseph Smith, yet it's ironic that the very spirits he was called to cast out among the Saints eventually overpowered him. For some reason he couldn't get over the fact that the Prophet would descend the steps of the revelation room (at the John Johnson farm), where he was recording the word of God, and then play with his little children.

Scot Facer Proctor and Maurine Jensen Proctor ed., *Autobiography of Parley P. Pratt* (Salt Lake City: Desert Book, 2000), n4 81

QUESTION:

50. Joseph Wakefield baptized George A. Smith in Potsdam, New York, as mentioned. What other relative of Joseph Smith did Brother Wakefield ordain and to what office?

    a. Joseph Smith Sr. to the office of elder
    b. Hyrum Smith to the office of Patriarch
    c. William Smith (younger brother of the Prophet) to the office of elder
    d. John Smith (brother to Joseph Smith Sr.) to the office of a elder

SECTION 51

BRIEF HISTORICAL BACKGROUND: Edward Partridge sought instruction from the Prophet regarding the New York Saints, who were migrating to the area. Joseph approached the Lord and received the following revelation at Thompson, Ohio, in May 1831.

THE STORY: It's not unreasonable to assume that Joseph was under a huge amount of stress. He and Bishop Partridge not only had the burden of placing two hundred New York Saints on lands, but also he and Emma had to deal with the personal tragedy of the death of their newborn twins who had passed away April 30, 1831.

LITTLE-KNOWN STORIES **111**

Nonetheless, the situations resolved themselves as the Lord sent the gospel message to men of means who owned enough land to settle the migrating Saints. A second tragedy—the death of Julia Murdock—on the same day that Emma's twins passed away blessed Emma and Joseph with a set of twins. Because John Murdock was on the verge of leaving on a mission, he knew he couldn't take care of the newborn twins. With his wife's passing just a few hours after the birth of the twins and realizing that Emma and Joseph had lost their twins, he asked the Prophet if he would consider adopting his newborn children. Of course Emma and Joseph jumped at the news and soon the Smith home was filled with the cooing of Joseph Murdock Smith and Julia Smith.

THE FACT: The following is from the journal of Sister Margarette McIntire Burgess. This journal entry gives us an indication of the Prophet's concern for his wife and his deep love for children (this is during the Nauvoo years):

> I will relate another incident which occurred. Joseph's wife, Sister Emma, had lost a young babe. My mother having twin baby girls, the Prophet came to see if she would let him have one of them. Of course it was rather against her feelings, but she finally consented for him to take one of them, providing he would bring it home each night. This he did punctually himself, and also came after it each morning. One evening he did not come with it at the usual time, and Mother went down to the mansion to see what was the matter, and there sat the Prophet with the baby wrapped up in a little silk quilt. He was trotting it on his knee, and singing to it to get it quiet before starting out, as it had been fretting. The child soon became quiet when my mother took it, and the Prophet came up home with her. Next morning when he came after the baby, Mother handed him Sarah, the other baby. They looked so much alike that strangers could not tell them apart; but as Mother passed him the other baby he shook his head and said, "This is not my little Mary." Then she took Mary from the cradle and gave her to him, and he smilingly carried her home with him. The baby Mary had a very mild disposition, while Sarah was quite cross and fretful, and by this my mother could distinguish them one from the other, though generally people could not tell them apart. But our Prophet soon knew which was

the borrowed baby. After his wife became better in health he did not take our baby anymore, but often came in to caress her and play with her. Both children died in their infancy, before the Prophet was martyred."

http://www.boap.org/LDS/Early-Saints/REC-JS.html

QUESTION:

51. Julia Clapp Murdock's uncle was a man by the name of Abner Clapp. He too was a member of the Church. What current and important piece of Church property was Abner Clapp the first white settler to own?

   a. The Columbus Ohio Temple lot
   b. The Kirtland Ohio Temple lot
   c. The Sacred Grove
   d. The Jackson County temple lot

SECTION 52

BRIEF HISTORICAL BACKGROUND: Revelation to Joseph Smith on June 7, 1831, at Kirtland, Ohio. This revelation was received a day after the conference of the Church. Many men are called to serve missions in this revelation, and some are ordained to the office of high priest.

THE STORY: In December 1830, Joseph Smith had announced that the Lord was in the process of forming a New Zion. From that time forward, the Prophet was constantly questioned by members concerning the location. To be honest, Joseph didn't know the exact spot, other than it was in the West by the borders of the Lamanites.

The arrival of Parley P. Pratt to the Kirtland area that spring, with his glowing reports of western Missouri, only added to the anticipation, and it caused Joseph to approach the Lord with inquiries.

A conference of the Church was called for June 3–6, a conference so important that elders serving missions were called home in order to attend. At the conference, men received for the first time the office of high priest. The day after the conference, Joseph Smith received section 52.

William E. Berrett, *The Restored Church,* 7th ed.
(Salt Lake City: Deseret Book, 1953), 118

THE FACT: In verses 2–3 the Lord declares: "I, the Lord will make known unto you what I will that ye shall do from this time until the next conference, which shall be held in Missouri, upon the land which I will consecrate unto my people, which are a remnant of Jacob and those who are heirs according to the covenant. Wherefore, verily I say unto you, let my servants Joseph Smith, Jun., and Sidney Rigdon take their journey as soon as preparations can be made to leave their homes, and journey to the land of Missouri."

Not just Joseph and Sidney Rigdon, but twenty-eight others were also called to travel to Missouri to teach by different routes as they traveled to the west. Levi Hancock and Zebedee Coltrin were called by the Lord to serve as companions on this journey. Levi shares the following:

> We then went to Winchester in Randolph County [Indiana], and stopped at the county seat on the head waters of the White River. We saw there a school master and introduced the Gospel to him. He was so well pleased with the message that he spread the news as fast as possible and called a meeting. After the meeting he wanted to be baptized, so we went to the water with him and baptized him. Soon after this we were happy to hear that nearly all the people wanted to hear us so we went to the courthouse and got permission to hold a meeting there. After this meeting we were able to baptize several others. . . . We continued to preach here in the region and around about, until we had raised a large branch of the Church . . . and in a short time we had . . . about one hundred members.

Autobiography of Levi Hancock, Historical Department,
The Church of Jesus Christ of Latter-day Saints, Salt Lake City

Some in town didn't understand the new religion and proceeded to persecute the elders. Levi and Zebedee had an appointment to meet with investigators the next day at 11:00 a.m., but they received a note telling them to leave town by 10:00 a.m. Initially, the two elders thought they would obey the order, but then they decided to keep their meeting. Levi records the following in his journal:

> The next morning Sunday came and we were prepared for the worst. It was my turn to speak and I sang too. Zebedee gave the prayer. Bill Walker placed himself at the door and looked as surly as a bull; he was my friend. He said nothing, but something said to me, that I should not be hurt. So I commenced talking and soon forgot myself and said what came to my heart. I mounted the bench and walked in among the same crows who had written that letter. I said, 'You wrote to warn me to leave this place before then, but you see I am still here. . . . I am a cousin to the first man who signed the Declaration of Independence. Now, if you want to reveal anything to me, come on I am ready.' Nothing was said, so I sat down, and Zebedee then took hold of the subject and gave a good sermon. He opened the door for baptism. We felt the spirit of the Lord there with us. After the meeting we went to the water and baptized seventeen of that crowd, who the day before were going to mob us.

Laureen Gaunt, "Research and Perspective:
The Pioneer Saints of Winchester, Indiana," *Ensign*, October 1992, 56

Question:

52. When the original schoolhouse in Winchester, Indiana, was showing its wear and tear, a new schoolhouse was built in 1879. What was this schoolhouse named?

   a. The Nauvoo School
   b. Levi Hancock Public School
   c. The Mormon School
   d. The School of the Prophets

SECTION 53

BRIEF HISTORICAL BACKGROUND: Revelation given June 1831 at Kirtland, Ohio, for Algernon Sidney Gilbert

THE STORY: Algernon Sidney Gilbert was the prosperous business owner of the Gilbert and Whitney store in Kirtland, Ohio, and he was curious what the Lord had in mind for him. Joseph Smith inquired and the Lord unveiled a plan that required Brother Gilbert to leave his business and business partner. The Lord instructs Sidney in verse 5, "And again, verily I say unto you, you shall take your journey with my servants Joseph Smith, Jun., and Sidney Rigdon." Unlike James Covill, Sidney Gilbert turned his back on worldly comfort for the life of a missionary in the untamed western edges of the country.

THE FACT: Brother and Sister Gilbert had the pleasure of raising one nephew and two nieces, the children belonging to Sister Gilbert's sister, Keziah Rollins. Keziah's husband had drowned in a shipwreck on Lake Erie. With no way to care for her children, Keziah sent James Henry, Mary Elizabeth, and Caroline to live with the childless Uncle Algernon and Aunt Elizabeth.

The Prophet Joseph was particularly fond of these children, having come to know them in his visits to the Gilbert and Whitney store in Kirtland. Joseph Smith placed his hands on the head of Mary Elizabeth and gave her a great blessing. He also, in a blessing, stated to James Henry, "Well the Lord has shown him great things."

Why do I speak of the children that Sidney and his wife raised? Because the children had great courage, which of course could only come from the teachings of great parents (or in this case, a great uncle and aunt). Later, Mary Elizabeth and Caroline would save the revelations meant for publication in the Book of Commandments from total destruction when the mob vandalized the printing shop in Jackson County.

http://suplibrary.org/stories/detail.asp?id=327

Question:

53. Sidney Gilbert served valiantly for the Church but did slip momentarily, which led to his death. What did he do?

    a. Ignore a mission call from the Prophet

    b. Refused to leave Jackson County

    c. He was the person guilty for the attempted murder of Governor Boggs

    d. Ate meat that the prophet told him to leave alone as it was poisoned by the mob

Section 54

BRIEF HISTORICAL BACKGROUND: During June 1831, in Kirtland, Ohio, Joseph Smith received the following revelation for Newell Knight on how to proceed with Leman Copley taking his land back from the Church.

THE STORY: The law of consecration is a perfect system, a system designed by the Lord for the benefit for all. Under such a system, the requirement of "one heart and one mind," by those engaged, resulted in "no poor among them." This system worked in the days of Enoch but has met limited success in this dispensation.

When Joseph first came to Kirtland, he realized that the Campbellites were practicing what was known at the time as "the family." This practice failed because of misunderstanding. You may have heard of the famous story about Heman Bassett (who eventually joined the Church as a sixteen-year-old and ordained to the office of elder at the age of seventeen). He took Levi Hancock's watch and sold it, claiming that the watch was his also because it belonged in "the family." Joseph had a better idea, as revealed by the Lord, but it would require selfless love on those who were to live under such a system. Leman Copley was all for the law of consecration at the outset, allowing the Colesville Saints to settle on his large farm, but two months later he forced them off the land, charging them sixty dollars damage for "fitting up his houses and planting his ground."

Karl Ricks Anderson, *Joseph Smith's Kirtland*
(Salt Lake City: Deseret Book, 1989), 131–32

THE FACT: To be honest, it didn't get any better in Utah. The law of consecration was referred to as the "united order." Remember Orderville, Utah, and the experimentation of this order? What some may not know is this order was practiced throughout Utah. The following is from the journal entry of Emily Dow Partridge Young, wife of Brigham Young, on May 12, 1875:

> I have got a woman to wash for me today. She lives in the united order. I sure . . . pity her.

Emily Dow Partridge Young Diary, 30 January 1878, LDS Church Archives;
Dan Barker, *Unique Stories and Facts From LDS History*
(Springville, Utah: Cedar Fort, 2010), 159

QUESTION:

54. How many united orders were set up in the West?

  a. 2
  b. Over 200
  c. 57
  d. 157

SECTION 55

BRIEF HISTORICAL BACKGROUND: At Kirtland, Ohio, during June 1831, the Prophet Joseph received the following revelation for nonmember William W. Phelps.

THE STORY: William Wines Phelps was a highly educated man, editor of a political newspaper, and considered for the position of lieutenant governor of New York when he first heard of the Church through the efforts of Sidney Rigdon. He said the following about the Book of Mormon:

> By that book I found a key to the holy prophets; and by that book began to unfold the mysteries of God, and I was made glad. Who can tell his goodness, or estimate the worth of such a book?

> The Church of Jesus Christ of Latter-day Saints, *Church History in the Fulness of Times* (Salt Lake City: The Church of Jesus Christ of Latter-day Saints, 1993), 103

On January 10, 1831, he wrote Eber D. Howe, editor of the *Painesville Telegraph* and author of the anti-Mormon book *Mormonism Unvailed* [sic], stating the following in reference to the Book of Mormon:

> I have read the book, and many others have, but we have nothing by which we can positively detect it as an imposition, nor have we any thing more than what I have stated and the book itself, to show its genuineness. We doubt—supposing, if it is false, it will fall, and if of God, God will sustain it.

> http://saintswithouthalos.com/b/phelps_ww.phtml

Because of the Book of Mormon, William Phelps and his family sought out the Prophet Joseph Smith in a move from New York to Kirtland. The Lord commanded William in section 55, "Thou art called and chosen; and after thou hast been baptized by water, which if you do with an eye single to my glory, you shall have a remission of your sins."

This revelation was received on June 15, 1831. The next day William W. Phelps was baptized into the Church.

THE FACT: The Lord instructed William in verse 4, "And again, you shall be ordained to assist my servant Oliver Cowdery to do the work of printing, and of selecting and writing books for schools in this church, that little children also may receive instruction before me as is pleasing unto me."

In addition to the above instructions, William is also called to "correct" the hymns selected by Emma Smith. In fact, William W. Phelps penned, and in some cases, wrote the music to twenty-nine of the ninety hymns in the first hymnal. He's responsible for such favorites as, "Adam-ondi-Ahman," "Gently Raise the Sacred Strain," "If You Could Hie to Kolob," "Now Let Us Rejoice," " Now We'll Sing with One Accord," "O God, the Eternal Father," "Praise to the Man," "Redeemer of Israel," and "The Spirit of God."

http://phelpsfamilyhistory.com/bios/w_w_phelps_hymns.asp

QUESTION:

55. In verse 6 of section 55, a man by the name of Joseph Coe is mentioned. Who is he?

    a. Joseph Smith's brother-in-law
    b. The Kirtland Branch executive secretary
    c. Member of the high council in Missouri
    d. Member of the high council in Kirtland

SECTION 56

BRIEF HISTORICAL BACKGROUND: Joseph Smith received the following revelation at Kirtland, Ohio, during June 1831. This revelation was an answer to Joseph's appeal for what he should do in the case of Ezra Thayre not being able to travel with Thomas B. Marsh to Missouri.

THE STORY: What was the holdup? Why wasn't Ezra ready to travel to Missouri with Thomas B. Marsh, his missionary companion, when Thomas was ready to depart? Even though Ezra had served and completed a successful mission earlier with Northrop Sweet in the fall of 1830, at least for the moment, he became temporarily sidetracked with the cares of the world.

THE FACT: When Oliver Cowdery, Ziba Peterson, Parley P. Pratt, and Peter Whitmer Jr. stopped in the Kirtland area on their way to Missouri and the Lamanites, they baptized Frederick G. Williams. Frederick then left his farm and family in the care of the Church and traveled on with the missionaries to teach the Lamanites. As the Saints began to arrive from New York in the Kirtland area, Joseph Smith Sr. and Ezra Thayre were living with Frederick's family on their 144-acre farm.

It's interesting that Joseph received the following revelation, a revelation that is not recorded in our current Doctrine and Covenants (not all of the revelations Joseph received are in the Doctrine and Covenants) in regard to the working relationship with the three families (possibly more) living on the Williamses' farm. The revelation states:

> *Revelation given through Joseph Smith at Kirtland, Ohio, in May 1831, concerning the farm owned by Frederick and also concerning Joseph and Ezra.*
>
> Behold ye are holden for the one even so likewise thine advisary (i.e. advisory) is holden for the other wherefore it must needs be that ye

pay no more money for the present time until the contract be fulfilled, and let mine aged servant Joseph (Smith Sr.) and his family go into the house after their advisary is gone.

And let my servant Ezra (Thayre) board with him and let all the brethren immediately assemble together to put up an house for my servant Ezra and let my servant Frederick's family remain and let the house be prepared and their wants be supplied and when my servant Frederick returns from the west behold and lo he desireth to take his family in mine own due time unto the west.

Let that which belongeth unto my servant Frederick be secured unto him by deed or bond and thus he willeth that the brethren reap the good thereof.

Let mine aged servant Joseph govern the things of the farm and provide for the families and let him have help inasmuch as he standeth in need.

Let my servant Ezra humble himself and at the conference meeting (D&C 52) he shall be ordained unto power from on high and he shall go from thence if he be obedient unto my commandments and proclaim my gospel unto the western regions with my servants that must go forth unto the borders by the Lamanites for behold I have a great work for them to do and it shall be given unto you to know what ye shall do at the conference meeting. Even so Amen.

What shall the brethren do with the moneys? Ye shall go forth and seek diligently among the brethren and obtain lands and save the money that it may be consecrated to purchase lands in the west for an everlasting inheritance. Even so, Amen."

Kirtland Revelation Book, 91–92,
Joseph Smith Collection, Church Historians Office

When Ezra left New York, he had a fair amount of cash, most likely obtained from the sale of his property. This he consecrated to the Church with the agreement to an interest in the Frederick G. Williams farm. When Ezra received his call to Missouri, he had not yet been given this interest and appears that he was not going to leave on his mission until his personal interest was secured. This attitude was what caused the Lord to state in verse 8, "And again, verily I say unto you, that my servant Ezra Thayre must repent of his pride, and of his selfishness, and obey the former commandment which I have given him concerning the place upon which he lives."

Dean Garrett, A Commentary on the Doctrine and Covenants
(Salt Lake City: Deseret Book, 2001) 2:134–35

56. What is the Kirtland Revelation Book that the above revelation was recorded in?

   a. A history of Kirtland and area

   b. A compilation of the early revelations received by the Prophet

   c. A book that predicted the end of the world

   d. A book with prophesy and revelation indicating Salt Lake City as the headquarters of the Church

SECTION 57

BRIEF HISTORICAL BACKGROUND: The first revelation received by Joseph Smith in Jackson County, Missouri, on July 20, 1831, after he asks the Lord, "Where will thy temple be built?"

THE STORY: Joseph Smith records the following, as found in the *History of the Church*:

> The meeting of our brethren [Oliver Cowdery, Peter Whitmer Jr., Ziba Peterson, and Frederick G. Williams, all of whom had gone to Missouri as missionaries], who had long awaited our arrival, was a glorious one, and moistened with many tears. It seemed good and pleasant for brethren to meet together in unity. But our reflections were many, coming as we had from a highly cultivated state of society in the east, and standing now upon the confines or western limits of the United States, and looking into the vast wilderness of those that sat in darkness; how natural it was to observe the degradation, leanness of intellect, ferocity, and jealousy of a people that were nearly a century behind the times, and to feel for those who roamed about

without the benefit of civilization, refinement, or religion; yea, and exclaim in the language of the Prophets: "When will the wilderness blossom as the rose? When will Zion be built up in her glory, and where will Thy temple stand, unto which all nations shall come in the last days?" Our anxiety was soon relieved by receiving the following [Doctrine and Covenants 57].

Joseph Smith, in *History of the Church*, 1:189

THE FACT: The Lord states in verse 3, "Behold, the place which is now called Independence is the center place; and a spot for the temple is lying westward, upon a lot which is not far from the courthouse."

The courthouse mentioned in the revelation is significant, not only in the history of the United States, but also of the Church. Algernon Sidney Gilbert, who was instructed by the Lord to travel with the Prophet to Missouri, purchased this courthouse in Independence, Missouri, for 371 dollars as a private residence and also as a mercantile store for the Saints in the area. A number of interesting facts surround this courthouse. First, it was constructed using 100 percent slave labor. Second, it's the oldest courthouse west of the Mississippi River. Third, it's the oldest Latter-day Saint dwelling west of the Mississippi River still in existence. Fourth, Harry S. Truman briefly held court in it. And fifth, see the question below.

Max H. Parkin, "Joseph Smith and the United Firm,"
BYU Studies 46, no. 3 (2007), 25

QUESTION:

57. Who supervised the construction of this courthouse?

    a. Lilburn W. Boggs

    b. Lyman Wight

    c. Ziba Peterson

    d. Alexander Doniphan

Section 58

BRIEF HISTORICAL BACKGROUND: Revelation given to Joseph Smith at Jackson County, Missouri, on August 1, 1831, in answer to some of the Saints' inquiry of what the Lord's will was for them.

THE STORY: In verse 50, the Lord commanded Sidney Rigdon to write a description of the land so that the members in the East could get a mental picture in their minds (remember, photography was yet to be invented). Sidney Rigdon paints the following description:

> The country is unlike the timbered states of the East. As far as the eye can reach the beautiful rolling prairies lie spread out like a sea of meadows; and are decorated with a growth of flowers so gorgeous and grand as to exceed description; and nothing is more fruitful, or a richer stockholder in the blooming prairie than the honey bee. Only on the water courses is timber to be found. There in strips from one to three miles in width, and following faithfully the meanderings of the streams, it grows in luxuriant forests. The forests are a mixture of oak, hickory, black walnut, elm, ash, cherry, honey locust, mulberry, coffee bean, hackberry, boxelder, and bass wood; with the addition of cottonwood, butterwood, pecan, and soft and hard maple upon the bottoms. The shrubbery is beautiful, and consists in part of plums, grapes, crab apple, and persimmons.
>
> The soil is rich and fertile; from three to ten feet deep, and generally composed of a rich black mould, intermingled with clay and sand. It yields in abundance, wheat, corn, sweet potatoes, cotton and many other common agricultural products. Horses, cattle and hogs, though of an inferior breed, are tolerably plentiful and seem nearly to raise themselves by grazing in the vast prairie range in summer, and feeding upon the bottoms in winter. The wild game is less plentiful of course where man has commenced the cultivation of the soil, than in the wild prairies. Buffalo, elk, deer, bear, wolves, beaver and many smaller animals here roam at pleasure. Turkeys, geese, swans, ducks, yea a variety of the feathered tribe, are among the rich abundance

that grace the delightful regions of this goodly land—the heritage of the children of God.

The season is mild and delightful nearly three quarters of the year, and as the land of Zion, situated at about equal distances from the Atlantic and Pacific oceans, as well as from the Alleghany and Rocky mountains, in the thirty-ninth degree of north latitude, and between the sixteenth and seventeenth degrees of west longitude, it bids fair—when the curse is taken from the land—to become one of the most blessed places on the globe. The winters are milder than the Atlantic states of the same parallel of latitude, and the weather is more agreeable; so that were the virtues of the inhabitants only equal to the blessings of the Lord which He permits to crown the industry of those inhabitants, there would be a measure of the good things of life for the benefit of the Saints, full, pressed down, and running over, even an hundredfold.

Sidney Rigdon, in *History of the Church*, 1:189

THE FACT: It's interesting that the Lord rejected this description (see Doctrine and Covenants 63:55–56). It was a much more positive perspective than an 1828 description of the Independence area by a Congregationalist and Presbyterian missionary. He wrote the following:

The prospects for our evangelical work appear less likely here than any place I have seen in my westward journeying. Such a godless place, filled with so many profane swearers, would be difficult to imagine. . . . There are a few so-called ministers of the gospel hereabouts, but they are a sad lot of churchmen, untrained, uncouth, given to imbibing spirituous liquors, and indulging as participants in the gambling which accompanies horse racing and cock fighting. There are many suspicious characters who headquarter here, but when intelligence arrives that a federal marshal is approaching this county, there is a hurried scurrying of many of this element to the Indian Territory on the west side of the Missouri. . . . one soon learns not to make inquiry concerning the names nor the home towns of this class of men. . . . Christian Sabbath observance here appears to be unknown. It is a day for merchandising, jollity, drinking, gambling, and general anti-Christian conduct. . . . There appears to be an overabundance of females here practicing the world's oldest profession. . . . Gouging and more serious forms of violence are common.

The sheriff has little support from the populace, except to prevent burglars breaking into the merchant's shops. He confided to me that the citizens do not care to have the lawless punished.

T. Edgar Lyon, "Independence, Missouri and the Mormons, 1827–1833," *Brigham Young University Studies* 13, no 1. (Autumn 1972): 10–19

QUESTION:

58. On the first Sunday after Joseph Smith and those traveling with him arrive in Jackson County, who preached to the Lamanites first?
   a. Joseph Smith
   b. William W. Phelps
   c. Ziba Peterson
   d. Ezra Booth

SECTION 59

BRIEF HISTORICAL BACKGROUND: Revelation given to Joseph Smith at Jackson County, Missouri, on August 7, 1831. The temple lot was dedicated a few days prior (August 3) to receiving this revelation.

THE STORY: On August 2, 1831, twelve men representing the twelve tribes of Israel laid the first log "as a foundation of Zion in Kaw township, twelve miles west of Independence." It was during this service that Sidney Rigdon dedicated the land to the Lord. The next day eight elders—Joseph Smith, Oliver Cowdery, Sidney Rigdon, Peter Whitmer Jr., Frederick G. Williams, William W.

Phelps, Martin Harris, and Joseph Coe—congregated at the temple lot where Sidney Rigdon dedicated lot to the Lord. Joseph Smith laid the cornerstone in the southeast corner and then Psalm 87 was read.

Church Educational System, *Church History in the Fulness of Times* (Salt Lake City: The Church of Jesus Christ of Latter-day Saints, 1993), 107; Richard L. Bushman, *Rough Stone Rolling* (New York City: Alfred A. Knopf, Random House, 2006), 163

THE FACT: Joseph Smith taught that not only is Jackson County, Missouri, the location for the New Jerusalem, but it is also the location of the Garden of Eden.

Church Educational System, *Church History in the Fulness of Times* (Salt Lake City: The Church of Jesus Christ of Latter-day Saints, 1993), 106.

QUESTION:

59. Of the original sixty-three acres of land [the temple block] the Church purchased in Independence, Missouri, in the early 1830s, how much of this land were they able to buy back after the Saints were expelled from the state?

    a. All 63 acres
    b. All 63 acres and then some
    c. 10 acres
    d. 20 acres

SECTION 60

BRIEF HISTORICAL BACKGROUND: The Lord instructed the Prophet to have the elders return home from Missouri to Kirtland, preaching along the way. Joseph received this revelation August 8, 1831, at Jackson County, Missouri.

THE STORY: Much success was realized as the elders preached along the way from Kirtland to Independence, Missouri. A number of congregations were established in western Ohio, in addition to Illinois and Indiana. Samuel Smith and Reynolds Cahoon were called as companions, and shortly after their call, they traveled to Reynolds' relatives in southern Indiana. Here they stayed for a brief period of time and experienced success. On the return trip from Missouri, the two missionaries stopped in the same area (Green County) for two weeks where they met and converted John Patten. Brother Patten wrote his brother David in Michigan, stating among other things, that he had received the Holy Ghost and explained to David the restored gospel. David wrote, "This caused my heart to leap for joy, and I resolved to go immediately and see for myself."

David Patten was baptized by his brother John in June of 1832 and three years later was ordained to the Quorum of the Twelve Apostles. He is also the first Apostle to die in this dispensation from a fatal wound received at the Battle of Crooked River in Missouri.

http://www.boap.org/LDS/Early-Saints/DPatten.html

THE FACT: The following is from the journal of David W. Patten:

> From this happy state I fell away and lived, in a measure, in darkness until the year 1830, when my mind became again aroused by the Spirit of God to a sense of my situation, and I began to pray mightily to God that he would pardon my sins and grant me his Holy Spirit. About this time the sound of the Book of Mormon came to my ears, and I was greatly agitated in mind about it, and desired to see it. I saw the book that same summer, but had no opportunity of reading it further than the preface and testimony of the witnesses. A fear came upon me, and I dare not say anything against it. From that time I began to cry to God for saving faith.
>
> Nothing took place worthy of note until May, 1832, when on receiving a letter from my brother in Indiana, giving me information of the rise of the Church of Christ, the reception of the Holy Ghost and the gifts thereof by the Saints. My brother informed me that he had received the Holy Ghost by the laying on of the hands of the

Elders of the Church. This caused my heart to leap for joy, and I resolved to go immediately and see for myself.

I soon became satisfied that the work was true, and was baptized on the 15th of June, 1832, in Greene Co., Indiana, by my brother, John Patten. I was ordained an elder on the 17th, under the hands of Elisha H. Groves in said county, when I was appointed, in company with brother Wood, to preach in the Territory of Michigan. We travelled and preached together, and I recorded many remarkable cases of healing, which occurred under my administration: in many instances I went to the sick, who said they had faith and promised to obey the Gospel when they got better, and commanded them in the name of the Lord to arise and be made whole; and they were immediately restored. Sixteen persons were baptized near the Maumee River.

http://www.boap.org/LDS/Early-Saints/DPatten.html

QUESTION:

60. What Biblical personality did David W. Patten encounter while on his mission to the south?

    a. Isaiah

    b. David

    c. Cain

    d. Adam

SECTION 61

BRIEF HISTORICAL BACKGROUND: Revelation received on the return trip home to Kirtland from Jackson County. Joseph Smith is given this revelation at McIlwaine's Bend (near present day Miami, Missouri) on the Missouri River, August 12, 1831.

THE STORY: During the first few days on the journey back to Kirtland, Joseph Smith and the missionaries paddled in canoes down the Missouri River toward St. Louis. On August 12, W. W. Phelps saw in vision the "destroyer riding in power upon the face of the waters." This situation ensued because the returning missionaries had bad feelings toward each other and disagreements had surfaced among them.

THE FACT: The following is another story of returning missionaries, a boat, and water:

> While no evidence yet suggests that Mormon converts were scheduled to sail to America on board the new queen of the White Star line, six young returning missionaries—Alma Sonne, George B. Chambers, Willard Richards, John R. Sayer, F. A. Dahle, and L. J. Shurtliff—all had been booked passage on the *Titanic* by Elder Sonne himself, who had served as emigration clerk in Liverpool for much of his mission. What a greater farewell for successful missionaries than to send them home on the world's greatest ship! The Church's British newspaper, the *Millennial Star*, saluted Elder Sonne for his fine work as emigration agent, wishing him "God speed and marked success in that wider field of endeavor to which the great ocean liner and overland express will swiftly carry him.
>
> "Then a strange thing happened," as Sonne's biographer reports. [Elder] Fred Dahle . . . sent a wire a day or two before their scheduled departure stating that he had been delayed and could not arrive by the 12th. He suggested that the other elders go on without him. Alma, for some inexplicable reason, cancelled their bookings on the *Titanic* and rebooked them on the *Mauretania* leaving a day later. "I did this on my own responsibility," he later said, "and the others in the group manifested a little resentment because they were not sailing on the *Titanic.*"

Prior to their missions Alma Sonne was the boyhood friend of the less-active Fred Dahle. When Alma received his call to serve in England, he convinced Fred to serve a mission also. Ironically, Fred was called to serve in the same mission as Elder Sonne. At the conclusion of their missions, when the two elders discovered the fate of the *Titanic*, Elder Sonne thanked Elder Dahle for saving his life, to which Fred responded, "No, I should thank you, for it was you who saved my life by convincing me to serve this mission."

The six elders were not the only members scheduled to board the *Titanic*—the Clifford family was as well. The Cliffords were on their way to America, where Brother Clifford had recently been hired to act as the caretaker and farmer to the Joseph Smith Memorial and farm in Sharon, Vermont. This LDS family of eleven from England never crossed the Atlantic on the doomed ship. As the day of departure neared, Brother Clifford felt extremely uneasy about the trip and canceled their boarding passes, obtaining passage a year later on another ship. Even though seventeen LDS lives were saved from the disaster, one Latter-day Saint, Irene C. Corbett, did go down with the *Titanic*. She had been studying in London and decided to return to Utah. Here's the sad side: she had heard there would be elders traveling on the *Titanic*, so she purchased passage knowing that with elders on board she would be safer. Unfortunately, she did not find out about the elders changing their plans.

Dan Barker, *Unique Stories and Facts From LDS History*
(Springville, Utah: Cedar Fort, 2010), 91

There are unsubstantiated rumors that Mormon missionaries were on board the *Carpathia*, the ship that saved several hundred *Titanic* passengers in lifeboats. Elder James Hamilton Martin was on board the *Virginian* en route from Halifax to Liverpool when it changed directions to help with rescue efforts if necessary. He wrote: "Shortly after 9 a.m. [April 15] we reached the iceberg that had caused the sinking of the largest steamship afloat and the death of 1,630 people and for six hours traveled along side of it. It was no more and no less than a mountain of ice. At 11 a.m. we passed the place where the *Titanic* went down.

A few Latter-day Saints interpreted the sinking as evidence of a long-held doctrine that Satan, the destroyer, rides upon the waters. An early 1831 revelation to the Prophet Joseph Smith had stated: "There are many dangers upon the waters, and more especially hereafter; for I, the Lord, have decreed in mine anger many destructions upon the waters; . . . nevertheless all flesh is in mine hand, and he that is faithful among you shall not perish by the waters (D&C 61:4–6)." In an article titled "Dangers Upon the Deep," Elder Orson Whitney wrote:

"One frightful feature of the unparalleled struggle that ended with the signing of the armistice (November 11, 1918), was the havoc wrought by the German U-boats, otherwise known as submarines. There had been, before the coming of the U-boat, dreadful dangers upon the waters, as the fate of the ill-starred *Titanic*—ripped open by an iceberg—testifies. But the submarine, the assassin of the *Lusitania*, multiplied those dangers a hundredfold. Did the proud world know that a prophet of God had foreseen these fearful happenings, and had sounded a warning of their approach?"

http://rsc.byu.edu/archived/regional-studies-latter-day-saint-church-history-british-isles/6-%E2%80%9Cnearer-my-god-thee%E2%80%9D-sinki

QUESTION:

61. Between the years 1840 and 1890, how many Latter-day Saint voyages were successfully completed over the Atlantic Ocean without losing one ship at sea?

    a. 50
    b. 625
    c. 132
    d. 550

SECTION 62

BRIEF HISTORICAL BACKGROUND: As Joseph Smith and his group of missionaries were heading east to Kirtland, they met elders headed west to Independence at Chariton, Missouri. Joseph received this revelation August 13, 1831.

THE STORY: In July 1831, Reynolds Cahoon and Samuel Smith stopped to preach in the town of Paris, Illinois. Their preaching attracted William McLellin, the town's schoolteacher, who wrote the following, "When I heard it, I made up my mind that there was more in it than any religion I had ever before heard advocated."

David Whitmer and Harvey Whitlock also stopped to preach in Paris. Listening to Harvey Whitlock, William wrote, "I never heard such preaching in all my life. The glory of God seemed to encircle the man, and the wisdom of God to be displayed in his discourse."

Despite having thirty students to teach, William joined David Whitmer and Harvey Whitlock on their journey to Independence. His purpose in traveling with the pair was to meet the Prophet Joseph Smith. On August 3, after William McLellin bought the last Book of Mormon from Harvey and David, he pursued the journey on his own. William stated his reasoning, "My object was to get to Independence before them and see if the testimony of the other witnesses would agree with theirs."

http://www.boap.org/LDS/Early-Saints/Mcllelin.html

THE FACT: On August 14, William rode three miles, where he stopped at the residence of Mr. William Ivy to eat breakfast and feed his horse. While here, William engaged in conversation with Mrs. Ivy. When she learned he had a Book of Mormon in his possession, she pleaded with him to sell the book to her, which he did. William then continued his trip to the ferry, just one mile from Chariton. He arrived there on August 15 and discovered that he had just missed the Prophet Joseph Smith by one day. William, though disappointed, continued on to Independence, Missouri. Brother McLellin would eventually meet the Prophet and enjoy serving two missions, serving with Parley P. Pratt on one of them. He was also part of the committee to settle the Saints' difficulties in both Jackson and Clay County, Missouri, and finally served on the Clay County High Council.

http://www.boap.org/LDS/Early-Saints/Mcllelin.html

62. William reached Independence on August 18. On the nineteenth, he traveled ten miles west to Kaw Township [present day Kansas City] and stayed the night with Joshua Lewis and his family. The next day Hyrum Smith baptized William into the Church. Who is Joshua Lewis?

   a. The first mayor of Kansas City
   b. Indian agent to the Delawares
   c. Most likely the first man baptized in the Independence area
   d. Famous Mormon persecutor

SECTION 63

BRIEF HISTORICAL BACKGROUND: The Prophet, and those traveling with him, arrived in Kirtland, Ohio, on August 27, 1831. Joseph Smith received this revelation in late August.

THE STORY: While Joseph and the elders were in Missouri on their missions, Lucy Mack Smith, mother of the Prophet, was on a mission of her own to visit her relatives in the Detroit (Pontiac, Michigan) area. Lucy returned home to Kirtland before Joseph. When he arrived, she requested that Joseph send missionaries to the Pontiac area. Joseph eventually called and sent Jared Carter on this mission.

THE FACT: On a visit to one of her nieces in the Pontiac area, Lucy Mack Smith had an opportunity of meeting and conversing with her niece's minister, Mr. Ruggles. Upon meeting the Prophet's mother, Mr. Ruggles extended his hand in friendship, yet at the same time rudely stated, "And you are the mother of that poor, silly, foolish boy, Joe Smith, who pretended to translate the Book of Mormon." When Lucy asked why he would say such things about her son, he answered, "Because, that he should imagine he was going to break down all the churches with the simple Mormon book." Lucy Smith left him with a prophecy that her son would send a minister to his congregation, and that this elder would succeed in converting one-third of his congregation including the very deacon.

As mentioned, Joseph sent Jared Carter, who baptized seventy of Mr. Ruggle's Presbyterian flock, including Samuel Bent, the deacon of the church.

Scot Facer Proctor and Maurine Jensen Proctor, eds., *The Revised and Enhanced History of Joseph Smith By His Mother* (Salt Lake City: Deseret Book, 1996), 292–94

QUESTION:

63. Colonel Stephen Mack, the founder of Pontiac, Michigan, and brother to Lucy Mack Smith, built a road from Pontiac to Detroit in hopes of attracting people to his new store. Today this road is known as Woodward Avenue. What building is found on this road?

    a. The Detroit Michigan Temple
    b. The hotel where Lucy stayed on her visit
    c. Colonel Mack's store incorporated into a shopping mall
    d. An LDS stake center

SECTION 64

BRIEF HISTORICAL BACKGROUND: Revelation given to Joseph Smith the day before he left for Hiram, Ohio, to resume the translation (revision) of the Bible. He received this revelation on September 11, 1831.

THE STORY: Section 119 is the first time in this dispensation when the Lord introduced the law of tithing to the Prophet Joseph Smith. Section 64 may very well be the first hint at the law when the Lord instructed in verse 23, "Behold, now it is called today until the coming of the Son of Man, and verily it is a day of sacrifice, and a day for the tithing of my people; for he that is tithed shall not be burned at his coming."

THE FACT: The following is from the autobiography of Sarah M. Kimball:

> My eldest son was born in Nauvoo, November 22nd, 1841; when the babe was three days old a little incident occurred which I shall mention. The walls of the Nauvoo Temple were about three feet above the foundation. The Church was in need of help to assist in raising the Temple walls. I belonged to the Church of Jesus Christ of Latter-day Saints; my husband did not belong to the Church at that time. I wished to help on the Temple, but did not like to ask my husband (who owned considerable property) to help for my sake. My husband came to my bedside, and as he was admiring our three days' old darling, I said, "What is the boy worth?" He replied, "O, I don't know, he is worth a great deal." I said, "Is he worth a thousand dollars?" The reply was "Yes, more than that if he lives and does well." I said, "Half of him is mine, is it not?" "Yes, I suppose so." "Then I have something to help on the Temple." He said pleasantly, "You have?" "Yes, and I think of turning my share right in as tithing." "Well, I'll have to see about that." Soon after the above conversation Mr. Kimball met the Prophet Joseph Smith, President of the Church, and said, "Sarah has got a little the advantage of me this time, she proposes to turn out the boy as Church property." President Smith seemed pleased with the joke, and said, "I accept all such donations, and from this day the boy shall stand recorded, *Church property*." Then turning to Willard Richards, his secretary, he said, "Make a record of this, and you are my witness." Joseph Smith then said, "Major, (Mr. Kimball was major in the Nauvoo Legion) you now have the privilege of paying $500 and retaining possession, or receiving $600 and giving possession." Mr. Kimball asked if city property was good

currency. President Smith replied that it was. Then said Mr. Kimball, "How will that reserve block north of the Temple suit?" President Smith replied, "It is just what we want." The deed was soon made out and transferred in due form. President Smith said to me, "You have consecrated your first born son, for this you are blessed of the Lord. I bless you in the name of the Lord God of Abraham, of Isaac, and of Jacob. And I seal upon you all the blessings that pertain to the faithful. Your name shall be handed down in honorable remembrance from generation to generation.

http://www.mormonwomenhistory.org/final/biographies/smk.html

QUESTION:

64. When Agnes Flake was ready to move to San Bernardino, California, in 1850 from the Salt Lake Valley, what did she use to settle her tithing account?

    a. Produce from her garden
    b. A cannon
    c. Her servant
    d. Her house

SECTION 65

BRIEF HISTORICAL BACKGROUND: The first of sixteen revelations received in Hiram, Ohio. This revelation is dated October 1831.

THE STORY: Joseph Smith referred to this revelation as "the prayer." It was discovered that when six journals of William McLellin were found in the Church archives, William acted as scribe at the time this revelation was given. His journal provides us with two important facts in regard to section 65.

THE FACT: Because of William McLellin journals, the Church now knows that section 65 was received on October 31, 1831. The Church also knows why it was referred to as "the prayer," because the Lord linked this revelation to Matthew 6:10, which is a verse in the Lord's Prayer: "Thy Kingdom come. Thy will be done in earth, as it is in heaven." This is especially prevalent in the last verse in section 65 and the last verse of the Lord's Prayer. Verse 6 reads, "for thine is the honor, power and glory, forever and ever, Amen."

Jack W. Welch and Trevor Packer, "The Document Corner: The Newly Found Manuscript of D&C Section 65," *BYU Studies* 33, no. 3 (1993)

QUESTION:

65. On September 12, 1831, Joseph and Emma and their four-month-old twins moved from Kirtland to Hiram. Also on this date, Ezra Booth and Symonds Ryder spoke out against the LDS Church at a Methodist Camp meeting. This led to the excommunication of the two men. Six months earlier Ezra, a Methodist minister, joined the Church at the time Joseph Smith healed the arm of Elsa Johnson. A doctor was present at the time of the healing. What was the doctor's explanation for the healing?

    a. Nothing was ever wrong with Elsa Johnson's arm—she was faking the injury.
    b. When Joseph stretched out her arm, perspiration began to flow, causing the cords in her arm to loosen.
    c. The doctor believed it was the power of Satan.
    d. The doctor believed it was his prescription of rubbing tobacco leaves on the arm for two weeks that caused the arm to heal.

SECTION 66

BRIEF HISTORICAL BACKGROUND: William E. McLellin inquired the Lord's will for himself through Joseph Smith and the following revelation was received October 25, 1831, at Orange, Ohio.

THE STORY: The following from the autobiography of William McLellin:

> I examined the book, the people, the preachers, and the old scripture and from the evidences which I had before me I was bound to believe the Book of Mormon to be a divine revelation and the people to be Christians. Consequently, I joined them.
>
> And on the 24th [August 1831] I was ordained an Elder in The Church of Christ and on the 25th I started to the east with brother Hyrum Smith, a brother to Joseph. On the 28th I preached my first discourse to the world. I spoke one hour and 1/2 which astonished the multitude! Some said I had been a preacher. Some said a lawyer etc, etc. But the secret was God assisted me by His spirit and it reached their hearts. Thence we traveled on proclaiming by the way until we got to Jacksonville, Ill. (in court term) on Friday and gave an appointment to preach the next day in the court house. We attended the house though it was largely full of judges, lawyers, doctors, priests and people. I think about 500 [attended]. I spoke 3 hours and when done I cannot describe the joy of some, the consternation of others and the anger of others. . . .
>
> We [William McLellin and Hyrum Smith] reached Kirtland [from Independence] on the 18th day of October, and on the 25th, I attended a general conference in the town of Orange, about 20 miles distant. Here I first and formed an acquaintance with Joseph Smith, Jr., Oliver Cowdery, Sidney Rigdon, John Whitmer, etc. About 40 ministers attended the conference. During its sittings, I, with nine others, was pointed out again by the spirit of revelation, as having the gifts and callings to the office of High Priest, and was ordained thereunto under the hands of Pres. Oliver Cowdery. Following this conference I went home with the Prophet, and on Saturday, the 29th,

I received through him, and wrote from his mouth a revelation concerning myself [Doctrine and Covenants 66]. I had expected and believed that when I saw Brother Joseph, I should receive one: and I went before the Lord in secret, and on my knees asked him to reveal the answer to five questions through his Prophet, and that too without his having any knowledge of my having made such request. I now testify in the fear of God, that every question which I had thus lodged in the ears of the Lord of Sabbath, were answered to my full and entire satisfaction. I desired it for a testimony of Joseph's inspiration. And I to this day consider it to me an evidence which I cannot refute." (William McLellin, Ensign of Liberty 1, 1848, 61)

http://www.dcsites.com/dc049.htm

THE FACT: It's sad, but with time William apostatized from the Church. On May 11, 1838, he appeared before a bishop's court and excommunicated. He played an active role in the mob persecution of the Saints and robbed Joseph's house of a number of items while the Prophet was confined to the Richmond Jail. While Joseph was in jail, William approached the sheriff and asked if he could flog (whip or beat with a stick) the Prophet. The sheriff was fine with this only if Joseph could fight back. The sheriff told Joseph of the arrangement, and Joseph agreed just so long as he could fight without his irons on. William refused to fight under these terms, unless he could have a club. Joseph was still fine with the arrangement; however, the sheriff did not let them fight under such unfair terms.

http://www.boap.org/LDS/Early-Saints/Mcllelin.html

QUESTION:

66. All offices in the priesthood as we currently know them today are represented at this conference. What office is being represented at this conference for the first time?

a. Deacon
b. Teacher
c. Priest
d. High Priest

SECTION 67

BRIEF HISTORICAL BACKGROUND: Joseph Smith receives the following revelation November 1831 at a conference of elders in Hiram, Ohio.

THE STORY: The revelation received prior to section 67 is our current section 1, or the preface to the Doctrine and Covenants. In the same conference, the Lord commanded the elders present to assemble together the revelations received thus far into the Book of Commandments. Section 67 is the second revelation received during this conference. During this conference, there was some criticism by the elders in attendance on the language of the revelations. The Lord challenged the elders to take the least of his commandments and try to duplicate it: "Now, seek ye out of the Book of Commandments, even the least that is among them, and appoint him that is the most wise among you; Or, if there be any among you that shall make one like unto it, then ye are justified in saying that ye do not know that they are true; But if ye cannot make one like unto it, ye are under condemnation if ye do not bear record that they are true" (vv. 6–8).

THE FACT: William McLellin took the challenge and failed, which prompted Joseph Smith to say:

> William E. McLellin, as the wisest man in his own estimation, having more learning than sense, endeavored to write a commandment like unto one of the least of the Lord's, but failed; it was an awful responsibility to write in the name of the Lord. The Elders and all present that witnessed this vain attempt of a man to imitate the language of Jesus Christ, renewed their faith in the truth of the commandments and revelations which the Lord had given to the Church through my instrumentality; and the Elders signified a willingness to bear testimony of their truth to all the world.
>
> http://saintswithouthalos.com/b/mclellin_weh.phtml

67. On the next day, Wednesday morning, November 2, as the conference reconvened, what was one of the first orders of business?

   a. The signing of a statement to appear at the back of the Book of Commandments that the revelations are true
   b. Sing a variety of hymns
   c. Break off two and two and tract throughout town
   d. Plan the next trip to Missouri

SECTION 68

BRIEF HISTORICAL BACKGROUND: Joseph Smith receives the following revelation for Orson Hyde, Luke S. Johnson, Lyman E. Johnson, and William McLellin at Hiram, Ohio, during November 1831.

THE STORY: When the original Twelve Apostles were chosen in this dispensation, Lyman Johnson was ordained February 14, 1835, at the young age of twenty-three. There were great blessings in store for Lyman. Then what he may have thought to be the impossible at one time—the thought of apostasy—became a reality. Wilford Woodruff records the following on May 29, 1837:

> I saw one of these Apostles in the Kirtland Temple, while the Sacrament was being passed, stand in the aisle and curse the Prophet of God to his face while he was in the stand, and when the bread was passed he reached out his hand for a piece of bread and flung it into his mouth like a mad dog. He turned as black in the face almost as an African with rage and with the power of the devil. What did he

do? He ate and drank damnation to himself. He did not hang himself; but he did go and drown himself, and the river went over his body while his spirit was cast into the pit, where he ceased to have the power to curse either God or His Prophet in time or in eternity."

http://saintswithouthalos.com/b/johnson_le.phtml

THE FACT: At a Council meeting, Brigham Young paraphrased the words of Lyman Johnson:

Brethren—I will call you brethren—I will tell you the truth. If I could believe Mormonism—it is not a matter whether it is true or not—but if I could believe Mormonism as I did when I traveled with you and preached, if I possessed the world I would give it. I would give anything. I would suffer my right hand to be cut off, if I could believe it again. Then I was full of joy and gladness. My dreams were pleasant. When I awoke in the morning, my spirit was cheerful. I was happy by day and by night, full of peace and joy and thanksgiving. But now it is darkness, pain, sorrow, misery in the extreme. I have never since seen a happy moment.

http://www.ldschurchnews.com/articles/19053
/Among-first-apostles-3-forgotten.html

QUESTION:

68. Luke Johnson was also ordained to the apostleship but left the Church in 1838, only to be rebaptized in Nauvoo shortly before the Saints left for the Salt Lake Valley. Luke is noted for arresting what individual and then helping him escape?

    a. Joseph Smith Sr.
    b. Joseph Smith Jr.
    c. Brigham Young
    d. Porter Rockwell

SECTION 69

BRIEF HISTORICAL BACKGROUND: Revelation received November 1831 at Hiram, Ohio, instructing Joseph Smith to call John Whitmer to travel with Oliver Cowdery to Missouri and help safeguard the revelations and the money donations for the Saints in the West.

THE STORY: It was necessary Joseph moved to the Johnson farm in Hiram to obtain the peace necessary to organize the revelations for publication and resume the translation of the Bible. Having Joseph in Hiram gave the young Church a presence in the area. Just as Newell K. Whitney and his wife prayed Joseph to Kirtland, so too was Samuel Smith prayed to Hiram.

THE FACT: In the fall of 1831, William McLellin and Samuel Smith were called to serve a mission to the Hiram area. Not yet ready to leave, according to Lucy Mack Smith, Samuel heard a voice in the middle of the night, saying to him, "Samuel, arise immediately and go forth on the mission which thou wast commanded to take to Hiram." He arose, wasted little time gathering some clothes, and left without eating. At Hiram, Samuel met up with William McLellin, and together they preached in the surrounding area. Shortly after their arrival, they were summoned by a young lady who had been sick for a number of months. She had prayed to the Lord that Mormon missionaries be sent to her home to lay their hands upon her head and heal her. This Samuel did for her. The young lady healed, and later was baptized into the Church.

Scot Facer Proctor and Maurine Jensen Proctor, eds., *The Revised and Enhanced History of Joseph Smith By His Mother* (Salt Lake City: Bookcraft, 1996), 294

QUESTION:

69. Oliver and John not only took the revelations to Missouri, but they also took the collected funds with them to help Edward Partridge purchase lands. How much money had Edward Partridge received from the eastern branches of the Church by January 1832?

    a. $451.89
    b. $6723.09
    c. $165.98
    d. $2694.70

SECTION 70

BRIEF HISTORICAL BACKGROUND: Revelation received by Joseph Smith on November 12, 1831 at Kirtland, Ohio. This revelation reiterated the importance of the Book of Commandments.

THE STORY: It's interesting that from November 1 to 12, six revelations were received by the Prophet during, or surrounding, conferences in relation to the Book of Commandments. Sections 67 through 70 are received in chronological order, whereas sections 1 and 133 were also received. But section 1 was placed as the preface to the Book of Commandments and also the Doctrine and Covenants, and the other was inserted as the appendix to the Book of Commandments.

Joseph recorded the following:

> My time was occupied closely in reviewing the commandments and sitting in conference, for nearly two weeks; for from the first to the twelfth of November we held four special conferences. In the

last which was held at Brother Johnson's, in Hiram, after deliberate consideration, in consequence of the book of revelations, now to be printed, being the foundation of the Church in these last days, and a benefit to the world, showing that the keys of the mysteries of the kingdom of our Savior are again entrusted to man; and the riches of eternity within the compass of those who are willing to live by every word that proceedeth out of the mouth of God—therefore the conference voted that they prize the revelations to be worth to the Church the riches of the whole earth, speaking temporally. The great benefits to the world which result from the Book of Mormon and the revelations which the Lord has seen fit in His infinite wisdom to grant unto us for our salvation, and for the salvation of all that will believe, were duly appreciated; and in answer to an inquiry, I received [section 70].

Joseph Smith, in *History of the Church*, 1:235–36

THE FACT: Howard W. Hunter states the following about the Doctrine and Covenants:

The Doctrine and Covenants is a unique book. It is the only book on the face of the entire earth with a preface composed by the Creator himself. Furthermore, this book of scripture contains more direct quotations from the Lord than any other existing book of scripture.

It is not a translation of an ancient document, but is of modern origin. It is a book of revelation for our day. It is a unique and divinely inspired selection of revelations that came through prophets of God in our day in answer to questions, concerns, and challenges they and others faced. It contains divine answers to real-life problems involving real people.

Doctrine and Covenants contains the word and will of the Lord as revealed to men and women in this dispensation of time. It is a book of scripture specifically for our day. It is a book for the entire world.

The Teachings of Howard W. Hunter, Clyde J. Williams, ed.
(Salt Lake City: Bookcraft, 1997), 55

70. Joseph Smith referred to the Book of Mormon as the "keystone of our religion." What did President Ezra Taft Benson call the Doctrine and Covenants?

   a. The cornerstone
   b. The sunstone
   c. The capstone
   d. The seer stone

SECTION 71

BRIEF HISTORICAL BACKGROUND: A call for Joseph Smith and Oliver Cowdery to preach the gospel in the area. Joseph Smith received this revelation December 1, 1831, at Hiram, Ohio.

THE STORY: Ezra Booth, because of his excommunication, was convinced by others to use his influence in spreading falsehoods to stop the growth of the Church. Ezra sent a series of letters to the Ohio Star in Ravenna, Ohio, in hopes of stemming the tide of Church conversions and also to create confusion with Church members, thus causing them to question or leave their newfound religion. To combat this, Joseph and Oliver served a mission from December 4, 1831, to approximately January 10, 1832, in the Ravenna and Kirtland area. Others are also called on similar missions.

Church Educational System, *Church History in the Fulness of Times* (Salt Lake City: The Church of Jesus Christ of Latter-day Saints, 1993), 114

In the introduction of the first of nine letters, Mr. Booth speaks of his "most singular and romantic undertaking" being that of his mission to Missouri. Then, referring to his mission, Ezra stated:

> It has taught me quite beyond my knowledge, the imbecility of human nature, and especially my own weakness. It has unfolded in its proper character, a delusion to which I had fallen a victim, and taught me the humiliating truth, that I was exerting the powers of both my mind and body, and sacrificing my time and property, to build up a system of delusion, almost unparalleled in the annals of the world.

Ezra's ninth and final letter concluded with these parting words:

> It is with pleasure I close this exposition, having in part accomplished, what I intended when I commenced it. The employment has been an unpleasant one to me, and from the first, I should have gladly avoided it, could I have done it, and maintained a conscience void of offence, toward God and man. — But should an individual by this exposition, be extricated or prevented from falling into the delusion, which has been the subject of consideration, I shall be amply compensated, for the painful task which I have performed.

http://saintswithouthalos.com/p/1831_booth8-9.phtml

THE FACT: The Lord stated in verse 7, "Wherefore, confound your enemies; call upon them to meet you both in public and in private; and inasmuch as ye are faithful their shame shall be made manifest."

Sidney Rigdon then issued the following challenge to Booth through a public notice:

> *Sir*—As you have publicly declared the book of Mormon to be an imposition, and I believing it to be otherwise, at present, deeming it my privilege to know it as well as you, do hereby present a request to you to meet me in the township of Hiram, Portage county, at such time and place as may be agreed upon hereafter, to investigate this subject, before the public; that if I am deluded in receiving this book as a revelation from God, I may be corrected, and the public relieved from anxiety. Your acceptance or rejection of this request, is desired through the medium of the Ohio Star.

http://saintswithouthalos.com/b/rigdon_s.phtml

Interestingly, Ezra did not show up for the debate. This may have been a wise choice though, since Sidney was known as an eloquent orator.

Joseph Smith stated in the *History of the Church* 1:241 that Sidney's and his mission "did much toward allaying the excited feelings which were growing out of the scandalous letters then being published."

QUESTION:

71. Who was the first apostate to write and publish false articles about the Church?
    a. Ezra Booth
    b. John Whitmer
    c. Symonds Ryder
    d. Sidney Rigdon

SECTION 72

BRIEF HISTORICAL BACKGROUND: Joseph Smith received this revelation on December 4, 1831, at Kirtland, Ohio. The calling of another bishop became necessary.

THE STORY: The Lord instructs in verses 7–8, "And the duty of the bishop shall be made known by the commandments which have been given, and the voice of the conference. And now, verily I say unto you, my servant Newel K. Whitney is the man who shall be appointed and ordained unto this power."

The Lord had appointed Edward Partridge to be bishop over Missouri and the western lands. Nevertheless, the need arose for a bishop to minister the needs of those in the Kirtland area and the lands to the east. Newell was the perfect fit, at least to the Lord, even though Newell wasn't so sure himself. After the call, Newell approached the Prophet and expressed his concerns of inadequacy and of feeling unqualified for such a position. Joseph Smith counseled Newell to go to his room and pray until he did feel qualified for the call. I'm sure Newell, upon receiving this instruction from Joseph, couldn't help but recollect the nights he and his wife, Elizabeth Ann, supplicated the Lord asking for the gospel truth to be sent to them. It was during one of these evening prayers that the Whitney home was surrounded as "a cloud of glory resting on our home." Joseph Smith was also a participant in this vision, although hundreds of miles away in New York, actually seeing Newell and Elizabeth praying him to Kirtland. It was because of this vision that Joseph could confidently state when he first arrived at the Whitney store, "Newell Whitney, thou are the man" when in fact he had never met him in person before.

Following Joseph's instructions, and while Brother Whitney was on his knees in earnest prayer, Newell heard the heavenly voice whisper, "Thy strength is in me."

http://lds.org/ensign/1978/12/the-newel-k-whitney-family?lang=eng

THE FACT: It's interesting that Elizabeth Ann joined the Church a number of months prior to Newell accepting the gospel. She joined in November 1830 at the time the four elders on the Lamanite mission came through the Kirtland area. Five years after Newell's baptism, his parents also joined the Church. Not everyone in the Whitney immediate family established a tie with the Church. Newell had a younger brother, Samuel, who idolized him. In fact, Samuel oversaw the finances of the Whitney store. He constantly tried to persuade Newell to leave the Church, so he was completely stunned when Bishop Whitney consecrated all he had to the church, including the store. Samuel was certain his brother was defrauded out of his business. Years later when Newell was living in Nauvoo, Samuel came to visit him. He couldn't get over the fact that many of the Saints lived in humble circumstances, yet they had a magnificent temple.

Regardless of their differences, the two men respected and loved each other. Samuel mourned over Newell's financial losses, while Newell mourned over his brother's constant rejection of the gospel.

http://lds.org/ensign/1978/12/the-newel-k-whitney-family?lang=eng

QUESTION:

72. Throughout the entire history of the Church, the keeping of records has been extremely important. In verse 17, the Lord spoke in reference to the issuing of certificates so that those traveling from branch to branch could show the leading authority their worthiness to belong to the Church. On June 3, 1844, just days prior to Joseph and Hyrum's deaths, Joseph instructs William Clayton to do what with the Church records?

    a. Burn them
    b. Bury them
    c. Take them to Carthage
    d. Load them in wagons and take them to the Salt Lake Valley

SECTION 73

BRIEF HISTORICAL BACKGROUND: Section 73 was a call for Joseph and Sidney to cease their preaching and again turn their attention to the translation of the Bible. Joseph and Sidney received this revelation on January 10, 1832, at Hiram, Ohio.

THE STORY: The Bible translation had its beginnings in New York and continued to July 2, 1833, when the Prophet stated confidently that he was "finished with the work."

Joseph Smith, in *History of the Church*, 1:368

THE FACT: The Bible translation project helped stimulate the Prophet's thinking to query the Lord on important Church organization and doctrinal issues, which resulted in the reception of such sections as Doctrine and Covenants 74, 76, 77, 84, 86, 88, 91, 93, 102, 104, 107, 113, and 132.

> The Church Educational System, *Church History in the Fulness of Times* (Salt Lake City: The Church of Jesus Christ of Latter-day Saints, 1993), 119

QUESTION:

73. During the Bible translation, Joseph read about Enoch and his people. Where did Joseph Smith state the City of Enoch was located prior to its ascension into heaven?

    a. Jackson County, Missouri
    b. Israel
    c. The area of current-day Iraq
    d. The Gulf of Mexico

SECTION 74

BRIEF HISTORICAL BACKGROUND: The Prophet received the following revelation as an explanation to 1 Corinthians 7:14. This revelation was given to Joseph in January 1832 at Hiram, Ohio.

THE STORY: At a BYU speech in 1984, Bruce R. McConkie answered the question why we as Latter-day Saints use the King James Version of the Bible. He stated:

As far as the Bibles of the world are concerned, the King James Version is so far ahead of all others that there is little comparison. . . It is the Bible that came into being to prepare the way for the translation of the Book of Mormon and to set a literary pattern and standard for the revelations in the Doctrine and Covenants. It is the official Bible of the Church.

http://emp.byui.edu/marrottr/GenlAuthorities/Bible-SealedBook.pdf

THE FACT: In the same speech Elder McConkie explains the importance of the Joseph Smith Translation of the Bible:

The Joseph Smith Translation, or Inspired Version, is a thousand times over the best Bible now existing on earth. It contains all that the King James Version does, plus pages of additions and corrections and an occasional deletion. It was made by the spirit of revelation, and the changes and additions are the equivalent of the revealed word in the Book of Mormon and the Doctrine and Covenants. . . .

. . . Reference to this section and to the footnotes themselves will give anyone who has spiritual insight a deep appreciation of the revelatory work of the Prophet Joseph Smith. It is one of the great evidences of his prophetic call.

http://emp.byui.edu/marrottr/GenlAuthorities/Bible-SealedBook.pdf

QUESTION:

74. During a time of persecution and trial in 1831, Joseph Smith said he did what for "great consolation?"
    a. Read a chapter from the Book of Mormon
    b. Read a chapter from the Bible and prayed
    c. Prayed
    d. Talked with his brother Hyrum

SECTION 75

BRIEF HISTORICAL BACKGROUND: This revelation was received on January 25, 1832, at a special conference of the Church at Amherst, Ohio. Joseph Smith is ordained as the President of the High Priesthood.

THE STORY: This revelation was actually received in two parts during the conference. Sidney Rigdon first recorded verses 1–22 and then later recorded verses 23–36. The fact there was a President of the High Priesthood actually came from instructions received previously by the Lord in section 107. This may seem confusing, except that some of section 107 (which was received March 28, 1835) was originally given to the prophet as early as November 1831. The Lord stated in verses 65–66, received in November 1831, the following, "Wherefore, it must needs be that one be appointed of the High Priesthood to preside over the priesthood, and he shall be called President of the High Priesthood of the Church; Or, in other words, the Presiding High Priest over the High Priesthood of the Church."

http://josephsmithpapers.org/paperSummary/revelation-25-january-1832%E2%80%93a-dc-751%E2%80%9322; http://saintswithouthalos.com/n/offices_p_hp.phtml

THE FACT: Some may question why this conference was held at Amherst, Ohio, rather than in Hiram or Kirtland. Joseph stated that not only was this the home of elders Gideon Carter and Sylvester Smith (no relation to the Prophet), but also that it provided a chance for the elders to preach "and promulgate the Gospel to the inhabitants of the surrounding country."

Verse 17 refers to a Major N. Ashley. He and an elder by the name of Burr Riggs were to take their mission "into the south country." It's not known whether this mission materialized, as six months later, on July 3, 1832, Major is found at the home of Edward Partridge in Independence, Missouri, working as a tanner.

At the conference in Amherst, he had confidence in his testimony. I state this only because the mission call with Burr Riggs was initiated by Major asking the Prophet what the Lord would have him do. When the persecutions became too much, Major left the Church. Sadly, we last read of Major Ashley as a member of the mob at Haun's Mill.

"D&C People Form Fascinating Mosaic: Some Were Tried and Remained," *LDS Church News,* Jan. 7, 1989

QUESTION:

75. Who was called to be Joseph's counselors during this meeting?
    a. Sidney Rigdon and Jesse Gause
    b. Sidney Rigdon and Frederick G. Williams
    c. He didn't have any at this time
    d. Sidney Rigdon only

SECTION 76

BRIEF HISTORICAL BACKGROUND: It's interesting that the heading to this section explains that this is a vision rather than a revelation. This was given to Joseph Smith and Sidney Rigdon at Hiram, Ohio, on February 16, 1832. While translating the Bible, Joseph realized that many points touching the salvation of man were lost. It was while inquiring of the Lord that the following vision was given.

THE STORY: Philo Dibble, an early Kirtland convert (October 1830), was present at the time section 76 was received. He gives the following account of the events of this vision as they transpired in the revelation room at the home of John Johnson:

> The vision which is recorded in the Book of Doctrine and Covenants was given at the house of "Father Johnson," in Hiram, Ohio, and during the time that Joseph and Sidney were in the spirit and saw the heavens open, there were other men in the room, perhaps twelve, among whom I was one during a part of the time—probably two-thirds of the time—I saw the glory and felt the power, but did not see the vision.
>
> The events and conversation, while they were seeing what is written (and many things were seen and related that are not written,) I will relate as minutely as is necessary.
>
> Joseph would, at intervals, say: "What do I see?" as one might say while looking out the window and beholding what all in the room could not see. Then he would relate what he had seen or what he was looking at. Then Sidney replied, "I see the same." Presently Sidney would say "what do I see?" and would repeat what he had seen or was seeing, and Joseph would reply, "I see the same."
>
> This manner of conversation was repeated at short intervals to the end of the vision, and during the whole time not a word was spoken by any other person. Not a sound nor motion made by anyone but Joseph and Sidney, and it seemed to me that they never moved a joint or limb during the time I was there, which I think was over an hour, and to the end of the vision.
>
> Joseph sat firmly and calmly all the time in the midst of a magnificent glory, but Sidney sat limp and pale, apparently as limber as a rag, observing which, Joseph remarked, smilingly, "Sidney is not used to it as I am."

http://www.boap.org/LDS/Early-Saints/REC-JS.html

THE FACT: Section 76, one of the most important revelations given to the Church, was received while Joseph was translating the Bible and Sidney acted as scribe. The two men were studying John 5:29 when the vision was received. Elder Tyler Daniels recorded in his journal the Prophet's love of the Bible and the ease with which he was able to explain the Bible's teachings to others:

> During his short stay he preached at my father's residence, an humble log cabin. He read the 3rd chapter of John, and explained much of

it, making it so plain that a child could not help understanding it, if he paid attention. I recollect distinctly the substance of his remarks on the 3rd verse— "Except a man be born again he cannot see the Kingdom of God". . .

His discourse was, I think, entirely on the first principles of the gospel, and he quoted many passages of scripture, but I do not recollect any other so clearly defined as those I have quoted. I have given his exact language, as near as I can recollect it, after a lapse of over fifty years—nearly sixty years. The joy that filled my juvenile soul no one can realize except those who have had a foretaste of heavenly things. It seemed as though the gates of heaven were opened and a living stream flowed directly to the holy man of God. It also filled the house where we were sitting. To this day, when I think of it, which is quite often, and always when I hear those scriptures referred to, a thrill of joy and of testimony permeates the inmost recesses of my soul.

http://www.boap.org/LDS/Early-Saints/REC-JS.html

QUESTION:

76. Joseph Smith described this vision as coming from where?
   a. Kolob
   b. The celestial kingdom
   c. A transcript from the records of the eternal world
   d. Heavenly Father

SECTION 77

BRIEF HISTORICAL BACKGROUND: Joseph Smith received this revelation at Hiram, Ohio, March 1832, clarifying the revelation of John in the book of Revelation. This section is unique in the sense that it was a question-and-answer session with the Lord.

THE STORY: It was during this question-and-answer session that Joseph Smith asked in verse 11 what was meant by the 144,000. I'm sure you'll agree that there has been a difference of opinion on this verse by various religious sects throughout the world. Some believe that the 144,000 will be saved in the Kingdom of God; others believe that it's linked to the Mayan Calendar and is indicative of 144,000 days. Some believe this number indicates the time Christ will come again—when their religion population matches 144,000. And finally, others believe that there will only be 144,000 people left on earth to carry on humanity after some huge, upcoming disaster wipes out the majority of the world's population.

http://en.wikipedia.org/wiki/144000_(number)

THE FACT: Orson Pratt explains who these 144,000 are:

> Before the Lord shall come . . . there is to be a great work among the nations. . . . The ten tribes will have to come forth and come to this land, to be crowned with glory in the midst of Zion by the hands of the servants of God, even the Children of Ephraim; and twelve thousand High Priests will be elected from each of these ten tribes, as well as from the scattered tribes, and sealed in their foreheads, and will be ordained and receive power to gather out of all nations, kindreds, tongues and people as many as will come unto the general assemblage of the Church of the first-born.
>
> The Church of Jesus Christ of Latter-day Saints, *Journal of Discourses*
> (Liverpool, England: Latter-day Saint Book Depot, 1874), 16:325

These 144,000, if you will, are missionaries called to find, teach, and gather the Lord's elect around the world. Right now there are just over 52,000 missionaries serving full-time missions in the Church. I'm sure you've already done the math and realize this number has to almost triple to reach a missionary force of 144,000!

77. Joseph Smith counseled the elders in the Church to teach like whom?

   a. Parley P. Pratt
   b. Nephi
   c. Porter Rockwell
   d. John the Baptist

SECTION 78

BRIEF HISTORICAL BACKGROUND: The purpose of establishing the Lord's storehouse is revealed to Joseph Smith during March 1832 at Hiram, Ohio.

THE STORY: If your Doctrine and Covenants was printed earlier than the 1981 edition, you will notice in this section that code names or pseudonyms were used to replace the names of some Church leaders and even places.

The reasoning behind the use of pseudonyms was to protect those individuals named in the revelation. Persecution was running high, and the Lord saw the need to protect his servants. Orson Hyde comments on the use of the pseudonyms:

> The law of Enoch is so named in the Book of Doctrine and Covenants, but in other words, it is the law given by Joseph Smith, Jr. The word Enoch did not exist in the original copy; neither did some other names. The names that were incorporated when it was printed, did not exist there when the manuscript revelations were given, for I saw them myself. Some of them I copied. And when the Lord was about to have the Book of Covenants given to the world it was

thought wisdom, in consequence of the persecutions of our enemies in Kirtland and some of the regions around, that some of the names should be changed, and Joseph was called Baurak Ale, which was a Hebrew word; meaning God bless you. He was also called Gazelam, being a person to whom the Lord had given the Urim and Thummim. He was also called Enoch. Sidney Rigdon was called Baneemy. And the revelation where it read so many *dollars* into the treasury was changed to *talents*. And the City of New York was changed to Cainhannoch.

The Church of Jesus Christ of Latter-day Saints, *Journal of Discourses* (Liverpool, England: Latter-day Saint Book Depot, 1874), 16:156

THE FACT: The following is a list of the pseudonyms used in the Doctrine and Covenants and the corresponding individual, place, or thing that the pseudonym replaced. Also included are the Doctrine and Covenants sections where the pseudonym was used and the interpretation of the Hebrew name.

Enoch—Joseph Smith (78, 82, 92, 96, 104)

Gazalem—Joseph Smith (78, 82, 104), The Light of the Lord

Baurak Ale— Joseph Smith (103, 105), Blessed of God

Ahashdah—Newell K. Whitney (78, 82, 96, 104), A close watcher

Alam—Edward Partridge (82), Everlasting helmet

Pelagoram—Sidney Rigdon (78, 82, 104)

Mahalaleel—Algernon S. Gilbert (82), He shined from God

Olihah—Oliver Cowdery (82, 103), God have mercy

Horah—John Whitmer (82), A conceiver

Mahemson—Martin Harris (82, 104), He turns back

Shalemanasseh—William W. Phelps (82), A tried broken pillar

Shinehah—Kirtland (82, 96, 104, 105), Kirtland Stake

Talents—dollars (104)

Cainhannock—New York (104)

Shederlaomach—Frederick G. Williams (92, 103), Unbound sheaf

Zombre—John Johnson (96, 104), Slow to hear

Seth—Joseph (96)

Tahhanes—the Tannery (96)
Laneshire House—Printing office (104)
Ozondah— Store (104), Ashery
Shule—Ashery (104), Ashery
Shinelah—print (104)
Shinelane—printing (104)
Baneemy—Sidney Rigdon (105), My sons

David J. Whittaker, "Substituted Names in the Published Revelations of Joseph Smith," *BYU Studies* 23, no. 1 (1983)

QUESTION:

78. Why were the pseudonyms no longer used in the 1981 edition of the Doctrine and Covenants?

    a. There was no longer a need to protect these individuals since all have passed on, including the persecutors.
    b. It was causing too many members to get sidetracked in Gospel Doctrine class.
    c. Too many members were inquiring their bishops what their code names were.
    d. The Church realizes that progress is impossible without change.

SECTION 79

BRIEF HISTORICAL BACKGROUND: In March 1832, Joseph Smith received this revelation for Jared Carter calling him on a mission. It was given at Hiram, Ohio.

THE STORY: Jared Carter served five missions for the Church: three to the eastern states, one to Michigan, and one to Canada. In verse 1 of this revelation, the Lord stated, "Verily I say unto you, that it is my will that my servant Jared Carter should go again into the eastern countries, from place to place, and from city to city, in the power of the ordination wherewith he has been ordained, proclaiming glad tidings of great joy, even the everlasting gospel."

This revelation was his call to serve his second mission to the eastern states.

http://josephsmithpapers.org/person?lastFirst=Carter%2C%20Jared

THE FACT: The following journal entry of Lyman Omer Littlefield describes a situation from Jared Carter's third mission, to Michigan. He mentions Brother Samuel Bent. Remember, Samuel was the deacon in the Presbyterian church belonging to Mr. Ruggles, who came in contact with Lucy Mack Smith, and she prophesied that the elders would convert a third of his congregation and take the deacon away too.

> My parents were members of the Methodist Church and did not wish to exchange that faith for another; but they went to hear what these strangers had to say. Their little son Lyman was permitted to bear them company. It was winter and of course a sleigh was our mode of conveyance. Their place of holding meeting was in a log schoolhouse built in the edge of some timber and as we turned from the main road to drive near we knew that meeting had commenced, for we heard the speaker in a full and animated tone of voice enunciating his doctrines. It is said in the scriptures: "Blessed are they who know the joyful sound;" so the writer must just then have been one of the favored, for at the very first sound of Jared Carter's voice—for it was he who was speaking—a strange, unaccountable feeling came over me, and before hearing one word pronounced by him, there was something connected with the tone of his voice that convinced me he was a man of God and was telling the truth. The writer went in that meeting prepared to believe all the speaker said, and your humble friend has been a believer in what many call Mormonism from that hour.
>
> After attending one or two more meetings and reading the Book

of Mormon all she could, my mother was fully convinced of the truth of the gospel. My father did not believe so readily, but after a few weeks he, too, was convinced and my parents became members of the Church of Jesus Christ of Latter-day Saints—they being baptized by immersion for the remission of sins and having hands laid upon them for the reception of the Holy Ghost. Quite a number of people in that vicinity embraced the new faith and a branch of the Church was organized and presided over by Elder Samuel Bent.

http://www.boap.org/LDS/Early-Saints/LLittlefield.html

QUESTION:

79. In verse 3 of this revelation, the Lord promised Jared, "And inasmuch as he is faithful, I will crown him again with sheaves." Brother Carter served six months and two days on this mission to the eastern states. How many people did he baptize?

    a. 21
    b. 95
    c. 43
    d. 105

SECTION 80

BRIEF HISTORICAL BACKGROUND: A call from the Lord was extended to two additional missionaries through the Prophet Joseph Smith, dated March 1832 at Hiram, Ohio.

THE STORY: Stephen Burnett and Eden Smith are called to serve a mission to wherever they desire. Stephen Burnett was eighteen years old and a high priest at the time of this call, possibly the youngest high priest in the early Church. Not much is known of the missionary labors of these two brethren, although Eden Smith did record the following:

> We traveled on north two miles and Cald with A presbyterian Priest and told him Concerning the Book of Mormon and Concerning the Gosple of Jesus Christ and he Cald for proof of the Book of Mormon and we cited him to the bible and he said he did not Receive that and we told the Cituation he was in and what he must do left him and went on our way.
>
> http://www.saintswithouthalos.com/b/burnett_s.phtml; http://www.gospeldoc-trine.com/DoctrineandCovenants/DC%2080.htm

It may seem odd that the Lord left it up to the two missionaries where they desired to serve. But it makes sense, given the following fact.

THE FACT: At a special conference of the Church on April 10, 1843, many elders received their mission calls. Here are a few of the noteworthy calls:

> William B. Brink—the interior of Pennsylvania, where the elders have not been.
> Eleazar Willis—wherever he chose.
> Moses Wade—a county in New York where there had not been any preaching by the Saints.
>
> Joseph Smith, in *History of the Church,* 5:349–49

At a conference of the Church, on September 17, 1837, in Kirtland, Ohio, another unique situation played out where 109 elders numbered themselves and then split into eight groups of thirteen missionaries each. Each group was designated a destination based on a point of the compass. Elders 105–109 were assigned a group. Then all present were instructed that if their call did not suit them, then they could trade with an elder from another group that was more to their liking.

> Joseph Smith, in *History of the Church,* 2:514.

80. Where did Stephen Burnett and Eden Smith serve their mission?

    a. Missouri

    b. New Hampshire

    c. Tennessee

    d. New York

SECTION 81

BRIEF HISTORICAL BACKGROUND: A revelation given to Joseph Smith calling Frederick G. Williams to the First Presidency of the Church. Joseph received this revelation March 1832 in Hiram, Ohio.

THE STORY: For one who held such a high position in the Church, so little is known of Jesse Gause. There is no record of his baptism, although some speculate that Reynolds Cahoon may have been the individual who performed this ordinance for Jesse in the later part of 1830. It's also known that Joseph Smith called Jesse to be a counselor on March 8, 1832, with Sidney Rigdon. Records show that he traveled with the Prophet to Missouri in April 1832 and later he was called to serve a mission with Zebedee Coltrin after Jesse returned from his trip to Missouri. Approximately three weeks into the mission, Zebedee experienced severe headaches, causing his return to Kirtland. Prior to Zebedee returning to Kirtland, the two missionaries prayed for each other. Brother Gause continued his mission to the east "and walked right out of the history of the Church, never again to return. There appears to be no other record on the man either in or out of the Church."

Robert J. Woodford, "Jesse Gause, Counselor to the Prophet,"
BYU Studies (Spring 1975), 362–64

THE FACT:

PRESIDENCY OF THE HIGH PRIESTHOOD AND FIRST PRESIDENCY 1832–1844

Italics: Left the Church for some time.

Date	President	First Counselor	Second Counselor	Other Counselors
Mar. 1832–Dec. 1832	Joseph Smith Jr	*Jesse Gause*	*Sidney Rigdon*	
Mar. 1833–Dec. 1834	Joseph Smith Jr	*Sidney Rigdon*	*Frederick G. Williams*	
Dec. 1834–Sept. 1837	Joseph Smith Jr *Oliver Cowdery (Asst.)*	*Sidney Rigdon*	*Frederick G. Williams*	
Sept. 1837–Nov. 1837	Joseph Smith Jr. *Oliver Cowdery (Asst.)*	*Sidney Rigdon*	*Frederick G. Williams*	*Oliver Cowdery (Asst.)* Hyrum Smith (Asst.) John Smith (Asst.) Joseph Smith Sr. (Asst.)
Nov. 1837–Apr. 1838	Joseph Smith Jr. *Oliver Cowdery (Asst.)*	*Sidney Rigdon*	Hyrum Smith	*Oliver Cowdery (Asst.)* Joseph Smith Sr. (Asst.) John Smith (Asst.)
Apr. 1838–Sept. 1840	Joseph Smith Jr.	*Sidney Rigdon*	Hyrum Smith	Joseph Smith Sr. (Asst.) John Smith (Asst.)
Sept. 1840–Jan. 1841	Joseph Smith Jr.	*Sidney Rigdon*	Hyrum Smith	John Smith
Jan. 1841–Apr. 1841	Joseph Smith Jr. Hyrum Smith (Asst.)	*Sidney Rigdom*	*William Law*	John Smith
Apr. 1841–May 1842	Joseph Smith Jr. Hyrum Smith (Asst.) *John C. Bennett (Asst.)*	*Sidney Rigdon*	*William Law*	John Smith
May 1842–Feb. 1843	Joseph Smith Jr Hyrum Smith (Asst.)	*Sidney Rigdon*	*William Law*	John Smith (Asst.)
Feb. 1843–Apr. 1844	Joseph Smith Jr. Hyrum Smith (Asst.)	*Sidney Rigdon*	*William Law*	John Smith (Asst.) *Amasa Lyman*
Apr. 1844–Jun. 1844	Joseph Smith Jr. Hyrum Smith (Asst.)	*Sidney Rigdon*		John Smith (Asst.) *Amasa Lyman*

http://www.splendidsun.com/wp/wp-content/uploads/2010/12/78-84.pdf

LITTLE-KNOWN STORIES 167

QUESTION:

81. Which of the following religions did Jesse Gause **not** belong to?

   a. The Church of Jesus Christ of Latter-day Saints
   b. Shaker
   c. Quaker
   d. Methodist

SECTION 82

BRIEF HISTORICAL BACKGROUND: Revelation given to Joseph Smith on April 26, 1832, at a conference of the Church in Jackson County, Missouri. Joseph was sustained as the President of the High Priesthood.

THE STORY: Again, pseudonyms were used in this section but dropped with the 1981 edition of the Doctrine and Covenants.

Just a week prior to Joseph Smith and his group leaving for Missouri, he and Sidney Rigdon had been tarred and feathered (March 24, 1832). Mob violence was at a fever pitch when the brethren left for Missouri on April 1, 1832. The following was recorded by Joseph Smith in his Annotated History. Pay attention to how far the mob followed them:

> April first, I started for Missouri, in company with Newel K. Whitney, Peter Whitmer, and Jesse Gause, to fulfil the revelation. Not wishing to go by Kirtland, as another mob existed in that neighborhood (and indeed, the spirit of mobocracy was very prevalent through that whole region of country at the time), brother George Pitkin took us in his wagon by the most expeditious route to Warren, where we arrived the same day, and were there joined by Elder Rigdon, who

left Chardon in the morning; and proceeding onward, we arrived at Wellsville the next day, and the day following at Steubenville, where we left the wagon; and on Wednesday, the 4th of April, we took passage on board a steam packet for Wheeling, Virginia; where we purchased a lot of paper for the press in Zion, then in care of W. W. Phelps.

After we left Hiram, fearing for the safety of my family, on account of the mob, I wrote to my wife (in connection with Bishop Whitney) suggesting that she go to Kirtland and tarry with Brother Whitney's family until our return. From Wheeling we took passage on board the steamer Trenton. While at the dock, during the night, the boat was twice on fire burning the whole width of the boat through into the cabin, but with so little damage that the boat went on in the morning; and when we arrived at Cincinnati, some of the mob which had followed us, left us, and we arrived at Louisville the same night. Captain Brittle offered us protection on board of his boat, and gave us supper and breakfast gratuitously.

At Louisville we were joined by Elder Titus Billings, who was journeying with a company of Saints from Kirtland to Zion, and we took passage on the steamer Charleston for St. Louis, where we parted from Brother Billings and company, and by stage arrived at Independence, Missouri, on the twenty-fourth of April, having traveled a distance of about three hundred miles from St. Louis. We found the brethren in Zion, generally enjoying health and faith; and they were extremely glad to welcome us among them."

http://www.boap.org/LDS/History/HTMLHistory/v1c19history.html

THE FACT: The Lord states in verse 20, "This order I have appointed to be an everlasting order unto you, and unto your successors, inasmauch as you sin not." Before the Saints could set in place the united order, they were persecuted and eventually driven out of Missouri. However, over the years there has been some success at establishing such an order, but for the most part, because of selfishness, the united order has never been fully established in this dispensation. The following is from the *Deseret News* dated May 2, 1874 in response to the Twentieth Ward in Salt Lake City at the suggestion of the order:

Even with this considerable concession only thirty of approximately six hundred raised their hands in support of the order. This visibly chagrined Brigham but he used control rather than fury until there were fifty hands raised. He said that would be enough for a start."

Deseret News, 2 May 1874

QUESTION:

82. What is the only pseudonym (verse 20 gives the proper name) that is still currently used in the Church?

    a. Gazelam
    b. Firm
    c. Baurak Ale
    d. Cainhannoch

SECTION 83

BRIEF HISTORICAL BACKGROUND: On April 30, 1832, at Independence, Missouri, Joseph Smith was given a revelation in regard to women and children having claims on their husbands and fathers for support.

THE STORY: It's difficult to know for certain what age the Lord had in mind when He stated in verse 4 that "children have claim upon their parents for their maintenance until they are of age." I understand what that age is today. With a tightened economy, the average age of children leaving home and getting married has definitely increased; however, this hasn't always been the practice. In the early 1800s, many states had laws for the minimum age to marry. That age was twelve, with even a few states allowing children as young as ten the right to marry.

THE FACT: As you read this next story from the autobiography of Mosiah Hancock, note that he was born April 9, 1834:

> After the death of the Prophet, the mob spent their fury on the Twelve and a few others. The Brethren pushed the work on the Temple; and the Gospel was preached; and every Saint was busy doing all he could to help the work along. Although I was very young, I was on guard many a night, and gladly did I hail with many of the Saints, the completion of the temple. On about January 10, 1846, I was privileged to go in the temple and receive my washings and anointings. I was sealed to a lovely young girl named Mary [Dunn], who was about my age, but it was with the understanding that we were not to live together as man and wife until we were 16 years of age. The reason that some were sealed so young was because we knew that we would have to go West and wait many a long time for another temple.
>
> We left the Indian Mills on May 14, 1848, and we left Winter Quarters on May 18th. While we were camped at Winter Quarters, Mary Dunn came to our camp and wanted to go with us, but mother said we could not take her because we had no room. Mary's mother had died and her father had gotten a stepmother for his children. She came with her bundle of clothes to our wagon, and with what joy I hailed my noble, beautiful wife! But Mary had to go, and oh what sorrow as I saw her depart. We were separated for life.
>
> http://www.boap.org/LDS/Early-Saints/MHancock.html

QUESTION:

83. Verse 4 reads, "All children have claim upon their parents for their maintenance until they are of age." This is often referred to as the "age of majority." What is this age in most states today?

   a. 21
   b. 16
   c. 18
   d. 19

SECTION 84

BRIEF HISTORICAL BACKGROUND: Joseph Smith designated this as a revelation on priesthood. The Prophet received this revelation September 22–23, 1832, at Kirtland, Ohio.

THE STORY: This revelation teaches men of all ages what is commonly referred to as the "Oath and Covenant of the Priesthood." The Lord stated in verse 33, "For whoso is faithful unto the obtaining these two priesthoods of which I have spoken, and the magnifying their calling, are sanctified by the Spirit unto the renewing of their bodies." Surprisingly, prior to 1854, boys were not usually ordained to the Aaronic Priesthood. However, in 1854 Wilford Woodruff recorded, "We are now beginning to ordain our young sons to the lesser priesthood here in Zion."

History of the Church, 4:540–41

THE FACT: Brigham Young provided this interesting perspective:

> Now will it cause some of you to marvel that I was not ordained a high priest before I was ordained an apostle? Brother Kimball and myself were never ordained high priests. How wonderful! I was going to say how little some of the brethren understood the priesthood, after the Twelve were called. In our early career in this Church, on one occasion, in one of our councils, we were telling about some of the Twelve wanting to ordain us high priests, and what I said to Brother Patten when he wanted to ordain me in York State: said I, "Brother Patten, wait until I can lift my hand to heaven and say. 'I have magnified the office of an elder." After that our conversation was over in the council, some of the brethren began to query, and said we ought to be ordained high priests; at the same time I did not consider that an apostle needed to be ordained a high priest and elder, or a teacher. I did not express my views on the subject, at that time, but thought I would hear what brother Joseph would say about

it. It was William E. McLellin who told Joseph that I and Heber were not ordained high priests, and wanted to know if it should not be done. Said Joseph, "Will you insult the Priesthood? Is that all the knowledge you have of the office of an apostle? Do you not know that the man who receives the apostleship receives all the keys that ever were, or that can be conferred upon mortal man? What are you talking about? I am astonished!" Nothing more was said about it.

Discourses of Brigham Young, John A. Widtsoe, comp.
(Salt Lake City: Deseret Book, 1954), 1:136

QUESTION:

84. What was one of the duties of a deacon during the Nauvoo years of the Church?

    a. Hand out programs at sacrament meeting
    b. Serve missions
    c. Chop wood for the widows
    d. Patrol Nauvoo City streets at night

SECTION 85

BRIEF HISTORICAL BACKGROUND: Joseph Smith received the following revelation on November 27, 1832, at Kirtland, Ohio. This revelation was written as a letter to answer questions about the Saints receiving their inheritances in Missouri.

THE STORY: Joseph Smith discovered that Bishop Edward Partridge was not always giving the Saints arriving in Missouri their inheritances (the necessary land to sustain their families), or that some of the Saints arriving in Missouri refused to live the law of

consecration, which, according to the Lord, was a necessary requirement to live with the Saints in Missouri. Joseph Smith sent a letter
to W. W. Phelps in hopes of alleviating some of the above concerns.

THE FACT: Brigham Young elaborated, as only he could, on
why the law of consecration failed among the Missouri Saints:

> When the revelation . . . was given in 1838, I was present, and recol-
> lect the feelings of the brethren. . . . The brethren wished me to go
> among the Churches, and find out what surplus property the people
> had, with which to forward the building of the Temple we were com-
> mencing at Far West. I accordingly went from place to place through
> the country. Before I started, I asked brother Joseph, "Who shall be
> the judge of what is surplus property?" Said he, "Let them be the
> judges themselves. . . ."
>
> Then I replied, "I will go and ask them for their surplus prop-
> erty;" and I did so; I found the people said they were willing to do
> about as they were counselled, but, upon asking them about their
> surplus property, most of the men who owned land and cattle would
> say, "I have got so many hundred acres of land, and I have got so
> many boys, and I want each one of them to have eighty acres, there-
> fore this is not surplus property." Again, "I have got so many girls,
> and I do not believe I shall be able to give them more than forty acres
> each." "Well, you have got two or three hundred acres left." "Yes, but
> I have a brother-in-law coming on, and he will depend on me for a
> living; my wife's nephew is also coming on, he is poor, and I shall
> have to furnish him a farm after he arrives here." I would go on to
> the next one, and he would have more land and cattle than he could
> make use of to advantage. It is a laughable idea, but is nevertheless
> true, men would tell me they were young and beginning [in] the
> world, and would say, "We have no children, but our prospects are
> good, and we think we shall have a family of children, and if we do,
> we want to give them eighty acres of land each; we have no surplus
> property." "How many cattle have you?" "So many." "How many
> horses, &c?" "So many, but I have made provisions for all these, and
> I have use for every thing I have got."
>
> Some were disposed to do right with their surplus property, and
> once in a while you would find a man who had a cow which he con-
> sidered surplus, but generally she was of the class that would kick
> a person's hat off, or eyes out. . . . You would once in a while find
> a man who had a horse that he considered surplus, but at the same

time he had the ringbone, was broken-winded, spavined in both legs, and had the pole evil at one end of the neck and a fistula at the other, and both knees sprung."

The Church of Jesus Christ of Latter-day Saints, *Journal of Discourses*
(Liverpool, England: Latter-day Saint Book Depot, 1874), 2:306–7

QUESTION:

85. The united order, or the law of consecration, was also known as what?

    a. Order of Enoch
    b. Order of John the Baptist
    c. Order of doubting Thomas
    d. Order of Abraham

SECTION 86

BRIEF HISTORICAL BACKGROUND: Revelation given to Joseph Smith while reviewing the translation of the Bible December 6, 1832, at Kirtland, Ohio.

THE STORY: The Prophet received this revelation on the Bible parable of the sower and the seed a day after he had called Noah Packard and Solomon Humphreys Jr. on a mission.

THE FACT: The following is Noah Packard's conversion story:

In the year 1831 a rumor was in circulation that a gold Bible had been dug out of the earth; and hearing the preachers of the day rail out against it, I believed the words of the Savior were about to be fulfilled in regard to false prophets and teachers arising in the last days, who, if it were possible would deceive the very elect. In the fall of this same year a man by the name of William Jolly and family moved into the neighborhood; who I was informed, were believers in the gold Bible. I felt in my heart to pity them, and told my wife we would go and make them a visit; accordingly as soon as they commenced conversation on the subject of religion, quoting the words of the Savior in regard to false prophets and teachers in the last days; on hearing this, Mrs. Jolly went and placed a stand in the middle of the floor and put a candle and a large family Bible upon it and said, "Now to the law and testimony." When she immediately turned to the passages of scripture I had quoted and read them, and applied them to the sects long extinct upon the earth, which I could not refute. I immediately commenced searching the Bible and found that in the last days God would set His hand the second time to gather Israel from all the earth.

About this time Mrs. Jolly presented the Book of Mormon to me and asked me if I would read it; I told her I would, and took it and carried it home and placing the book against my forehead asked secretly the Lord if that work was His, He would make it manifest to me. I then opened the book and commenced reading aloud that my wife might also hear it. We read it through and I commenced reading it the second time and the Lord poured out His spirit upon me and the scriptures were opened to our understanding, and we were convinced that the Book of Mormon was a true record of the Aborigines of America containing the fullness of the gospel of Jesus Christ which was to come forth at the time of the restitution of the house of Israel.

Accordingly I and my wife were baptized in the town of Parkman by Parley P. Pratt and were confirmed in the Church of Jesus Christ of Latter-day Saints, under his hands and Hyrum Smith's hands, the day I am unable to state, but think it was between the first and fifth of June 1832. Between this time and January following I went to Kirtland and was ordained a priest under the hands of Joseph Smith, the Prophet, and Sidney Rigdon.

http://www.boap.org/LDS/Early-Saints/NPackard.html

86. Which individual served the most missions in the Church?
    a. Joseph Smith Jr.
    b. Samuel Smith
    c. Parley P. Pratt
    d. Orson Pratt

SECTION 87

BRIEF HISTORICAL BACKGROUND: While the Brethren were discussing American slavery, this revelation was received December 25, 1832, at or near Kirtland, Ohio. Not only is it a revelation but also a prophecy on war.

THE STORY: There are those who ridiculed the fact that Joseph Smith not only predicted the "War Between the States," but also the location of the first shots. At the time this revelation and prophecy were proclaimed, it was obvious to some the country was heading in that direction anyways. In November 1831, South Carolina met in convention and voted to be a "free and separate nation," with full intent to sever all ties with the United States on February 1, 1833. President Andrew Jackson sent troops to quell the uprising. Those not necessarily claiming prophetic powers were cognizant of the eventual outcome of war. These individuals felt that anyone could have predicted the forthcoming war.

Those that scoff Joseph Smith misunderstand this prophecy, for it predicted not only the Civil War but also all wars. Verse 2 states, "And the time will come that war will be poured out upon all nations, beginning at this place." Could Joseph Smith also foresee that Great Britain would ally to the cause of the southern states? No one, unless inspired by the Spirit of the Lord, could have predicted this three decades before the actual outbreak. The revelation states in verse 3, "And the Southern States will call on other nations, even the nation of Great Britain, as it is called, and they shall also call upon other nations, in order to defend themselves against other nations; and then war shall be poured out upon all nations."

THE FACT: As if it were the days of Noah when the rain began to fall, a Philadelphia newspaper printed the following in relation to Joseph Smith's prophecy:

> At the outset of the Civil War, the *Philadelphia Sunday Mercury* published the revelation stating, "In view of our present troubles, this prediction seems to be in progress of fulfillment, whether Joe Smith was a humbug or not" and concluding with the question, "Have we not had a prophet among us?"

> "A Mormon Prophecy," *Philadelphia Sunday Mercury* May 5, 1861, facsimile in Woodford, "The Historical Development of the Doctrine and Covenants," 1110

QUESTION:

87. What did Joseph Smith prophesy would happen to Jackson County as a result of the Saints' expulsion?

   a. It will blossom as the rose.
   b. It will grow and expand until its influence is felt around the world.
   c. They would experience the same devastation they handed the Saints.
   d. Prior to the Second Coming, the people would all convert to the Church.

SECTION 88

BRIEF HISTORICAL BACKGROUND: Revelation received at Kirtland, Ohio, on December 27, 1832. This revelation is known as the "Olive Leaf."

THE STORY: Just two days prior on December 25, Joseph Smith received the revelation on war. On December 27, the Prophet received the Lord's revelation on peace. Joseph Smith, in a letter to W. W. Phelps, referred to this revelation as the "Olive leaf . . . plucked from the Tree of Paradise, the Lord's message of peace to us." This title is fitting for two reasons: first, the olive tree is a symbol of peace, and second, many of the teachings within this revelation are instructions that can give us spiritual peace. This revelation was received over three days: December 27, 28, and January 3, 1833.

http://institute.lds.org/manuals/doctrine-and-covenants
-institute-student-manual/dc-in-081-88.asp

THE FACT: As the Lord instructed in section 88, the School of the Prophets first meeting was held January 23, 1833. The following is the observations of Zebedee Coltrin:

> The salutation as written in the Doctrine and Covenants [D&C 88:136–41] was carried out at that time, and at every meeting, and the washing of feet was attended to, the sacrament was also administered at times when Joseph appointed, after the ancient order; that is, warm bread to break easy was provided and broken into pieces as large as my fist and each person had a glass of wine and sat and ate the bread and drank the wine; and Joseph said that was the way that Jesus and his disciples partook of the bread and wine. And this was the order of the church anciently and until the church went into darkness. Every time we were called together to attend to any business, we came together in the morning about sunrise, fasting and partook of the sacrament each time, and before going to school we washed ourselves and put on clean linen.

At one of these meetings after the organization of the school, (the school being organized on the 23rd of January, 1833), when we were all together, Joseph having given instructions, and while engaged in silent prayer, kneeling, with our hands uplifted each one praying in silence, no one whispered above his breath, a personage walked through the room from east to west, and Joseph asked if we saw him. I saw him and suppose the others did and Joseph answered that is Jesus, the Son of God, our elder brother. Afterward Joseph told us to resume our former position in prayer, which we did. Another person came through; he was surrounded as with a flame of fire. He (Brother Coltrin) experienced a sensation that it might destroy the tabernacle as it was of consuming fire of great brightness. The Prophet Joseph said this was the Father of our Lord Jesus Christ. I saw Him.

http://www.boap.org/LDS/Early-Saints/ZebC.html

QUESTION:

88. Who is considered the father of adult education in America?
   a. Benjamin Franklin
   b. Joseph Smith
   c. Karl Maeser
   d. Professor Charles Anton

SECTION 89

BRIEF HISTORICAL BACKGROUND: At Kirtland, Ohio, on February 27, 1833, Joseph Smith received the revelation known as the Word of Wisdom.

THE STORY: Verse 3 reads, "Given for a principle with promise, adapted to the capacity of the weak and the weakest of all saints, who are or can be called saints." Most understood this revelation was given as a commandment at the time it was received, but really was given as a "principle with promise." Because of this misunderstanding the following incident occurred:

> [May 26, 1833] . . . we arrived at Kirtland, Ohio, having travelled 500 miles . . . on the next day we hired a house ~~in the City~~ of Brother Joseph Coe & moved into it. ~~Brother~~ Cousin Joseph took Brother Brown's family home with him—his Wife asked Sister Brown if she would like a cup of tea or coffee after her long journey—in a few days ~~they settled~~ in company with Elder Jos. H Wakefield they purchased a large wagon . . . & settled [in Chagrin] contrary to the council of the Prophet & they all afterward apostatized, assigning as a reason that the Prophet's Wife had offered them tea & coffee <w[hi]ch was> contrary to the word of wisdom, & that they had actually seen Joseph the Prophet <come down out of> the translating room & go to play with his children.
>
> History of George A. Smith, LDS Church Archives MS 1322

THE FACT: At a meeting on February 7, 1837, in Far West, Missouri, the elders in attendance voted to boycott ships or stores that sell "spirituous liquors, tea, coffee or tobacco."

> http://saintswithouthalos.com/n/wow.phtml

Patriarch John Smith spoke on the Word of Wisdom during the September general conference in 1851. While he was at the pulpit, Brigham Young approached the stand and made a motion that from this point on all members abstain from alcohol, coffee, tea, and tobacco. The motion was unanimous and became a binding commandment for all members.

> *Millennial Star*, Feb. 1 1852, 35

Some of the early Brethren explained what was meant by this phrase. Hyrum Smith, brother of the Prophet, wrote: "And again, 'hot drinks are not for the body, or belly;' there are many who wonder what this can mean; whether it refers to tea, or coffee, or not. I say it does refer to tea, and coffee."

"The Word of Wisdom," Times and Seasons, June 1, 1842, 800

The Prophet Joseph Smith said: "I understand that some of the people are excusing themselves in using tea and coffee, because the Lord only said 'hot drinks' in the revelation of the Word of Wisdom. . . .

"Tea and coffee . . . are what the Lord meant when He said 'hot drinks.'"

In Joel H. Johnson, Voice from the Mountains
(Salt Lake City: Juvenile Instructor Office, 1881), 12

The Doctrine and Covenants does not specifically mention heroin, cocaine, marijuana, ecstasy, other illegal drugs, or the abuse of pre-scription drugs. President Joseph Fielding Smith said: "Such revelation is unnecessary. The Word of Wisdom is a basic law. It points the way and gives us ample instruction in regard to both food and drink, good for the body and also detrimental. If we sincerely follow what is written with the aid of the Spirit of the Lord, we need no further counsel. . . .

"Thus by keeping the commandments we are promised inspiration and the guidance of the Spirit of the Lord through which we will know what is good and what is bad for the body, without the Lord presenting us with a detailed list separating the good things from the bad that we may be protected. We will learn by this faithful observance that the promises of the Lord are fulfilled."

Improvement Era, Feb. 1956, 78–79

QUESTION:

89. When did the Word of Wisdom become a question in the temple recommend interview?

   a. The early 1920s
   b. 1851
   c. 1951
   d. 1833

SECTION 90

BRIEF HISTORICAL BACKGROUND: Revelation given to Joseph Smith. The Lord provided additional instructions on the First Presidency. This revelation was received March 8, 1833.

THE STORY: A year prior, Joseph Smith had organized the First Presidency. With the excommunication of Jesse Gause in December 1832, it became necessary to call Frederick G. Williams to fill the vacancy, but this time the organization of the Presidency would be different. In verse 6 the Lord instructed, "And again, verily I say unto thy brethren, Sidney Rigdon and Frederick G. Williams, their sins are forgiven them also, and they are accounted as equal with thee in holding the keys of this last kingdom."

THE FACT: Verse 28 mentions a woman by the name of Vienna Jaques, a convert to the Church who remained true and faithful to her dying day in Salt Lake City at the age of 96.

She was many things to the Church, including serving as a witness at the first baptism for the dead in Nauvoo:

> It is not known precisely when the first proxy baptism or baptisms were performed, however, the first documented baptism for the dead was performed on 12 September 1840. On that occasion Jane Neyman requested that Harvey Olmstead baptize her in behalf of her deceased son Cyrus Livingston Neyman. Vienna Jacques witnessed the proxy baptism by riding into the Mississippi River on horseback to hear and observe the ceremony.
>
> A short while later, upon learning the words Olmstead used in performing the baptism, Joseph Smith gave his approval of the ordinance.
>
> http://www.mormonhistoricsitesfoundation.org/publications/studies _spring2002/MHS3.1Spring2002Baugh.pdf

90. Verse 11 reads, "For it shall come to pass in that day, that every man shall hear the fulness of the gospel in his own tongue, and in his own language, through those who are ordained unto this power, by the administration of the Comforter, shed forth upon them for the revelation of Jesus Christ." What was the original MTC of the Church?

    a. The Language Training Mission in Provo, Utah
    b. The Peter Whitmer Sr. cabin in Fayette, New York
    c. The Gilbert and Whitney Store in Jackson County, Missouri
    d. The School of the Prophets in Kirtland, Ohio

SECTION 91

BRIEF HISTORICAL BACKGROUND: Revelation given to Joseph Smith concerning the Apocrypha in the Old Testament. This revelation was received at Kirtland, Ohio, on March 9, 1833.

THE STORY: It's understood that the Bible has undergone numerous translations, and as result, errors have been introduced. Regardless, we still use the Bible and view it as being the word of God. The question then is why wouldn't Joseph Smith include the Apocrypha as a part of the Bible? The following from Elder Bruce R. McConkie:

> Scholars and Biblical students have grouped certain apparently scriptural Old Testament writings, which they deem to be of doubtful authenticity or of a spurious nature, under the title of the *Apocrypha*. There has not always been agreement as to the specific writings

which should be designated as apocryphal, but the following are now generally so listed: 1st and 2nd Esdras (sometimes called 3rd and 4th Esdras, because in the Douay Bible, Ezra is 1st Esdras, and Nehemiah, 2nd Esdras); Tobit; Judith; the rest of the chapters of Esther; Wisdom of Solomon; Wisdom of Jesus the Son of Sirach or Ecclesiasticus; Baruch and the Epistle of Jeremiah; additional parts of Daniel, including the Song of the Three Holy Children, the History of Susanna, and the History of the Destruction of Bel and the Dragon; Prayer of Manasses; 1st and 2nd Maccabees (called in the Douay Version, 1st and 2nd Machabees).

These apocryphal writings were never included in the Hebrew Bible, but they were in the Greek Septuagint (the Old Testament used by the early apostles) and in the Latin Vulgate. Jerome, who translated the Vulgate, was required to include them in his translation, though he is quoted as having decided they should be read "for example of life and instruction of manners" and should not be used "to establish any doctrine." Luther's German Bible grouped the apocryphal books together (omitting 1st and 2nd Esdras) at the end of the Old Testament under the heading: "Apocrypha: these are books which are not held equal to the sacred scriptures, and yet are useful and good for reading."

The Apocrypha was included in the King James Version of 1611, but by 1629 some English Bibles began to appear without it, and since the early part of the 19th century it has been excluded from almost all Protestant Bibles. The American Bible Society, founded in 1816, . . . and the British and Foreign Bible Society [excluded the Apocrypha from most of their Bibles during the 19th century].

From these dates it is apparent that controversy was still raging as to the value of the Apocrypha at the time the Prophet began his ministry. Accordingly, in 1833, while engaged in revising the King James Version by the spirit of revelation, the Prophet felt impelled to inquire of the Lord as to the authenticity of the Apocrypha. From the answer it is clear that the books of the Apocrypha were inspired writings in the first instance, but that subsequent interpolations and changes had perverted and twisted their original contexts so as to leave them with doubtful value.

Speaking of the Apocrypha the Lord says: "There are many things contained therein that are true, and it is mostly translated correctly; There are many things contained therein that are not true, which are interpolations by the hands of men. Verily, I say unto you, that it is not needful that the Apocrypha should be translated. Therefore, whoso readeth it, let him understand, for the Spirit manifesteth truth; And whoso is enlightened by the Spirit shall obtain benefit therefrom; And whoso receiveth not by the Spirit, cannot be benefited. Therefore it is not needful that it should be translated.' (D&C 91) . . .

Obviously, *to gain any real value from a study of apocryphal writings, the student must first have an extended background of gospel knowledge, a comprehensive understanding of the standard works of the Church, plus the guidance of the Spirit.*

Bruce R. McConkie, *Mormon Doctrine*
(Salt Lake City: Bookcraft, 1959), 41–42

THE FACTS: Verse 2 reads, "There are many things contained therein that are not true, which are interpolations by the hands of men." For example, in 2 Esdras, the writer blamed the consequences of the fall on Adam:

For the first Adam, burdened with a wicked heart, transgressed and was overcome, as were also all who were descended from him.

So weakness became permanent, and the Law was in the heart of the people with the evil root; and what was good departed, and what was evil remained. (2 Esdras 3:21–22)

It would have been better for the earth not to have produced Adam, or when it had produced him compelled him not to sin.

For what good is it to all men to live in sorrow and expect punishment after death?

O Adam, what have you done? For although it was you who sinned, the fall was not yours alone, but also ours for we are descended from you. (2 Esdras 7:46–48)

QUESTION:

91. The Apocrypha is only useful when what is used when reading them?

    a. A Bible commentary
    b. A colored pencil
    c. Your ward gospel doctrine teacher's interpretation
    d. The Spirit

SECTION 92

BRIEF HISTORICAL BACKGROUND: Revelation directed to Frederick G. Williams through the Prophet Joseph Smith at Kirtland, Ohio, on March 15, 1833.

THE STORY: Frederick G. Williams moved from Connecticut to the Cleveland area with his family as a twelve-year-old boy. I'm sure Frederick thought his father had moved his family right off the map of the United States since Cleveland, in the year 1799, had only one house.

With time, Frederick would serve during the War of 1812 as a pilot on an American war ship, marry, study to become a doctor, move to Kirtland, and establish a successful medical practice.

THE FACT: In 1830, Parley P. Pratt, Oliver Cowdery, Peter Whitmer Jr., and Ziba Peterson arrived in the Kirtland area. It didn't take long for the influential Williams family to attend the meetings of these missionaries. As interested as Frederick was in the gospel message, it was necessary for him to ponder it over in his mind for some time. In fact, his wife and children made the move to be baptized before Brother Williams did. Nevertheless, once he was baptized, he immediately felt a desire to share the gospel message with others. At the invitation of the four missionaries, Frederick agreed to accompany them on their journey to Missouri. It was agreed that he would travel to the Lamanites and after three weeks of teaching he was to return to his family and medical practice. He became so engrossed in his missionary labors that he didn't return home for ten months, having shared the gospel message first to his unresponsive parents, the Lamanites, and the people in the Independence, Missouri, area.

Joseph Smith had this to say about his good friend:

Brother Frederick G. Williams is one of those men in whom I place the greatest confidence and trust, for I have found him ever full of love and brotherly kindness. He is not a man of many words, but is ever winning, because of his constant mind. He shall ever have place in my heart, and is ever entitled to my confidence. He is perfectly honest and upright, and seeks with all his heart to magnify his Presidency in the Church of Christ, but fails in many instances, in consequence of a want of confidence in himself. Blessed be Brother Frederick, for he shall never want a friend, and his generation after him shall flourish. The Lord hath appointed him an inheritance upon the land of Zion: yea, and his head shall blossom, and he shall be as an olive branch that is bowed down with fruit."

http://saintswithouthalos.com/b/williams_fg.phtml

QUESTION:

92. Frederick G. Williams was Joseph Smith's closest friend, second counselor in the First Presidency, physician, scribe, and what else?

    a. Drove Joseph's carriage
    b. Body guard to the Prophet
    c. Sermon writer for Joseph Smith
    d. Spiritual advisor

SECTION 93

BRIEF HISTORICAL BACKGROUND: Revelation received May 8, 1833, at Kirtland, Ohio, by Joseph Smith. Men learn and go from grace to grace. Leading men in the Church to set their homes in order.

THE STORY: It was both a time of rejoicing in the Church and also a time of trials—a time when members were apostatizing in both Kirtland and Independence because of increased opposition and persecution from those outside the Church.

A special conference was organized on April 6, 1833, in the Independence area commemorating 1800 years since the Savior laid down his life and also three years since the organization of the young Church. This was the state of the Church at the time of this revelation.

http://institute.lds.org/manuals/doctrine-and-covenants
-institute-student-manual/dc-in-091-93.asp

THE FACT: In verse 50, Newell K. Whitney is chastised by the Lord for letting spiritual matters slide in his family. The Lord counseled, "And set in order his family, and see that they are more diligent and concerned at home, and pray always."

In desiring to fulfill Church responsibilities, members may push what really matters most to the backseat. Family prayer and scripture study can be neglected simply because we are "to busy on the Lord's errand." I don't think the Lord ever meant it to be this way. Whatever was going on in Newell's life at the time of this revelation, I do know he had a good heart and meant to do the right thing as the next story illustrates. Newell began his career during the War of 1812. As a nineteen-year-old, he became an army sutler, following the American troops and Native Americans by selling alcohol, food, and day-to-day necessities. On one occasion a customer approached Newell interested in buying alcohol. Brother Whitney realized the man was drunk and had a dependency on alcohol, so he refused to sell. Newell placed the best interest of those he sold to regardless of the loss of financial gain. It was during his refusal that an altercation broke out. This man was intent on killing Newell, and if it wasn't for the actions of a young Native American girl grabbing the attacker and holding him, giving Newell the necessary time to leave the situation, it's possible he could have been injured or killed by the attacker. Because of this incident, Brother and Sister Whitney named one of their daughters Moudalina after this brave Native girl.

http://byustudies.byu.edu/PDFLibrary/42.1StakerThou
-a8f4b834-fa8f-4e84-87c2-f6acbd2e735b.pdf

QUESTION:

93. As the Saints were crossing the plains, what was N. K. Whitney doing at 11:00 p.m. one night, creating alarm for both the guards and Porter Rockwell?

   a. Snoring
   b. Hunting rattlesnakes
   c. Washing his horses
   d. Singing

SECTION 94

BRIEF HISTORICAL BACKGROUND: Revelation given with instructions to form a building committee for the Kirtland Temple. This revelation was received at Kirtland, Ohio, on May 6, 1833.

THE STORY: I remember years ago as a young boy, my dad receiving a call to supervise the building of the Olds Alberta chapel partway through its construction. My father was a contractor and familiar with the construction of buildings. The labor on this chapel was volunteer help by individuals who had either a limited knowledge or those who lacked the ability to swing a hammer but had a desire to help in any way they could. I don't remember much—basically just the off flavor of the water in that town and the wonderful lunches provided by the sisters, but I did gain an appreciation for my dad and his ability to get everyone involved in the chapel's construction to its completion.

As part of the building committee, Hyrum Smith also understood the necessity of having a man on the temple site that could organize and bring the temple to fruition. It was determined that this man was to be Artemus Millet from Canada. Some speculation surrounds this story and has evolved into what can be referred to as "Mormon Myth" (it could be true, but there's not enough fact to support the story). The story goes that Joseph Smith sent Brigham Young on a mission to Canada to baptize Artemus and bring him to Kirtland to supervise the building of the temple.

THE FACT: It is true that Brigham and Lorenzo Young were called on missions to Canada, arriving in December 1832. It's also correct that Brigham records Brother Millet's baptism as January 1833. However, there is no record indicating if Brigham performed the baptism and definitely nothing indicating that Brigham Young extended an invite from Joseph Smith to move to Kirtland and assist in the temple's construction. What did occur though is that Hyrum Smith sent a letter to Artemus early in the summer of 1833, extending this invitation. Artemus arrived in the fall of that year and contracted the exterior work on the temple, for which he and Lorenzo Young received one thousand dollars.

http://byustudies.byu.edu/PDFLibrary/41.2ErecksonNewellConversion-659235e2-77d7-44c7-af6c-5ae19b6f30a4.pdf

QUESTION:

94. The reason so much confusion surrounds the conversion of Artemus Millet is partly due to his journals being burned shortly after his death. How did his journals burn?

    a. His house burned
    b. A woman trying to help clean his house accidentally burned them
    c. They were accidentally burned trying to start a fire in the fireplace.
    d. They were being stored in a barn and were destroyed in a barn fire

SECTION 95

BRIEF HISTORICAL BACKGROUND: On June 1, 1833, Joseph Smith received this revelation at Kirtland, Ohio. The Lord reprimanded the Saints for neglecting his commandment to begin work on the Kirtland Temple.

THE STORY: Even though the Saints were making preparations to build the temple, efforts to actually build the temple was nonexistent. The Saints were poor, a definite possibility as far as the lack of action. It's also possible that the Saints had their minds set on building the temple in Jackson County, since that really was the gathering place anyways. Whatever the reason, I'm sure their efforts were buoyed with the Lord's statement as found in verse 11, "Verily I say unto you, it is my will that you should build a house. If you keep my commandments you shall have power to build it." Immediately, Hyrum Smith and Reynolds Cahoon began digging the foundation and George A. Smith brought in the first load of stone from the rock quarry.

THE FACT: The perfect example of building a temple and the Lord giving "power to build it" is the Freiberg Temple in what was then East Germany. Thomas S. Monson shares the following:

> The announcement of the temple continued a series of miracles: for example, private ownership of property is not permitted in that country and yet we have been granted private ownership. The building of a temple has never before been permitted in a communist nation. In this case, the government itself suggested the building of the temple as an alternative to considering our request that members be permitted to visit the temple in Zollikofen, Switzerland. A third miracle is that land was purchased with German Democratic Republic Marks rather than with currency from the western nations. All in all, the event had been miraculous.
>
> Thomas S. Monson, *Faith Rewarded* (Salt Lake City: Deseret Book, 1996)

QUESTION:

95. After the Saints left the Kirtland area, the temple had a variety of uses, one of which was a public school. Which President of the United States attended school in the Kirtland Temple as a young man?

a. Andrew Jackson

b. James Garfield

c. Abraham Lincoln

d. Calvin Coolidge

[handwritten note in margin: Cousin John F Boynton—one of the original 12 apostles]

SECTION 96

BRIEF HISTORICAL BACKGROUND: Revelation given to Joseph Smith at Kirtland, Ohio, on June 4, 1833, showing the organization of the stake at Kirtland.

THE STORY: The Church has just purchased the Peter French farm and, by so doing, acquired the Peter French Tavern and a brick kiln, both of which were located on the farm. The members originally thought with the purchase of the brick kiln that they could construct the temple of bricks. This probably would have been the plan except that a stone quarry was discovered just two miles south of town, providing the Saints with all the stone necessary to erect the temple. After the stone walls were completed, they were plastered and marked to give the appearance of brick.

Karl Ricks Anderson, *Joseph Smith's Kirtland*
(Salt Lake City: Deseret Book, 1989), 133, 159

THE FACT: Karl R. Anderson, a recognized Kirtland area historian, states that little is known of the cornerstone laying ceremony on July 23, 1833, where twenty-four priesthood holders assembled. Brother Anderson shares the following story:

> Joseph Kingsbury, 21, was one of the priesthood holders who participated in laying the cornerstones. His biographer, Lyndon W. Cook, wrote: "The Prophet had designated Kingsbury one of the 24 men to participate in the service, but at the last minute it was learned that [Kingsbury] was not a Melchizedek Priesthood holder. Instead of giving the honor to another with proper authority, Joseph Smith took young Kingsbury aside and ordained him an elder. . . and [Kingsbury] fondly remembered the occasion for the rest of his life."
>
> http://www.ldschurchnews.com/articles/23458/Kirtland-Temple-Scarcely-a-scrap-of-history-exists-to-document--laying-of-cornerstones.html

QUESTION:

96. When the Church bought the Peter French farm they became the owners of the Peter French Tavern. What one thing did *not* happen at the tavern?

    a. The first patriarchal blessing
    b. The site of the first printing operation in Kirtland
    c. The organization of the Relief Society
    d. The Twelve Apostles left here for their missions

SECTION 97

BRIEF HISTORICAL BACKGROUND: The Saints in Missouri were facing severe persecution. Unaware of the situation, Joseph Smith received revelation on August 2, 1833, at

Kirtland, Ohio, indicating the Lord's will for the Jackson County Saints.

THE STORY: On August 6, 1833, Joseph Smith, in response to the revelation just received a few days prior, wrote a letter to the leaders of the Church in regard to the School in Zion. Verse 3 of this revelation states, "Behold, I say unto you, concerning the school in Zion, I, the Lord, am well pleased that there should be a school in Zion, and also with my servant Parley P. Pratt, for he abideth in me."

THE FACT: Parley P. Pratt gives a description of the school:

> In the latter part of summer and in the autumn [1833], I devoted almost my entire time in ministering among the churches; holding meetings; visiting the sick; comforting the afflicted, and giving counsel. A school of Elders was also organized, over which I was called to preside. This class, to the number of about sixty, met for instruction once a week. The place of meeting was in the open air, under some tall trees, in a retired place in the wilderness, where we prayed, preached and prophesied, and exercised ourselves in the gifts of the Holy Spirit. Here great blessings were poured out, and many great and marvelous things were manifested and taught. The Lord gave me great wisdom, and enabled me to teach and edify the Elders, and comfort and encourage them in their preparations for the great work which lay before us. I was also much edified and strengthened. To attend this school I had to travel on foot, and sometimes with bare feet at that, about six miles. This I did once a week, besides visiting and preaching in five or six branches a week.

> Parley P. Pratt Jr. ed., *Autobiography of Parley P. Pratt*
> (Salt Lake City: Deseret Book, 1985), 93–94

97. On July 23, 1833, the day the Saints were laying the cornerstones
of the Kirtland Temple, the Saints in Jackson County, Missouri,
were doing what?

    a. Enjoying a Branch picnic
    b. Forced to sign an agreement to leave the county
    c. Laying cornerstones at the Far West Temple site
    d. Attending the School of Zion

SECTION 98

BRIEF HISTORICAL BACKGROUND: Revelation
given to Joseph Smith August 6, 1833, at Kirtland, Ohio, in relation
to the Missouri persecutions.

THE STORY: It was during July 1833 that Edward Partridge
and Charles Allen were tarred and feathered. Emily Partridge,
daughter of Bishop Partridge, tells the story:

> In the summer of 1833, my youngest brother was born. When he was
> about three weeks old, mother sent me with Harriet to the spring for
> water, when I looked back and saw the house surrounded by an armed
> mob. We remained at the spring until they had gone. Then we got
> our water and went up to the house. They had taken father (George
> Simpson was their leader) up to Independence. We did not know what
> they were going to do with him; it might be kill him, as they had
> threatened. He had been put in prison once or twice before. After he
> had been gone awhile I was standing by the window looking the way
> the mob had gone, thinking of father, when I saw two men coming
> toward the house. One I knew. It was Albert Jackson, a young man.

He was carrying a hat, coat, and vest. The other I thought was an Indian, and as they were coming right to the house, I was so frightened that I ran upstairs. When they came in, it was our dear father who had been tarred and feathered, giving him the appearance of an Indian. (Charles Allen was also tarred and feathered the same day.) They had done their work well for they had covered him with tar from head to foot except his face and the inside of his hands. I suppose hundreds witnessed the outrage. I have heard one woman affirm that she saw a bright light encircle his head while the mob was tarring him. I very well remember the clothes he had on when he went away. They were dark blue. I remember blankets were hung up around the fireplace to screen him while the tar was being scraped from him."

http://www.boap.org/LDS/Early-Saints/EmPart.html

THE FACT: The persecutions in Jackson County started in 1833. It would have started a year earlier in 1832, except that a non-Mormon Indian agent put a stop to it. The agent's name was William Clark from Lewis and Clark fame:

> As the Church increased the hostile spirit of the people increased also— The enemies circulated from time to time, all manner of false stories against the saints, hoping thereby to stir up the indignation of others. In the spring of 1832 they began to brick-bat or stone the houses of the saints, breaking in window, &c., not only disturbing, but endangering the lives of the inmates. In the course of that season a county meeting was called at Independence, to adopt measures to drive our people from the county; but the meeting broke up, without coming to any agreement about them; having had too much confusion among themselves, to do more than to have a few knock-downs, after taking a plentiful supply of whiskey. The result of this meeting may be attributed in part, to the influence of certain patriotic individuals; among whom General Clark, a sub-Indian agent, may be considered as principal. He hearing of the meeting, came from his agency, or from home, some thirty or forty miles distant, a day or two before the meeting.
>
> He appeared quite indignant, at the idea of having the constitution and laws set at defiance, and trodden under foot, by the many trampling upon the rights of the few. He went to certain influential mob characters, and offered to decide the case with them in single combat: he said that it would be better for one to two individuals to die, then for hundreds to be put to death.

Times and Seasons, Vol. 1 No. 2. December, 1839

QUESTION:

98. Who did the Partridges first rent from when they came to Independence?

    a. Governor Dunklin (Governor of Missouri at this time)
    b. Lieutenant Governor Lilburn W. Boggs
    c. Joseph Smith Sr.
    d. General Clark

SECTION 99

BRIEF HISTORICAL BACKGROUND: This is the last revelation that Joseph Smith would receive in Hiram, Ohio. The revelation was directed to John Murdock in August 1832.

THE STORY: John Murdock's life is one laid in a foundation of faith and trust in the Lord. He not only lost his wife, Julia Clapp Murdock, at the time she gave birth to twins, but also, as the following story indicates, he had to find other members willing to take care of his three oldest children. Brother Murdock referred to the above mission in his autobiography:

> I then continued with the Church preaching to them and strengthening them and regaining my health till the month of August when I received the revelation recorded in the Book of Covenants [D&C], page 806, at which time I immediately commenced to arrange my business and provide for my children and send them up to the Bishop in Zion, which I did by the hand of Bro. [Brother] Caleb Baldwin in September. I gave him 10 dollars a head for carrying up my three eldest children. I then settled my business and on the 24th of September I visited Father Clapp's family, preached the gospel to

them. They were very unbelieving and hard. I returned to the brethren in Kirtland on the 25th and on the 27th started, in company with Brother Zebedia [Zebedee] Coltrin, and on that day called on Mr. Conning's family, Father Clapp's family and Benjamin Brich's family; all unbelieving. Stayed with Bro. [Brother] Kingsbury, in Painesville, preached in the evening. He gave us each 75 cents, God bless him. Met with a Dr. Matthews, a very wicked man, and [he] reviled against us, the Book of Mormon, and the doctrine we taught. We bore testimony according to the commandment and the Lord helped us in tending to the ordinance.

http://www.boap.org/LDS/Early-Saints/JMurdock.html

THE FACT: One of these three older children was a son by the name of John Riggs Murdock. This man holds a special distinction in Church history. It is said that he crossed the plains eleven times and is responsible for leading more Saints to the Salt Lake Valley than any other individual.

http://www.ldschurchnews.com/articles/37735
/Carriage-house-memorializes-faithful-wagon-train-captain.html

QUESTION:

99. The two twins that John permitted Joseph and Emma to adopt were named Julia and Joseph. Joseph died after being exposed to the weather the night Joseph Smith was tarred and feathered in Hiram, Ohio. John refers to his son's death as what?

   a. The beginning of his mission on the other side
   b. A reminder to despise our enemies
   c. My little guardian angel
   d. The first martyr for the gospel

SECTION 100

BRIEF HISTORICAL BACKGROUND: Revelation given to the Prophet and Sidney Rigdon October 12, 1833, at Perrysville, New York. Both Joseph and Sidney were on a mission and felt concern for their families.

THE STORY: Joseph Smith had had open communication with Heavenly Father for ten years. In this ten-year period, Joseph received enough revelation to produce one hundred sections in the Doctrine and Covenants. On average, the Prophet received ten revelations per year. It may not sound like much; however, remember that the majority of these revelations were given since the organization of the Church three and a half years earlier, primarily in 1831. A quick comparison with other scripture and their first one hundred chapters might amaze you.

THE FACT:

> The Old Testament—the first 100 chapters cover 28 centuries.
> The Book of Mormon—the first 100 chapters (in chronological order beginning with the Jaredites) cover 20 centuries.
> The New Testament—the first 100 chapters cover a time span of 44 years.
> As you can see, the frequency of revelation in this dispensation was significant enough to establish the Lord's Church again to man.

http://www.gospeldoctrine.com/DoctrineandCovenants/DC%20100.htm

QUESTION:

100. Joseph and Sidney stopped at the home of Freemen Nickerson in Mount Pleasant, Ontario. When Freeman learned that his parents had joined the Church and that they were responsible for sending the Prophet and Sidney to his home, what did he say to his father?

    a. "I will welcome them for your sake, but I would much rather have a nest of vipers turned loose on us."

    b. "If you believe, I'll believe."

    c. "Thanks, but no thanks."

    d. "Whatever!"

SECTION 101

BRIEF HISTORICAL BACKGROUND: Joseph received revelation from the Lord about the Missouri persecutions. This revelation is given at Kirtland, Ohio, on December 16, 1833.

THE STORY: The situation in Missouri had turned ugly. Fueled by prejudice and hatred, those responsible for their protection (the state government) turned their backs on the Saints. Even those who preached Christlike love to their congregations on the Sabbath spread falsehoods throughout the community during the week. The Reverend Finnis Ewing said, "The 'Mormons' are the common enemy of mankind and ought to be destroyed." Other ministers went "from house to house seeking to destroy the Church by spreading slanderous falsehoods, to incite the people to acts of violence against the Saints." But not all opposed the Saints, a sympathetic newspaper in Fayette, Missouri, the *Western Monitor* suggested that the Saints seek redress through political avenues in a series of articles published repressing the mob and its actions, but seeking of government aid also led to frustration on the part of the Missouri Saints.

http://seminary.lds.org/manuals/church-history -institute-student-manual/chft-11-15-11.asp

THE FACT: The Saints were frustrated because they had to give up their weapons, yet their enemies were permitted to retain their guns. Most of the members complied with this order, except the Hancock brothers (Solomon, Joseph, and Levi), who weren't about to submit. The mob knew the Hancock brothers had their guns, all sixteen of them. Mosiah Hancock writes the following in his autobiography, "There were 16 guns that were not surrendered. The owners taking their 16 guns into the thicket caused more consternation against the mob than all the mobber's guns caused against the Saints." Fearful of their reputations, the Missourians left them alone. Again, from the autobiography of Mosiah Hancock:

> It is a fact which should be remembered. . . . The Hancock brothers, Levi, Joseph, and Solomon, with their guns, guarded and fed 600 men, women, and children while camped in the woods after they had been driven from their homes. They were waiting for an opportunity to get away. I saw the Prophet marched away; and I saw, oh, the scenes I witnessed! I do not think people would believe them. So I will forbear. The howling fiends, although they wore the uniforms of the U.S., they were not to be trusted! So some of the brethren made three hundred tomahawks for protection.

http://www.boap.org/; Autobiography of Mosiah Hancock, Typescript, BYU-S

QUESTION:

Nathan Porter states this in his journal:

> Duering the following Spring and Summer [1833] they entered into a Cecret Combination binding them selves in the most wicked oaths, to stand by each other in driving evry Man Woman & child that would not renounce Mormonism from the County, this they did, But not without Some Sharp resistence [on] the part of the Brethren who felt it their duty, to defend themselves their Wives & Children

a gainst sutch inhuman outrages which resulted in the Death of several of the Mob, and one on the part of the Brethren."

101. What battle was Nathan referring to?
  a. The Battle of Crooked River
  b. Bulls Run
  c. The Battle above the Blue
  d. The Utah War

SECTION 102

BRIEF HISTORICAL BACKGROUND: On February 17, 1834, the organization of the first high council in Kirtland, Ohio, is recorded.

THE STORY: From early February 1834, Joseph was instructed by the Lord "according to the law of heaven" and the organization of the ancient Church was established. Disciplinary councils were an important function of this organization. The Prophet gave the following picture on such ancient councils:

> In ancient days councils were conducted with such strict propriety, that no one was allowed to whisper, be weary, leave the room, or get uneasy in the least, until the voice of the Lord, by revelation, or the voice of the council by the Spirit, was obtained, which has not been observed in this Church to the present time. It was understood in ancient days, that if one man could stay in council, another could; and if the president could spend his time, the members could also; but in our councils, generally, one will be uneasy, another asleep; one praying, another not; one's mind on the business of the council, and another thinking on something else.
>
> *Teachings of the Prophet Joseph Smith*, selected and arranged by Joseph Fielding Smith (Salt Lake City: Deseret Book, 1976), 69.

THE FACT: Disciplinary councils at the time of the Prophet were far more stringent than what would be experienced today. This may cause some to question the propriety of such a course of action when the Church was so small. Yet we can only assume the Prophet and early Church leaders understood the impact of cynical attitudes. Joseph Smith experienced this shortly after the organization of the Church with Hiram Page and his influence due to the "revelations" he claimed to have. George A. Smith shared the following experience:

> In June, 1833 . . . the Bishop's Council, and a Council of twelve High Priests, was organized. . . It was at the same Council that Daniel Copley, a timid young man, who had been ordained a Priest, and required to go and preach the Gospel, was called to an account for not going on his mission. The young man said he was too weak to attempt to preach, and the Council cut him off the Church. I wonder what our missionaries now would think of so rigid a discipline as was given at that time thirty one years ago, under the immediate supervision of the Prophet.
>
> *Journal of Discourses*, Tuesday, November 15, 1864, 11:8

QUESTION:

102. Who is the only person listed below who was a member of Kirtland's first high council?

    a. Parley P. Pratt
    b. Joseph Knight Sr.
    c. Christian Whitmer
    d. Luke Johnson

SECTION 103

BRIEF HISTORICAL BACKGROUND: The command from the Lord to organize Zion's Camp. Revelation given to Joseph Smith February 24, 1834, at Kirtland, Ohio.

THE STORY: In an earlier revelation, the Lord stated that he would fight the battles for the Saints. This promise was literally fulfilled at the encampment of Zion's Camp at Fishing River, Missouri, on June 19, 1834, as illustrated in the following story:

> On June 19, the group had reached Daviess County and began to set up camp between the Little and Big Fishing Rivers. Five armed men rode into camp and told them that a group of Missourians were amassing with the intent of killing 'Joe Smith and his army.' A tremendous storm soon arose in which rain, hail, thunder and lighting came down upon the mob and prevented them from attacking the members of the camp. Joseph and the others took refuge for the night in a small Church not far away.
>
> When Colonel Sconce met Joseph Smith on June 21, he acknowledged "there is an Almighty power that protects this people, for I started from Richmond, Ray county, with a company of armed men, having a fixed determination to destroy you, but was kept back by the storm, and was not able to reach you.
>
> http://www.mormonhistoricsitesfoundation.org/USA
> /missouri/daviess/zionsCamp/history.htm

THE FACT: For a time, the Lord also provided His protecting hand over what would become known as the Battle of Far West:

> They came on the direction of our city; which produced some little stir in the place, and in a few minutes there was about two hundred men both old and young, mustered to the public square in the city; the rest of the men living absent. We were immediately marched to the south boundary line of the city in the direction of the mob to defend our wives and children and property from destruction. When

we arrived to our post the mob was coming down on to a low piece of ground on the borders of Goose Creek where there was some scattering timber that took them out of our sight but some of them climbed up in to the trees and looked over into the city and swore that they saw an army of men that would number thousands. This we learned from our brethren that was prisoner then in their camp; the sight of this great army brought terror to their camp which caused them to halt for a little time.

Autobiography of William Draper, Typescript, HBLL; http://www.boap.org/

QUESTION:

103. Since we're on the topic of battles, who was the first Latter-day Saint to become a general in the US Army?

    a. George Hinckle
    b. Eph Hanks
    c. Richard W. Young
    d. Lyman Wight

SECTION 104

BRIEF HISTORICAL BACKGROUND: Revelation given with instructions pertaining to the united order. This revelation was received by the Prophet on April 23, 1834, at Kirtland, Ohio.

THE STORY: Not all were satisfied with the united order. Some desired its success, while others were driven by greed, selfishness, and misunderstanding. In fact, one disgruntled member took the Church to a Missouri court in May 1833 and sued for the return of a fifty-dollar donation.

James B. Allen and Glen M. Leonard, *The Story of the Latter-day Saints* (Salt Lake City: Deseret Book, 1992), 86.

THE FACT: As much as the Lord would have us live the law of consecration, we currently abide by the law of tithing and the Church welfare system. The following story tells of the welfare system at work during the "Dirty Thirties":

> In April of 1936, every bishop was asked to have in store enough food and clothing to help each family in his ward make it through the next winter. The Relief Society was a huge factor in this undertaking. In southern Utah the Relief Society put up 14,000 cans of peaches and ingeniously shelled their peas by running the pods through the "clothes wringers on [two] brand new Speed Queen washing machines" loaned by generous Sisters for the purpose.

Louise Y. Robison, "Relief Society's Contribution to the Church Welfare Program," *Relief Society Magazine* 25 (November 1938): 765–66

"Notes from the Field," *Relief Society Magazine* 23 (November 1936): 775

Relief Society in the St. George Stake, 28; *New Views of Mormon History,* edited by Davis Bitton and Maureen Ursenbach Beecher (Salt Lake City, University of Utah Press, 1987), 259

QUESTION:

104. During the winter 1930, how much food was given to the poor in Salt Lake City?

    a. 420,000 pounds

    b. 50,000 pounds

    c. 110,000 pounds

    d. 200,000 pounds

SECTION 105

BRIEF HISTORICAL BACKGROUND: Revelation received at Fishing River, Missouri, by the Prophet Joseph Smith on June 22, 1834, while he was encamped with Zion's Camp.

THE STORY: John M. Chidster, a member of Zion's Camp, shared the following recollection:

> My first recollection of seeing the Prophet Joseph Smith was at a place about sixty or seventy miles from Kirtland, where two companies of Zion's Camp met. My impression on beholding the Prophet and shaking hands with him was, that I stood face to face with the greatest man on earth. I testify he was a Prophet of God.
>
> Zion's Camp, in passing through the state of Indiana, had to cross very bad swamps, consequently we had to attach ropes to the wagons to help them through, and the Prophet was the first man at the rope in his bare feet. This was characteristic of him in all times of difficulty.
>
> We continued our journey until we reached the Wakandaw River, having traveled twenty-five miles without resting or eating. We were compelled to ferry this stream; and we found on the opposite side of it a most desirable place to camp, which was a source of satisfaction to the now weary and hungry men. On reaching this place the Prophet announced to the camp that he felt impressed to travel on; and taking the lead, he invited the brethren to follow him.
>
> This caused a split in the camp. Lyman Wight and others at first refused to follow the Prophet, but finally came up. The sequel showed that the Prophet was inspired to move on a distance of some seven miles. It was reported to us afterwards that about eight miles below where we crossed the river a body of men was organized to come upon us that night.
>
> http://www.boap.org/LDS/Early-Saints/REC-JS.html

THE FACT: Joseph was continually plagued by bad press. For whatever reason, newspapers had a way of embellishing the facts, and never in favor of the Church or its leaders. The next story is an example of Joseph versus the press. On May 17, 1834, the 205 members of Zion's Camp passed through Richmond, Wayne County, Indiana—twenty-five miles south of Winchester—on their trek from Ohio to Missouri. The *Richmond Palladium* carried the story of their arrival in the Saturday, 24 May 1834 edition:

> Mormonites, on Monday morning last, a caravan of about 200 Mormonites with a long train of wagons, passed through this place on their way to the "Far West." There were but few women among them, and the men were generally (if not all) supplied with firearms. A stout, hardy looking set of fellows they were too, and many of them quite intelligent. From their equipment it had been suspected that they intend joining the defending of their brethren in Jackson County, Missouri.

The Prophet Joseph Smith was with the group, and when Zion's Camp again passed through Richmond on July 27, 1834, on their return trek to Ohio, the Prophet visited Winchester after a short stay in Richmond. Seventeen-year-old George A. Smith recorded in his journal the events that took place when Zion's Camp arrived in Richmond:

> We all arrived at Richmond, Ind. The Richmond newspaper published that day had announced to the world the astounding news that Joe Smith, the Mormon leader, had had a battle with the mob in Jackson County and had been wounded in the leg. The limb had to be amputated, and three days later he died of mortification. Joseph and Hyrum visited the editor, but had difficulty to convince him he was not really dead. Here our party separated, making different routes. (Journal of George A. Smith, Historical Department, The Church of Jesus Christ of Latter-day Saints, Salt Lake City)

> http://lds.org/ensign/1992/10/research-and-perspectives
> -the-pioneer-saints-of-winchester-indiana?lang=eng

105. Joseph Smith was commanded to organize a force of 500 men if he could, but to go with no less than 100. How large was Zion's Camp?

    a. 101
    b. 207
    c. 500
    d. 499

SECTION 106

BRIEF HISTORICAL BACKGROUND: Revelation directed from Joseph Smith to Warren A. Cowdery, older brother of Oliver Cowdery, at Kirtland, Ohio, dated November 25, 1834.

THE STORY: Before the Book of Mormon was even bound, while pages were being lifted from the press and hung to dry, a few individuals had the opportunity to copy from these pages with the desire to teach others. David Whitmer said, "The Book of Mormon was still in the hands of the printer, but my brother, Christian Whitmer, had copied from the manuscript the teachings and the doctrine of Christ, being the things which we were commanded to preach."

Thomas B. Marsh is another who accepted the gospel when he saw the proof sheets in the Grandin Print Shop pulled from the press. However, the story of Solomon Chamberlain is amazing. Solomon resided in Lyons, New York. In 1829, while traveling on the Erie Canal, he felt the Spirit, which convinced him to leave the boat and venture into the town of Palmyra. He walked three miles south of the canal and stayed the night in a farmhouse. In the morning, his host asked him if he was familiar or had heard of the "gold bible." Solomon recorded, "There was a power like electricity went from the top of my head to the end of my toes." Why would the mere mention of a book that he had never heard of before stir him to the core? Because in 1816 he received a visitation from an angel declaring, "there would be a book come forth, like unto the Bible and the people would be guided by it, as well as the Bible." The angel also taught him that the true gospel was not on the earth, but that it would soon be restored. For a few years, Solomon had kept a constant watch for this book and now realized he was less than a mile from the Smith home. After receiving directions, Solomon eagerly made his way "across lots" to the Smith home. Arriving at the residence, Solomon found Joseph Smith Sr., Hyrum Smith, and Christian Whitmer. For two days Solomon received instructions from these men who also shared teachings from the Book of Mormon. Hyrum took him to the E. B. Grandin Printing Office, where he was given sixty-four pages from the ancient record. He immediately recognized the pages in his hands as the book he had been searching for. Hyrum Smith and Oliver Cowdery permitted him to take the pages to Canada, and there he taught the gospel truths that he had learned from an angel, the men at the Smith home, and the loose Book of Mormon transcript pages. Even though unordained, Solomon wrote the following about his mission to Canada:

> I took [the pages] with their leave and pursued my journey to Canada, and I preached all that I knew concerning Mormonism, to all both high and low, rich and poor. . . . I did not see any one in traveling for 800 miles, that had ever heard of the Gold Bible (so called) I exhorted all people to prepare for the great work of God that was now about to come forth, and it would never be brought down nor confounded.

http://lds.org/ensign/1988/07/from-a-book-coming-forth?lang=eng

THE FACT: Warren Cowdery joined the Church not by seeing a bound copy of the Book of Mormon but rather by reading the proof sheets. He shared these proof sheets with others in the town of Freedom, New York. William Hyde told the following:

In the year 1830 or '31, we began to hear something concerning the Book of Mormon, and the setting up of the Kingdom of God on earth in the last days. The little information that we gained upon this subject, until the Elders came preaching, was through Warren A. Cowdery, whose farm joined with ours. Warren A. obtained from his brother Oliver, at an early date, some of the proof sheets to the book of Mormon some of which we had the privilege of perusing, and we did not peruse any faster than we believed.

http://lds.org/ensign/1988/07/from-a-book-coming-forth?lang=eng

QUESTION:

106. While the Book of Mormon was still in print, what proof sheets did Joseph Smith take with him to Harmony, Pennsylvania?

    a. 3 Nephi
    b. Words of Mormon
    c. 1 and 2 Nephi
    d. Mosiah and Alma

SECTION 107

BRIEF HISTORICAL BACKGROUND: Revelation given to Joseph Smith the Prophet March 28, 1835, at Kirtland, Ohio, in regards to priesthood.

THE STORY: In mid January 1835, the prophet approached Brigham and Joseph Young and asked them to gather as many of the men who served in Zion's Camp to attend a meeting on February 14, 1835. At this meeting, according to the commandment in Doctrine and Covenants 18:37, the Three Witnesses were ordained and blessed with the Spirit to enlighten their minds so they could choose the Twelve Apostles. The selections were made with seniority within the Quorum based on age. Those chosen were Thomas B. Marsh, David W. Patten, Brigham Young, Heber C. Kimball, Orson Hyde, William E. McLellin, Parley P. Pratt, Luke S. Johnson, William Smith, Orson Pratt, John F. Boynton, and Lyman E. Johnson.

Two weeks later on February 28, 1835, the Quorum of the Seventy, along with the seven presidents of the Quorum were selected. At this meeting, Joseph taught the Brethren that the purpose of Zion's Camp was not about guns and revenge, but rather a test of sacrifice. The Lord wanted to know who were willing to place all things before the Lord, even their own lives if necessary.

By March 12, it was determined to send the Quorum of the Twelve on missions to the eastern states. On March 28, the Quorum of the Twelve met with the Prophet, shortly before the Twelve departed on their mission. During this meeting, the Twelve desired Joseph Smith to approach the Lord and seek revelation, and the Prophet received verses 1–58. The remainder of the verses had already been received beginning as early as November 1831. This revelation was compiled and placed in the 1835 edition of the Doctrine and Covenants.

THE FACT: The following provides some information about the preparations and mission of the Quorum of the Twelve:

> Later entries confirm that they largely followed this itinerary, regulating branches, teaching members, and preaching and proselytizing along the way. Among the several preparatory meetings held late April and early May was a 26 April assembly of the Twelve and some of the Seventy, held in the unfinished temple in Kirtland, convened "in order to receive our charge and instructions from President Joseph Smith Jun. relative to our mission and duties." Two days later they made the decision not only to leave on 4 May, as earlier proposed, but to depart at 2:00 a.m. that day, ensuring arrival at Fairport Harbor in time to catch a lake steamer for New York.
>
> Traveling east on their quorum mission "to the Atlantic," the newly organized quorum normally met as a group with members along the way, though occasionally one or another had a different assignment (and in early June, Brigham Young and Orson Hyde had to leave their brethren for a time and return to Kirtland as witnesses

in a court case on behalf of JS). Through their 7 August conference in Bradford, Massachusetts, the schedule of conferences unfolded largely as had been planned in the 12 March meeting. That day, however, they decided to alter plans for the remainder of the mission and return home a month earlier. One conference was canceled and the last two moved up, changes, say the minutes, dictated by "the Spirit of God." The record thereafter documents only two more conferences, both in Maine: Saco on 21 August and Farmington on 28 August. With the account of the latter, presumably the final gathering before quorum members returned home, the record abruptly ends.

The Record of the Twelve is the only known record created by the Quorum of the Twelve Apostles during its first several years of existence. This can be explained by practical difficulties but also by the fact that most activities of quorum members over the next several years were undertaken either as individual assignments or in connection with the activities of other leadership quorums. In the fall and winter of 1835–1836, members of the Twelve joined with other quorums in finishing the House of the Lord in Kirtland, Ohio, and in preparing for and participating in the March 1836 dedication and solemn assembly. JS's journal for 30 March 1836 reports that rather than undertaking a quorum mission, "the 12 are at liberty to go wheresoever they will and if one shall say, I wish to go to such a place let all the rest say Amen." The quorum mission to England planned for 1837 was postponed because of division within the church and within the quorum, although Heber C. Kimball and Orson Hyde of the Twelve did make the journey. The mass migration of leadership and members from Kirtland to Far West, Missouri, in 1838 made a mission impractical that summer. Not until 1839–1840, after the violent expulsion from Missouri, would the Twelve again undertake a mission as a quorum.

http://josephsmithpapers.org/paperSummary/
record-of-the-twelve-14-february%E2%80%9328-august-1835

107. How many missions would the Quorum of the Twelve serve in unison throughout the history of the Church in the last dispensation?

    a. 5
    b. 1
    c. 6
    d. 2

Section 108

Brief Historical Background: Joseph Smith received revelation at the request of Seventy Lyman Sherman. This revelation was given at Kirtland, Ohio, on December 26, 1835

The Story: The day after Christmas, Lyman approached the prophet and said, "I have been wrought upon to make known to you my feelings and desires, and was promised that I should have a revelation which should make known my duty." Within the hour, Joseph Smith received the revelation as promised to Brother Sherman.

http://byustudies.byu.edu/PDFLibrary/19.1CookLyman
-d25407a7-adc6-4656-962f-bf64c724b7e9.pdf

The Fact: Of the ninety-seven men who have served in the Quorum of the Twelve Apostles in this dispensation, one would fail to find the name of Lyman Sherman, the man noted for being called but not actually being ordained to the holy apostleship. What may be even more peculiar is the fact that Lyman was never notified of his call.

While Joseph Smith, Hyrum Smith, and Sidney Rigdon were confined to Liberty Jail, they sent a letter to Brigham Young and Heber C. Kimball on January 16, 1839, instructing them to call George A. Smith and Lyman Sherman to the apostleship. The letter instructed both Brigham and Heber to "get the Twelve together, [and] ordain such as have not been ordained." George A. Smith was chosen to replace the fallen Thomas B. Marsh, and Sherman was to replace the momentarily sidetracked Orson Hyde.

Don Carlos Smith, Joseph's younger brother, informed George A. Smith late in January 1839 of his call. Yet Lyman, who was suffering with an illness at that time, was never notified. It is not entirely clear why Brigham and Heber did not pass the news of his appointment on to Brother Sherman.

Lyndon W. Cook, "Lyman Sherman—Man of God, Would-be Apostle,"
BYU Studies 19, (Fall 1978), 121–24

QUESTION:

108. Why did Lyman Sherman set fire to the Church's printing office in Kirtland?

   a. To thwart the apostates' plans of using the printing office to spread their slander toward the Prophet and the Church
   b. He was a pyromaniac
   c. Joseph asked him to before Brother Sherman left Kirtland to join the rest of the Church in Missouri
   d. He was not yet a firm believer in the Word of Wisdom and ash from his pipe ignited a barrel of ink

SECTION 109

BRIEF HISTORICAL BACKGROUND: Dedicatory prayer given at the Kirtland Temple on March 27, 1836. This prayer was received by revelation.

THE STORY: Building the Kirtland Temple was an act of faith. In April 1832, the United Firm had secured a five-year, $15,000 loan to purchase lands and provisions in the Jackson County area yet had lost it all when the Saints were forced off their properties during the Missouri persecutions of 1833. The Saints were impoverished and deep in debt. The Lord had always provided a means, whether through the conversion of wealthy members—such as John Tanner and his wife, who gave unselfishly to the cause until they gave their all. The Lord also protected the Saints from their enemies during the temple's construction. These situations added to the joy the Saints felt at the dedication of the first temple in this dispensation.

THE FACT: During the construction of the temple, Roger Orton recorded seeing:

> A mighty angel riding upon a horse of fire, with a flaming sword in his hand, followed by five others, encircling the house, and protecting the Saints . . . from the power of Satan and a host of evil spirits, which were striving to disturb the Saints.

> Roger Orton, in *History of the Church*, 2:386–87

QUESTION:

109. How did the Kirtland Saints refer to the Kirtland Temple?
   a. The Lord's House
   b. The Temple
   c. The Mountain of the Lord
   d. The Kirtland Temple

SECTION 110

BRIEF HISTORICAL BACKGROUND: Visions given to Joseph Smith and Oliver Cowdery in the Kirtland Temple, on April 3, 1836. Joseph and Oliver see the Lord Jehovah!

THE STORY: Verse 8 reads, "Yea, I will appear unto my servants, and speak unto them with mine own voice, if my people will keep my commandments, and do not pollute this holy house." This promise has been fulfilled on a number of occasions. Melvin J. Ballard shared the following vision/dream he had of the Savior:

> As I entered the door, I saw, seated on a raised platform, the most glorious Being my eyes have ever beheld or that I ever conceived existed in all the eternal worlds. As I approached to be introduced, he arose and stepped toward me with extended arms, and he smiled as he softly spoke my name. If I shall live to be a million years old, I shall never forget that smile. He took me into his arms and kissed me, pressed me to his bosom, and blessed me, until the marrow of my bones seemed to melt! When he had finished, I fell at his feet, and, as I bathed them with my tears and kisses, I saw the prints of the nails in the feet of the Redeemer of the world. The feeling that I had in the presence of him who hath all things in his hands, to have his love, his affection, and his blessing was such that if I ever can receive that of which I had but a foretaste, I would give all that I am, all that I ever hope to be, to feel what I then felt!

Melvin J. Ballard, *Melvin J. Ballard—Crusader for Righteousness*
(Salt Lake City: Bookcraft, 1966), 65–66

THE FACT: The following is Lorenzo Snow's vision of the Savior:

> Upon learning of the death of President Wilford Woodruff, President Snow dressed in his holy temple robes, retired to the sacred altar in the Salt Lake Temple, and poured out his heart to the Lord. He reminded the Lord how he had pleaded that President Woodruff

outlive him, that he might not be called to bear the heavy burdens and responsibilities of Church leadership. "Nevertheless," he prayed, "Thy will be done. I have not sought this responsibility, but if it be Thy will I will present myself before thee for Thy guidance and instruction. I ask that Thou show me what Thou wouldst have me do."

After finishing the prayer, he expected a reply, some special manifestation from the Lord. He waited—and waited—and waited. There was no reply, no voice, no manifestation. He left the room in deep disappointment, passed through the celestial room and out into the large corridor leading to his own room, where a most glorious manifestation was given him. One of the most beautiful accounts of this experience is given by his granddaughter, Allie Young Pond: One day she and President Snow were walking in the Salt Lake Temple, and she tells of the following conversation:

After we left his room and while we were still in the large corridor, leading into the Celestial room, I was walking several steps ahead of Grandpa when he stopped me, saying, "Wait a moment, Allie, I want to tell you something. It was right here that the Lord Jesus Christ appeared to me at the time of the death of President Woodruff. . . ."

Then grandpa came a step nearer and held out his left hand and said, "He stood right here, about three feet above the floor. It looked as though He stood on a plate of solid gold."

Grandpa told me what a glorious personage the Savior is and described His hands, feet, countenance and beautiful white robes, all of which were of such a glory of whiteness and brightness that he could hardly gaze upon Him.

Then grandpa came another step nearer me and put his right hand on my head and said: "Now, granddaughter, I want you to remember that this is the testimony of your grandfather, that he told you with his own lips that he actually saw the Savior here in the Temple, and talked with Him face to face."

Ivan J. Barrett, "He Lives! For We Saw Him," *Ensign*, Aug. 1975, 19–20

QUESTION:

110. What is significant about Sunday, April 3, 1836, the day the Savior, Moses, Elijah, and Elias appeared to Joseph Smith and Oliver Cowdery in the Kirtland Temple?

    a. Sidney Rigdon's birthday
    b. Porter Rockwell is placed in jail
    c. The first PEC meeting in the Kirtland ward
    d. The Jewish Passover

SECTION 111

BRIEF HISTORICAL BACKGROUND: The Prophet Joseph Smith received the following revelation at Salem, Massachusetts, on August 6, 1836. A man named Burgess had convinced the Prophet that there was treasure in Salem that only he (Burgess) knew about.

THE STORY: The following from early member Ebenezer Robinson:

> The revelation [Doctrine and Covenants 111] put the best face on a misbegotten venture. Long after the event, Ebenezer Robinson, a printer in Nauvoo, remembered that a convert named Burgess had persuaded Church leaders that a large sum of money was hidden in the cellar of a Salem house. Perhaps Joseph believed he could identify the site. . . . Less than encouraging, the Salem revelation opened with the words "I the Lord your God am not displeased with your coming this journey, notwithstanding your follies," and tried to deflect the men to missionary work. "There are more treasures than one for you in this city." The "wealth pertaining to gold and silver" could be obtained "in due time," implying that meanwhile they should

concentrate on people. For two weeks, the men taught from house to house, taking time out to visit the famous east India marine Society museum like ordinary tourists. On August 20, Rigdon lecture on "Christianity" at the lyceum. All the while they looked for the treasure-house. On August 19, Joseph wrote Emma that "we have found the house since Bro. Burgess left us, very luckily and providentially, as we had one spell been most discouraged." They were plotting how to get possession. "The house is occupied, and it will require much care and patience to rent or buy it." Joseph said they were willing to wait months if necessary, but by September, the party was back in Kirtland with no treasure for their pains.

http://www.boap.org/LDS/Early-Saints/ERobinson.html

THE FACT: Verse 2 reads, "I have much treasure in this city for you, for the benefit of Zion, and many people in this city, whom I will gather out in due time for the benefit of Zion, through your instrumentality." Joseph Smith and those with him may not have seen the fulfillment of the Lord's promise on this trip, but other elders would reap the benefits as the following story indicates:

This promise was at least partially fulfilled in 1841, when Erastus Snow and Benjamin Winchester were called to preach the gospel in Salem. They were given a copy of this revelation along with a charge to fulfill the prophecy to gather out many people for the benefit of Zion. Snow and Winchester arrived in Salem in September of 1841. They preached at public meetings, published a pamphlet addressed to the citizens of Salem, and challenged the notorious Mormon apostate John C. Bennett to debate. Their efforts bore fruit. By March 1842 they had organized the Salem Branch with 53 members. By the end of that summer, the branch had 90 members. In his private journal, Erastus Snow indicated that he baptized more than one hundred people in Salem from September 1841 until he returned to Nauvoo on 11 April 1843.

Stephen E. Robinson, H. Dean Garrett, *A Commentary on the Doctrine and Covenants* (Salt Lake City: Deseret Book, 2001), 4:75

QUESTION:

111. The Prophet's purpose in journeying to Salem, Massachusetts, was the hope of relieving the Church of extremely deep debt. What was the debt owed on the Kirtland Temple?

    a. $13,000
    b. $5,000
    c. $11,000
    d. $17,000

SECTION 112

BRIEF HISTORICAL BACKGROUND: On July 23, 1837, at Kirtland, Ohio, Joseph Smith received this revelation for Thomas B. Marsh. This is the last revelation the Prophet received in Kirtland.

THE STORY: Elders David Patten and Thomas B. Marsh resided in Missouri while the remainder of the Twelve lived in the Kirtland area. When Thomas B. Marsh found out about the failure of the Kirtland Safety Society and news of fellow apostles John Boynton, Lyman Wight, Orson Hyde, Orson Pratt, Parley P. Pratt, William McLellin, and Luke Johnson all sliding away from the Prophet (some in open rebellion), both Thomas and David Patten journeyed to Kirtland. Thomas left with good intentions, hoping to reunite the Twelve, but once in Kirtland, he was offended. Joseph Smith called Heber C. Kimball and Orson Hyde to England. The two apostles, along with Willard Richards and Joseph Fielding, left Kirtland June 13, 1837. Since Thomas B. Marsh was the President of the Quorum of the Twelve, he felt it was his place to inform the

Twelve of mission calls or be the one to introduce the gospel in foreign lands. Brigham Young shared the outcome of the ensuing situation:

> As soon as they came I got Marsh to go to Joseph But Patten would [not]. . . . He got his mind prejudiced & when He went to see Joseph David insulted Joseph & Joseph slaped him in the face & kicked him out of the yard this done David good. It appears that Marsh himself desired to introduce the gospel abroad.
>
> https://ojs.lib.byu.edu/spc/index.php/BYUStudies/article/viewFile/5159/4809

THE FACT: Thomas B. Marsh apostatized from the Church in 1838 for a time. This was the man who searched for the truth in Boston, and miraculously, was led by the Spirit to Palmyra, where he walked into the Grandin Printing Shop when the first sixteen pages of Book of Mormon proof were being pulled from the press. He was called to lead the Quorum of the Twelve. How could he, having such a calling, separate himself from the Church? Thomas's life proved that regardless of position in the Church, when one speaks out against the Lord's anointed, then those blessings are withdrawn and he or she is left to endure the buffetings of Satan. But unlike most dissenters, Thomas would eventually shed his pride and come back.

QUESTION:

112. On the day this revelation was received, what other great event took place in Church history?

   a. The first day the gospel was preached on English soil in the first England mission
   b. The Far West Temple site was dedicated
   c. The Adam-ondi-Ahman Temple site was dedicated
   d. Adam's altar was found at Adam-ondi-Ahman

SECTION 113

BRIEF HISTORICAL BACKGROUND: Revelation given from the Lord to Joseph Smith in March 1838 at Far West, Missouri. The Lord answered questions on the writings of Isaiah.

THE STORY: In verse 7 of this section, an individual by the name of Elias Higbee asked one of the questions that the Lord would answer during the revelation. Who was he and what was his role in the Church?

> As a Church historian, Elias Higbee helped collect affidavits regarding the Saints' losses in Missouri, and in October 1839 he accompanied Joseph Smith and Sidney Rigdon to Washington, D.C., to present them to U.S. officials. After President Van Buren rebuffed them in February 1840, Higbee stayed on, trying unsuccessfully for a hearing before the Senate Judiciary Committee. His documents relating to this Washington mission, later incorporated in the "History of Joseph Smith," were his main contribution to Church history.
>
> http://www.lightplanet.com/mormons/people/church_historians.html

THE FACT: The relationship between the Church and the United States White House runs rich and deep as the following facts attest.

— James A. Garfield was sworn into office and became the only president to utter the phrase "Mormon Church" in an inaugural address.

Michael K. Winder, *Presidents and Prophets*
(American Fork, Utah: Covenant Communications, 2007), 143

— Having just suffered a major stroke, Woodrow Wilson became the only president blessed by name in a temple dedicatory prayer. In Hawaii, President Heber J. Grant prayed, "We pray Thee to bless Woodrow Wilson, the president of these United States. Touch him with the healing power of thy holy spirit and make him whole. We pray that his life may be precious in Thy sight, and may the inspiration that comes from thee ever abide with him."

N. B. Lundwall, *Temples of the Most High*
(Salt Lake City: Bookcraft, 1949), 148

— Abraham Lincoln is the only US president to check out the Book of Mormon from the Library of Congress while in office. He signed the Book of Mormon out in November of 1861.

Cyril D. Pearson, "Abraham Lincoln and Joseph Smith,"
Improvement Era 48, no. 2 (February 1945)

— Benjamin Harrison asked LDS leaders for their prayers on behalf of his ill and dying wife, Caroline. "Who even heard," President Woodruff wrote in his diary, "of such a thing in this generation as [a] president of the United States asking their [the First Presidency's] prayers for himself and wife? May God grant it." The Mormon leaders obliged, but Carrie Harrison died on October 25.

Susan Staker ed., *Waiting for World's End: The Diaries of Wilford Woodruff*
(Salt Lake City: Signature Books, 1993)

— When Stephen A. Douglas spoke out against the Church in speeches from 1857 to 1860, Lincoln responded by pointing out the inconsistency between Douglas's idea of popular sovereignty and his denunciation of the Mormons as "alien enemies and outlaws." Lincoln also saw Douglas's advocating the repeal of Utah's territorial status as a way of trying to destroy Mormonism.

George U. Hubbard, "Abraham Lincoln as Seen by the Mormons,"
Utah Quarterly 31 (Spring 1963), 91–108

QUESTION:

113. Who is the only ex-US president to ask for a LDS blessing?

    a. Abraham Lincoln
    b. Calvin Coolidge
    c. James Garfield
    d. Martin Van Buren

SECTION 114

BRIEF HISTORICAL BACKGROUND: Revelation given to Joseph Smith at Far West, Missouri, on April 17, 1838.

THE STORY: The Lord mentioned David Patten by name in this short two-verse section, stating, "that he perform a mission unto me next spring." David had performed a number of missions up to this point and seemed to have been blessed with the gift of healing because he was able to relieve much sickness and suffering. During his mission to Pennsylvania in the fall and winter of 1832–1833, he recorded the following in his autobiography:

> When we arrived at the Springfield (Pa.) Branch we met with brothers Hyrum and William Smith. We held a meeting and had a joyful time together, brother Hyrum baptized six at the close of the meeting: next day two were baptized. When we found any sick I preached to them faith in the ordinances of the Gospel, and where the truth found place in their hearts, I commanded them in the name of the Lord Jesus Christ to arise from their beds of sickness and be made whole; in many instances the people came after me to lay hands on their sick, because of this gift which the Lord had bestowed upon me, and almost daily, the sick were healed under my hands: a woman

who had an infirmity for nearly twenty years was instantly healed. I arrived home in Kirtland, Feb. 25, 1833.

A healing of a different sort as recorded by Elder Patten:

March 25. The Elders were sent out from Kirtland to preach the Gospel, and counsel the Saints to gather to Kirtland. I started with brother Cahoon east, and on reaching Avon I preached at father Bosley's, where there was a man present who had disturbed several of our meetings, and would not be civil or quiet; he had defied any man to put him out of the house or make him be still. I felt stirred up in spirit, and told him to be quiet, or I certainly would put him out; he said I could not do it; I replied, "In the name of the Lord I will do it," whereupon I walked up to him, and seizing him by the neck with one hand and by the seat of the breeches with my other hand, I carried him to the door, and threw him about ten feet on to a pile of wood, which quieted him for the time being. From this circumstance the saying went out that David Patten had cast out one Devil, soul and body.

http://www.boap.org/LDS/Early-Saints/DPatten.html

THE FACT: David Patten was a man of great faith, realizing that the Lord would bless whatever he laid his hands on as the Spirit dictated. He believe he could heal not only God's children, but also His creatures to outperform their normal limits. The following is from the autobiography of Gilbert Belnap. He was a spy for the Prophet during the Nauvoo years, attending many meetings of Joseph's enemies in disguise.

I afterward sat in council with delegates from different parts of the country and secured the resolutions passed by that assembly. I then returned in safety to Nauvoo, but not without a close pursuit by those demons in human shape, uttering the most awful imprecations, and bawling out to meet almost every jump to stop or they would shoot. My greatest fear was that my horse would fall under me. I thought of the instance of David Patton administering to a mule which he was riding when fleeing before a similar band of ruffians. I placed my hands on either side of the animal and as fervently as I ever did, I prayed to God that his strength might hold out in order that I might bear the information which I had obtained to the Prophet. There were no signs of failure in accomplishing this purpose until just opposite the tomb. My horse fell on his side in the mud. This seemed to be a rebuke for me for urging him on to such a tremendous speed. We were entirely out of danger and covered with mud by reason of the fall. I rushed into the presence of the Prophet and gave him a minute detail of all that had come under my observation during that short mission.

http://www.boap.org/LDS/Early-Saints/GBelnap.html

QUESTION:

114. Why was David Patten placed in the number-two spot in seniority in the Quorum of the Twelve Apostles rather than as the President of the Quorum?

    a. He didn't feel his testimony was strong enough to hold the position of president
    b. He did not serve as many missions as Thomas B. Marsh
    c. He wasn't certain of his birth date
    d. He had missed to many priesthood meetings

SECTION 115

BRIEF HISTORICAL BACKGROUND: Revelation given to Joseph Smith making known the Lord's plans for the building up of Far West, Missouri. This revelation was received April 26, 1838 at Far West.

THE STORY: In verse 4, the Lord gave the name of his Church. He instructed, "For thus shall my church be called in the last days, even the Church of Jesus Christ of Latter-day Saints." This was the first time in this dispensation that the Lord revealed the official title of his Church. Other titles of the Church previous to this revelation are found in the following:

> A concise answer to this question is found by comparing the name of the Church on the title pages of the first three printings of the revelations: "The Church of Christ" (Book of Commandments, 1833), "The Church of the Latter Day Saints" (Doctrine and Covenants, 1835), and "The Church of Jesus Christ of Latter Day Saints" (Doctrine and Covenants, 1844).

> The Savior told the Nephites that his church should be called in his name. (See 3 Ne. 27:8.) As a result, the restored Church's official title from 1830 to 1834 was "The Church of Christ." That title is found in the revelation on the organization and government of the Church (D&C 20:1) and in early minute books. During this period, however, members of the Church regularly called themselves "saints"; the word *saint* is used approximately three dozen times in the D&C before 1834.

> On 3 May 1834, official action modified the name of the Church. In a priesthood conference presided over by Joseph Smith, a motion passed "by unanimous voice" that the Church be known as 'The Church of the Latter Day Saints.' (See *The Evening and the Morning Star*, May 1834, 2:160.) This alteration was not seen as a de-emphasis of Christ; on the contrary, it was done in hopes that the name of the Church would more clearly reflect the fact that Christ was at its head.

> In the same issue of the Kirtland newspaper in which the announcement appeared, an editorial explained that the change stemmed from a misleading nickname: the "Mormonite" church. The new name also had these advantages: (1) Since American Christians, including Congregationalists and reformers, frequently designated themselves as "The Church of Christ," that title did not distinguish the restored gospel from a host of Protestant sects. (2) Since Paul and Peter used the Greek word Saint ("a holy person") to refer to believers in Christ, the term *Latter-day Saints* implied that Church members were modern followers of Christ. Thus it also asserted the claim of restoration.

> Just as the term *saint* flourished when the official name was "The Church of Christ," the name of Christ regularly supplemented the official name of "The Church of the Latter Day Saints." For example,

in 1835, the Church was referred to as "the church of Christ" and the Twelve apostles were commissioned as "special witnesses of the name of Christ." (D&C 107:59, 23) The Saints certainly did not feel that the Church was leaving out the name of Christ.

Sometimes during this period the first and second titles would be combined—"the church of Christ of Latter Day saints"—as they were in priesthood minutes (*Messenger and Advocate*, Feb. 1836, 2:266) and in the publication of the first high council minutes (see headnote, D&C 5, 1835 edition).

A vivid illustration of the way members then understood the official name of the Church is found in a letter from John Smith, the Prophet's uncle, to his son Elias before the latter was converted. Writing 19 Oct. 1834, Uncle John answers the question of why the name could be changed:

"The Church of Christ is the Church of Saints and always was. This is the reason why the apostle directed letters sometimes to the Church of God, others to the Church, and again to the Brethren, sometimes to the Saints, always meaning the Church of Christ." (Archives, University of Utah)

Thus, the final version of the Church's name was no radical shift from the previous practice of using both "Christ" and "Saints" in designating the restored Church and its members. Revealed on 26 April 1838 (D&C 115:4), the full title, "The Church of Jesus Christ of Latter-day Saints," is striking by comparison to the names of the scores of churches that obscure their Christianity under the label of their founders or of some characteristic belief or aspect of church organization. It is a highly effective name, for while it is distinctive, it indicates that Jesus is at its head. It is also descriptive of divine restoration. And it is more than a name—it is a public commitment to a holy life through the Savior's power.

Richard Lloyd Anderson, "I Have a Question," *Ensign*, Jan. 1979, 13–14

THE FACT: In verses 7 and 8, the Lord commands, "Let the city, Far West, be a holy and consecrated land unto me; and it shall be called most holy, for the ground upon which thou standest is holy. Therefore, I command you to build a house unto me, for the gathering together of my saints, that they may worship me." The Saints wasted little time. On July 3, 1838, five hundred men excavated the trench for the foundation (80 x 120 feet) in half a day.

On July 4, 1838, during the cornerstone-laying ceremony, Sidney Rigdon gave his famous Independence Day speech that incited the mob and eventually led to the Saints expulsion from the state. Five of the Twelve Apostles and other members also met on the temple site, just after midnight on the early morning of April 26, 1839. In spite of the risk of personal danger (the Saints were now pushed out of the state and any member caught faced imprisonment and even the fear of death), they came together to fulfill the prophecy that the mission to England would depart from the temple site. A meeting was held and part of the foundation laid.

http://www.ldschurchtemples.com/farwest/

QUESTION:

115. Far West became the Church headquarters from the time the Prophet arrived in 1838 to the Saints' expulsion in 1839. It's estimated that Far West had a population of between three thousand and five thousand people. Who was the only person living in Far West for many years after the Saints were pushed out?

    a. William McLellin
    b. Parley P. Pratt
    c. David Whitmer
    d. John Whitmer

SECTION 116

BRIEF HISTORICAL BACKGROUND: On May 19, 1838, at Spring Hill, Missouri, Joseph Smith received the revelation indicating the name Adam-ondi-Ahman.

THE STORY: This is most likely the shortest section in the Doctrine and Covenants: only one verse with thirty-nine words. Yet it is extremely significant in its place in Church history. It was here that Adam called his posterity and blessed them. It is here that Adam will call the righteous Saints again, and not just those alive upon the earth at the time of his call. All righteous Saints from all ages will be present. It was here that a temple was to be built, but the site was never officially dedicated because a few days later the Church was forced from the area. Some may argue and claim that the temple site was dedicated; however, some evidence indicates the town square, not the temple lot, was dedicated.

http://www.ldschurchtemples.com/adamondiahman/

THE FACT: It may be obvious to you that I spend much of my time plowing through books and navigating my way through various Church websites. It constantly amazes me that no matter how much I read, Book of Mormon–like, I bump into facts I never knew. There's a wealth of this knowledge. The following story is one such fact:

> On Saturday, September 1, 1838, the First Presidency made its way from Far West toward Littlefield's halfway house—about halfway between Adam-ondi-Aham and Far West—for the purpose of appointing a city of Zion. It was named the City of Seth in honor of Adam's son. The center of this city, which could have been the site of a public square and future temple, was never established due to the expulsion of the Saints from Missouri shortly after the city was appointed.

http://www.ldschurchtemples.com/adamondiahman/

QUESTION:

116. What was the original name of Adam-ondi-Ahman?

    a. Adamville
    b. The Garden of Eden
    c. Spring Hill
    d. Lyman's Settlement

SECTION 117

BRIEF HISTORICAL BACKGROUND: Revelation given concerning some of the duties of the Brethren. Joseph Smith received this revelation at Far West, Missouri, on July 8, 1838.

THE STORY: The Lord instructs in verse 1: "Verily thus saith the Lord unto my servant William Marks, and also unto my servant Newel K. Whitney, let them settle up their business speedily and journey from the land of Kirtland, before I, the Lord, send again the snows upon the earth." Oliver Granger was instructed by Joseph Smith to carry this revelation to Kirtland and deliver it to William Marks and Newel K. Whitney. Just two days prior to receiving this revelation, what is known as Kirtland Camp left Ohio on route to Missouri in fulfillment of the command as stated in section 115 to gather to Zion. Records indicate that 515 members left with 260 actually making it to Far West. Many dropped out in Springville, Illinois, mostly due to illness, staying there until they could meet up with the Church in Nauvoo. Joseph Smith had no way of knowing who was part of Kirtland Camp. However, the Lord knew that Newel K. Whitney and William Marks decided to stay in Kirtland to protect investments. Because of this, the Lord gave what is known as section 117 to Joseph Smith.

http://institute.lds.org/manuals/Doctrine-and-Covenants
-institute-student-Manual/dc-in-111-117.asp

THE FACT: William Marks was the stake president of Kirtland and would hold this position in Missouri and in Nauvoo. On August 8, 1844, after the prophet's death and during a meeting of the members, William Marks tried to convince those in attendance that Sidney Rigdon was to be the new "guardian" for the Church. This is the same meeting where Brigham Young both sounded and looked like the Prophet Joseph Smith. Later, Marks was instrumental in convincing Joseph Smith's son, the young Joseph Smith III, to lead the Reorganized Church of Jesus Christ of Latter-day Saints.

http://lds.org/ensign/1979/09/nineteenth-century-break-offs?lang=eng

QUESTION:

117. Verse 12 states, "And again, I say unto you, I remember my servant Oliver Granger; behold, verily I say unto him that his name shall be had in sacred remembrance from generation to generation, forever and ever, saith the Lord." How is Oliver's name "held in scared remembrance"?

   a. A Church movie was made of his life
   b. The sister missionaries at Temple Square tell his story
   c. A monument is erected to honor him at Far West, Missouri
   d. His name has been canonized in scripture (section 117)

SECTION 118

BRIEF HISTORICAL BACKGROUND: Revelation given on July 8, 1838, at Far West, Missouri. The Lord instructed concerning the Twelve Apostles.

THE STORY: Referring to the Twelve Apostles, the Lord instructed, "And next spring let them depart to go over the great waters, and there promulgate my gospel, the fulness thereof, and bear record of my name. Let them take leave of my saints in the city of Far West, on the twenty-sixth day of April next, on the building-spot of my house, saith the Lord." It's also in this section that we are introduced to John Taylor, Wilford Woodruff, John E. Page, and Willard Richards as they are to "be appointed to fill the places of those who have fallen, and be officially notified of their appointment."

At the time of the call, John E. Page was en route to Missouri with a group of Canadian Saints. He had served in Canada on a mission for two years, traveling over five thousand miles and baptizing over six hundred converts.

http://institute.lds.org/manuals/church-history
-institute-student-manual/chft-11-15-15.asp

THE FACT: The mission to England was inspired because it infused the Church with many new members at a time when a number of people had apostatized in America. Wilford Woodruff labored successfully throughout the cities of Britain, converting many. The following are two of Elder Woodruff's missionary experiences.

Wilford Woodruff just seemed to have a way with ministers. Whether preaching from their pulpits or at baptisms, he just seemed to have the knack to get them baptized. On one occasion, while baptizing new converts into the Church, he had two ministers ride up and also request baptism. These ministers went away rejoicing.

Wilford Woodruff, Matthias F. Cowley ed.,
(Salt Lake City: Bookcraft, 1964), 109

As the Church was growing in the Hawcross area of England, so was the opposition. A number of the residents requested baptism. Wilford told them that if they had the faith to be baptized that he had the faith to administer the ordinance. Surrounded by a mob, and threatened with physical violence, the small group headed off for the pond. Wilford Woodruff reported, "I walked into the water with my mind stayed on God and baptized five persons while they were pelting my body with stones, one of which hit me on the head and came very near knocking me down."

"Elder Woodruff's Letter," *Times and Seasons,* Mar. 1, 1841, 330

QUESTION:

118. Like the Saints in America, those in Britain also experienced trials through persecution. Who was the individual that saved the Church from being expelled from this country prior to WWI?

    a. Sir Alexander Fleming
    b. Winston Churchill
    c. Joseph F. Smith
    d. Queen Victoria

SECTION 119

BRIEF HISTORICAL BACKGROUND: The Lord revealed the law of tithing to Joseph Smith at Far West, Missouri, on July 8, 1838.

THE STORY: When the Lord spelled out the law of tithing, it was different from what we are expected to pay as "members in good standing." The Lord taught the Prophet Joseph in verses 4 and 5 that they were not only to tithe "one-tenth of all their interest annually" but also "be tithed of their surplus properties."

THE FACT: By the time the Saints entered the Salt Lake Valley, the expectations were increased as explained by Parley P. Pratt:

> Once they had become established in their Great Basin communities, LDS pioneers were expected to pay three types of tithes: property, increase, and labor. Apostle Parley P. Pratt, on October 7, 1849, gave perhaps the first Utah discourse that details the triple tithe. First, he said, "To fulfill the law of tithing a man should make out and lay before the [Presiding] Bishop [then Newell K. Whitney] a schedule of all his property, and pay him the tenth of it." That is, he should pay a one-time initiatory tithe on all property he possessed. "When he has tithed his principal once," Pratt continued, "he has no occasion to tithe again" on that property. But the next year he must pay one-tenth of his increase of "cattle, money, goods and trade." A member also owed "the tenth of his time"—a labor tithe of each tenth day of man, young man, and work animals and wagons for the days not devoted to producing income or increase.
>
> *Journal History,* 7 October 1849, Archives, Historical Department,
> The Church of Jesus Christ of Latter-day Saints, Salt Lake City

QUESTION:

119. Brother Douglas M. Todd Sr. stated that his bishop wanted to change the name from tithing to what so more people would pay?

    a. Fire insurance
    b. Donation
    c. The Lord's pay
    d. The Lord's tenth

SECTION 120

BRIEF HISTORICAL BACKGROUND: The last of four revelations received by Joseph Smith on July 8, 1838, at Far West, Missouri.

THE STORY: The practice of the Church at all levels was to operate with councils rather than just one or two men making decisions. The Lord meant it to be this way because there is safety in councils. The following story illustrates the outcome when councils are neglected:

> Internal difficulties were brewing as the Saints poured into Caldwell County, where they constructed log houses and prepared the soil for spring planting. Thomas Marsh and Elisha Groves returned early in 1837 from their fund-raising mission in Kentucky and Tennessee and turned $1450 over to W. W. Phelps and John Whitmer, counselors in the stake presidency, since President David Whitmer was in Ohio. The counselors used the money to buy more land, but they purchased it in their own names and then sold it to the Saints at a small profit, which they retained. Several members of the Church immediately protested, and some of the high council complained that the counselors were also making decisions regarding Far West without consulting them. At a series of meetings in Far West in April, these brethren acknowledged their wrongs, and reconciliation was achieved. It was decided that Edward Partridge, acting with the counsel of the stake presidency, the high council, and two Apostles who were in Missouri—Thomas B. Marsh and David Patten—would distribute the lands.

A month later, however, Phelps and Whitmer again offended the high council and the Apostles with further attempts to profit from land deals. . . . Early in February 1838 the high council tried John Whitmer and W. W. Phelps for misusing Church funds. . . . Therefore, on 10 February the high council, with the assistance of two Apostles, excommunicated W. W. Phelps and John Whitmer.

> *Doctrine and Covenants Student Manual*, (Salt Lake City: The Church of Jesus Christ of Latter-day Saints, 1981), 183–84.

THE FACT: Elder Thomas B. Marsh provided additional information:

> You undoubtedly remember the visit which I, in company with Elder Groves, made to the churches in Kentucky and Tennessee in the summer of 1836. You may also recollect the nature and result of our visit. We came to solicit assistance for poor bleeding Zion. And we obtained through the goodness of the children of God in those regions, the sum of fourteen hundred and fifty dollars, which we delivered unto William W. Phelps and John Whitmer on our arrival at this place. But these men, instead of laying out the money for the benefit of poor bleeding Zion, purchased land for their own emolument. They generally did their business independently of the aid or counsel of either the bishop or high council. This gave some uneasiness to the two authorities of Zion, not only because they purchased land with church funds in their own name for their own aggrandizement, but because they selected the place for the city Far West and appointed the spot for the house of the Lord to be built on, drew the plan of said house, and appointed and ordained a committee to build the same, without asking or seeking counsel at the hand of either bishop, high council, or first presidency, when it was well understood that these authorities were appointed for the purpose of counseling on all important matters pertaining to the Saints of God.

Elders' Journal of the Church of Latter Day Saints, vol. 1 (October 1837–August 1838), no. 3, Far West, Missouri, July 1838, 37

QUESTION:

120. Thomas B. Marsh indicated that he served his mission to Kentucky and Tennessee with Elisha Groves. David Osborn in his autobiography stated that he and Elisha were hunting for what?

    a. Converts
    b. The mob
    c. Honeybees
    d. Deer

SECTION 121

BRIEF HISTORICAL BACKGROUND: Revelations received in answer to Joseph Smith's petitions while in jail at Liberty, Missouri, March 20, 1839.

THE STORY: This obviously was a dark time for the Prophet. Those jailed knew they were held against their will unjustly, just as those that placed them there understood this also. Some of those placed over to guard the Mormon prisoners were sympathetic at their misfortune and sufferings. The following is a statement from one of the guards, when the prisoners were in Jackson County, just days after being ripped from their families in Far West:

> While the prisoners were at Independence, Missouri, they were given the free hand to walk throughout town as they pleased with "a certain keeper being appointed merely to look to us." In fact, after only a few days in Independence they were moved from the house that they were being kept in to a more comfortable hotel which Parley P. Pratt refers to as "in the best style of which the place was capable." At one point Pratt "walked out of town and visited the desolate lands" which used to be inhabited by the Latter-day Saints and also the place dedicated seven years previously for the building of a temple, "it being a beautiful rise of ground, about half a mile west of Independence. When we saw it last it was a wilderness, but now our enemies had robbed it of every stick of timber, and it presented a beautiful rolling field of pasture, being covered with grass." Parley also mentioned the attitudes of General Wilson and those who were assigned to guard them as "politeness and attention on their part, and much cheerfulness and good feeling on our own."

> Parley P. Pratt, *History of the Late Persecution Inflicted by the State of Missouri upon the Mormons* (Detroit: Dawson and Bates, Printers, 1839), 46–47

THE FACT: James H. Ford, one of the guards in the Liberty Jail, shared the following:

When interviewed by Andrew Jenson and Joseph S. Black in September 1888 during a visit to Church history sites in Missouri, James H. Ford, the Clay County deputy sheriff in charge at the Jail when the Mormon prisoners were there, said he had, "On many occasions," taken the men out one at a time for walks around the town, in order to give them an opportunity "to enjoy the fresh air and get better meals then the jail fare allowed." He said he never looked upon Joseph Smith and his friends as "real criminals" but ascribed their incarceration mainly to "the excitement and bigotry of the times." Ford added that he took the best care of the prisoners he could, and "it was a lie that they had been fed on human flesh."

Dairy of Joseph Smith Black, September 18, 1888, Ms. BYU Archives, 40

QUESTION:

121. Elder Brigham. H. Roberts referred to the Liberty Jail as what?

    a. The "Pen"
    b. The "Rock"
    c. Liberty Jail
    d. The "Prison-temple"

SECTION 122

BRIEF HISTORICAL BACKGROUND: Revelation given to Joseph Smith while in Liberty Jail during March 1839.

THE STORY: Verse 1 reads, "The ends of the earth shall inquire after thy name, and fools shall have thee in derision, and hell shall rage against thee." To say that Joseph Smith was a curiosity among the outside world of the Latter-day Saints would be a gross understatement. Many sought him out, including the politicians of his day. The following is from Josiah Quincy, mayor of Boston, who, while traveling, was convinced by another traveler to stop in Nauvoo, Illinios, and seek out Joseph Smith:

> It is by no means improbable that some future textbook, for the use of generations yet unborn, will contain a question something like this: What historical American of the nineteenth century has exerted the most powerful influence upon the destinies of his countrymen? And it is by no means impossible that the answer to that interrogatory may be thus written: Joseph Smith, the Mormon prophet. And the reply, absurd as it doubtless seems to most men now living, may be an obvious commonplace to their descendants. History deals in surprises and paradoxes quite as startling as this. The man who established a religion in this age of free debate, who was and is today accepted by hundreds of thousands as a direct emissary from the Most High,—such a rare human being is not to be disposed of by pelting his memory with unsavory epithets. Fanatic, imposter, charlatan, he may have been; but these hard names furnish no solution to the problem he presents to us. Fanatics and impostors are living and dying every day, and their memory is buried with them; but the wonderful influence which this founder of a religion exerted and still exerts throws him into relief before us, not as a rogue to be criminated, but as a phenomenon to be explained. The most vital questions Americans are asking each other today have to do with this man and what he has left us. Is there any remedy heroic enough to meet the case, yet in accordance with our national doctrines of liberty and toleration, which can be applied to the demoralizing doctrines now advanced by the sect which he created? The possibilities of the Mormon system are unfathomable. Polygamy may be followed by still darker "revelations." Here is a society resting upon foundations which may at any moment be made subversive of every duty which we claim from the citizen. Must it be reached by that last argument which quenched the evil fanaticisms of Mulhausen and Munster? A generation other than mine must deal with these questions. Burning questions they are, which must give a prominent place in the history of the country to that sturdy self-asserter whom I visited at Nauvoo.
>
> http://www.boap.org/LDS/Early-Saints/JQuincy.html

THE FACT: While Joseph Smith and others were in Washington, DC, from December 1839 to early January 1840, seeking redress for the wrongs committed against the Saints in Missouri, the prophet had a chance to rub shoulders with the politicians of the day. Joseph Smith recorded the following on February 6, 1840 (*History of the Church*):

> I had previously preached in Washington, and one of my sermons I find reported in synopsis, by a member of Congress; which I will insert entire.

Matthew L. Davis wrote the following to his wife (I give only the first paragraph of his letter. In a sense, the second sentence is partial fulfillment of the promise in verse 1):

> Washington 6th February 1840 My Dear Mary—I went last evening to hear Joe Smith, the celebrated Mormon, expound his doctrine. I with several others, had a desire to understand his tenets as explained by himself. He is not an educated man: but he is a plain, sensible strong minded man. Everything he says, is said in a manner to leave an impression that he is sincere. There is no levity, no fanaticism, no want of dignity in his deportment. He is apparently from forty to forty-five years of age, rather above the middle stature, and what you ladies would call a very good looking man. In his garb there are no peculiarities, his dress being that of a plain unpretending citizen. He is by profession a Farmer; but is evidently well read.
>
> http://www.boap.org/LDS/Parallel/1840/5Feb40.html

QUESTION:

122. How does Joseph Smith rate on America's most influential list?

    a. 52

    b. 74

    c. 1

    d. 127

SECTION 123

BRIEF HISTORICAL BACKGROUND: A letter written by Joseph Smith to the Church, dated March 1839 while in jail at Liberty, Missouri. Joseph asked the members of the Church to start compiling accounts of their losses in Missouri.

THE STORY: It was Joseph's hope that the Church could take their grievances and losses to the Federal government to familiarize the leading politicians in the nation with the Church's persecution and, in the end, be compensated for their losses. As the following article indicates, reimbursement lay heavy on the conscience of Missouri:

> First, the Mormons suffered severe property losses for which their attempts to receive compensation failed. Their losses were not just in Caldwell County but were compounded losses incurred during eight years of living in and being forced from several counties. Their petitions for redress, filed between 1839 and 1845, included a thousand claims. Losses in Caldwell alone, as listed in these petitions, included ten thousand acres of land and big losses of crops, livestock, tools, plows, wagons, bridles, harnesses, saws, axes, rifles, pistols, swords, fence rails, beds, blankets, quilts, tin plates, chairs, and tents. Affidavits said that the army under Clark destroyed large amounts of timber, lumber, cattle, and hogs—even the shooting of some animals for sport. The flip side of Mormon losses was that Missouri dodged having to compensate the victims, which saved the state hundreds of thousands of dollars.
>
> http://mormonhistoricsitesfoundation.org/publications
> /studies_spring_01/MHS2.1Hartley.pdf

THE FACT: Although the Saints had incurred heavy losses previous to 1838, the final attempt at any recourse was significantly dimmed with Lilburn W. Boggs infamous Executive Order 44, otherwise known as the extermination order. Alvah Boggs, the great-grandson to Lilburn W. Boggs and convert to the Church in 1956, had this to say about his great-grandfather:

> My Brothers and Sisters, I indeed feel humble. I am just a recent convert to The Church of Jesus Christ of Latter-day Saints, to be exact, just one week. . . . My great-grandfather should have done everything in his power to protect any group of people or persons who wanted to worship God in any manner that they cared to worship him. This he certainly denied The Church of Jesus Christ of Latter-day Saints. I feel very remorseful for my parental linage for that particular thing. . . . I joined the Church because I believe in my heart this is the Church of God.

> Alvah Boggs, "Testimony, 1956," typescript on microfilm, LDS Church Archives

QUESTION:

123. Close to the time that the Saints were removed from Missouri, what other removal was taking place in this country?

    a. All British subjects loyal to the king sent back to England

    b. All Canadians sent back to Canada as a result of the War of 1812

    c. The Trail of Tears

    d. The Puritans sent to Oregon

SECTION 124

BRIEF HISTORICAL BACKGROUND: Revelation given to Joseph Smith at Nauvoo, Illinois, on January 19, 1841. Joseph Smith was commanded to make a proclamation of the gospel to the president of the United States.

THE STORY: Joseph Smith was commanded by the Lord to make a proclamation to the leaders of the world. W. W. Phelps worked on this project, but with everything else happening in Nauvoo, it was put aside for a time. It wasn't until 1845 that the Quorum of the Twelve Apostles, mostly because of Parley P. Pratt, sent out the proclamation. It begins:

> PROCLAMATION of the Twelve Apostles of the Church of Jesus Christ of Latter-day Saints.
>
> To all the Kings of the World;
> To the President of the United States of America;
> To the Governors of the several States;
> And to the Rulers and People of all Nations:
> GREETING:
> KNOW YE THAT the kingdom of God has come: as has been predicted by ancient prophets, and prayed for in all ages; even that kingdom which shall fill the whole earth, and shall stand for ever.
>
> The great Eloheim Jehovah has been pleased once more to speak from the heavens: and also to commune with man upon the earth, by means of open visions, and by the ministration of HOLY MESSENGERS.
>
> By this means the great and eternal High Priesthood, after the Order of his Son, even the Apostleship, has been restored; or, returned to the earth.
>
> http://www.physics.byu.edu/faculty/rees/325/documents/Proclamation1845.pdf

This proclamation is extensive and covers numerous pages. For those interested in reading the entire proclamation, visit the above website.

THE FACT: President Ezra Taft Benson felt it essential to issue a similar proclamation to the leaders of nations in 1975. It reads as follows:

> Today I shall speak doctrine, by way of warning and of testimony, and shall do so as one holding the holy apostleship, whose responsibility it is to proclaim the Lord's message in all the world and to all people. Each of my brethren of the Council of the Twelve has the same responsibility I have to declare these things to the world and to bear record of them before all men.

Toward the end of his mortal ministry, the Lord commanded the Prophet Joseph Smith as follows:

"Make a solemn proclamation of my gospel . . . to all the kings of the world, to the four corners thereof . . . and to all nations of the earth." (D&C 124:2–3.) He was to invite them to come to the light of truth, and use their means to build up the kingdom of God on earth.

In the spirit of this divine direction, on the sixth day of April 1845, and shortly after the Prophet Joseph Smith and his brother Hyrum had mingled their blood with that of the other martyrs of true religion, the Council of the Twelve made such a proclamation. . . .

It seems fitting and proper to me that we should reaffirm the great truths pronounced in this declaration and that we should proclaim them anew to the world.

To the rulers and peoples of all nations, we solemnly declare again that the God of heaven has established his latter-day kingdom upon the earth in fulfillment of prophecies. Holy angels have again communed with men on the earth. God has again revealed himself from heaven and restored to the earth his holy priesthood with power to administer in all the sacred ordinances necessary for the exaltation of his children. His church has been reestablished among men with all the spiritual gifts enjoyed anciently. All this is done in preparation for Christ's second coming. The great and dreadful day of the Lord is near at hand. In preparation for this great event and as a means of escaping the impending judgments, inspired messengers have gone, and are now going, forth to the nations of the earth carrying this testimony and warning.

The nations of the earth continue in their sinful and unrighteous ways. Much of the unbounded knowledge with which men have been blessed has been used to destroy mankind instead of to bless the children of men as the Lord intended. Two great world wars, with fruitless efforts at lasting peace, are solemn evidence that peace has been taken from the earth because of the wickedness of the people. Nations cannot endure in sin. They will be broken up, but the kingdom of God will endure forever.

Therefore, as humble servants of the Lord, we call upon the leaders of nations to humble themselves before God, to seek his inspiration and guidance. We call upon rulers and people alike to repent of their evil ways. Turn unto the Lord, seek his forgiveness, and unite yourselves in humility with his kingdom. There is no other way. If you will do this, your sins will be blotted out, peace will come and remain, and you will become a part of the kingdom of God in preparation for Christ's second coming. But if you refuse to repent or to accept the testimony of his inspired messengers and unite yourselves with God's kingdom, then the terrible judgments and calamities promised the wicked will be yours. . . .

When the voice of warning goes forth it is always attended by testimony. In the great declaration issued by the apostles of the Lord Jesus Christ in 1845, this is the testimony which was borne, and we who are the apostles today renew it as our witness:

"We say, then, in life or in death, in bonds or free, that the great God has spoken in this age.— *And we know it.*

"He has given us the Holy Priesthood and Apostleship, and the keys of the kingdom of God, to bring about the restoration of all things as promised by the holy prophets of old.— *And we know it.*

"He has revealed the origin and the Records of the aboriginal tribes of America, and their future destiny.— *And we know it.*

"He has revealed the fulness of the gospel, with its gifts, blessings, and ordinances.— *And we know it.*

"He has commanded us to bear witness of it, first to the Gentiles, and then to the remnants of Israel and the Jews.— *And we know it.*

"He has also said that, if they do not repent, and come to the knowledge of the truth, . . . and also put away all murder, lying, pride, priestcraft, whoredom, and secret abomination, they shall soon perish from the earth, and be cast down to hell.— *And we know it.*

"He has said, that when . . . the gospel in all its fulness [is] preached to all nations for a witness and testimony, He will come, and all Saints with him, to reign on the earth one thousand years.— *And we know it.*

"He has said that he will not come in his glory and destroy the wicked, till these warnings were given and these preparations were made for his reception.— *And we know it.*

"Heaven and earth shall pass away, but not one jot or tittle of his revealed word shall fail to be fulfilled.

"Therefore, again we say to all people, Repent, and be baptized in the name of Jesus Christ, for remission of sins; and you shall receive the Holy Spirit, and shall know the truth, and be numbered with the house of Israel."

http://lds.org/ensign/1975/11/a-message-to-the-world?lang=eng

124. On whose birthday was the proclamation to government leaders sent in 1845?

    a. Joseph Smith Jr.
    b. Jesus Christ
    c. Martin Van Buren
    d. Porter Rockwell

SECTION 125

BRIEF HISTORICAL BACKGROUND: Revelation given to Joseph Smith at Nauvoo, Illinois, in March 1841.

THE STORY: The Lord saw a need for the Saints to populate both sides of the Mississippi River and commanded Joseph Smith to establish a community, which he was to name Zarahemla.

> Zarahemla is within Lee County, Iowa and was founded by the Latter-Day Saints in the early 1840s. The settlement was inspired by a revelation given to the Prophet Joseph Smith Jr. after Joseph's visit in 1839 when he crossed the Mississippi River to look over the land west of Nauvoo. He said that a "town for Mormons should be developed just West of Montrose and given the name Zarahemla." Almost a year later in March 1841, the Doctrine and Covenants 125:1–3 revelation concerning Iowa reads:
>
> What is the will of the Lord concerning the saints in the Territory of Iowa?
>
> 2 Verily, thus saith the Lord, I say unto you, if those who call themselves by my name and are essaying to be my saints, if they will do my will and keep my commandments concerning them, let them gather themselves together unto the places which I shall appoint unto

them by my servant Joseph, and build up cities unto my name, that they may be prepared for that which is in store for a time to come.

3 Let them build up a city unto my name upon the land opposite the city of Nauvoo, and let the name of a Zarahemla be named upon it.

The construction of Zarahemla was quickly accomplished after this revelation but the Saints' stay was brief. George W. Gee surveyed the city under Joseph's direction and in a short period of time an Iowa Stake was soon couched on the western side of the Mississippi River. There were over 300 members of the Church settled in Zarahemla by August 7, 1841. Within the surrounding areas of Zarahemla, the Iowa Stake totaled around 750 members of the Church. About 30 houses were built in Zarahemla but by 1846 the Saints deserted the area. In the end abandoning Zarahemla was to be a good thing because the Supreme Court ruled in favor of the land shareholders of the Half-Breed Tract, which deposed any person not mentioned therein, the Mormons. Persecution and the big push West aided in the build up and desertion of this town.

This site was one of the two stakes of The Church of Jesus Christ of Latter-Day Saints at the time (it is also one of the eleven pre-Utah Stakes). John Smith was called to be the Stake President over eight Branches. However, the Stake was dissolved into Branch status within 27 months of its inception. This could be due to the gathering to Nauvoo or the legal issues the Zarahemla Mormons faced with their neighbors.

http://winterquarters.byu.edu/pages/Other.aspx

THE FACT: It didn't take long for enough Church membership to live in Zarahemla to establish a new stake. At the conference, George A. Smith opened the meeting by announcing the death of Don Carlos Smith, younger brother of Joseph Smith. John Taylor then spoke and then a number of notable men, including Joseph Meacham, John Smith, William Clayton, and George W. Gee, were called to form the Zarahemla Stake organization.

Another reason for the formation of Zarahemla was to take care of those individuals and families in need:

Sara King Hillman at the age of 43 was a widow who struggled with her sons Ira and Silas. This deed for land in Iowa gave Sara the assurance of a place to stay and the security of land without payments. Whether there were many other cases like Sara or not it shows the generosity of Joseph Smith and the difference in the population of Zarahemla, wealthy and poor.

http://winterquarters.byu.edu/pages/Other.aspx

QUESTION:

125. What one event did *not* take place in Zarahemla?
    a. The conference in which Brigham Young both appeared and sounded like the Prophet Joseph Smith
    b. The miraculous healings on July 22, 1839
    c. The Miracle of the Quail
    d. Joseph Smith's prophecy of the Saints relocating to the Rocky Mountains

SECTION 126

BRIEF HISTORICAL BACKGROUND: Revelation given to Joseph Smith instructing Brigham Young that it was no longer required for him to leave his family. This revelation was received July 9, 1841, at the home of Brigham Young in Nauvoo, Illinois.

THE STORY: By studying the missionary service of Elder Young, one might comprehend in a small way his unselfishness in the spreading the gospel in spite of personal discomfort.

THE FACT: The following are a few quick facts of the Quorum of the Twelve's mission to England:

— Brigham Young was well aware of the prophecy in section 118 declaring that the Quorum of the Twelve would leave for their mission to England from the temple site in Far West, Missouri. Brigham was also equally cognizant of Governor Boggs's extermination order. Undaunted at the possibility of death or imprisonment, Brigham Young, as president of the Quorum of the Twelve, executed the Lord's will as set out in section 118. "In the pre-dawn hours of April 26, Brigham Young led two dozen Latter-day Saints in prayer and song on the temple block in Far West, Missouri. Elder Young would state in reference to the situation, 'because the Lord God had spoken and it was our duty to obey, and the Lord would take care of us.' It was during this meeting that Wilford Woodruff and George A. Smith would be set apart as Apostles, completing, for the first time in months, the Quorum of the Twelve."

— While a prisoner at Liberty Jail, the Prophet had written about a Abrahamic-type test in which the Quorum of the Twelve would leave as a united group overseas trusting in the Lord for their own personal and families' well-being. Most of the Quorum of the Twelve left for their missions between August and September 1839 sick with fevers and chills. Not only did they leave sick, but sick families were also left behind.

— Brigham Young and Heber C. Kimball set foot on English soil April 6, 1840, the ten-year anniversary of the organization of the Church.

— Brigham Young saw the immediate need for a patriarch to the sixteen hundred members in England. Peter Melling was ordained the first patriarch in England on April 17, 1840.

— Brigham Young was fiercely loyal to the Prophet. While on his mission, he would ask the Prophet's permission before he acted. This could take months waiting for the correspondence to be sent and then an answer received from the prophet. Brother Brigham would write the Prophet on numerous occasions asking, "If you see any thing in, or about the whole affair, that is not right: I ask, in the name of the Lord Jesus Christ, that you would make known unto us the mind of the Lord, and his will concerning us. I believe that I am as willing to do the will of the Lord, and take counsel of my brethren . . . as ever I was in my life."

On May 18, traditionally a feast day among the United Brethren, Elder Young, "clothed with the power of God," addressed the Saints gathered at a large banquet. It was apparently on this occasion that a "notable miracle was wrought by faith & the power of God." Writing two weeks later, Elder Woodruff recorded that the three Apostles had blessed Sister May Pitts, confined to bed for six years and unable to walk without crutches for eleven, "& her ancle bones received strength & she now walks without the aid of crutch or staff."

— At the first conference on British soil, held in Preston, the membership voted on an ambitious missionary and publication program as presented by Brigham Young. This would include a British edition Book of Mormon, a Church newspaper, and a hymnal. With time there would also be a British edition Doctrine and Covenants.

It is interesting to contemplate the self-educated, unpolished Brigham toiling long hours editing, proofreading, and indexing the book. He was not unaware of his own meager "book learning" and phonetic spelling. "Now my Dear Brother," he wrote to Willard Richards, "you must forgive all my nonscense and over look erours." And another time: "excuse erours and mistakes you must remember its from me.

"Nineteenth-century Spelling," *Ensign*, Aug. 1975

— Brigham Young and Elder Kimball set in place policy for the emigration of British members to America. The first such group organized by the apostles set sail for America on June 1, 1840.

Our motto is go ahead. Go ahead.—& ahead we are determined to go—till we have conquered every foe. So come life or come death we'll go ahead, but tell us if we are going wrong & we will right it.

On 6 April 1841, one year after their arrival in England, the Twelve met with the Latter-day Saints in conference. President Young presided over and conducted the conference. Brigham Young and the

Twelve organized branches throughout the mission into conferences, each with a presiding elder, and appointed Elder Parley Pratt to preside over the whole. Reports from areas throughout the British Isles showed more than four thousand members; counting those who had emigrated or been cut off from the Church, more than five thousand people had been baptized in the British Isles to this point.

Ronald K. Esplin, "Brigham Young in England," *Ensign*, June 1987, 28–33

QUESTION:

126. What did Brigham Young die from in August 1877?

    a. Old age
    b. The flu
    c. Pneumonia
    d. Peritonitis, the affects of a ruptured appendix

SECTION 127

BRIEF HISTORICAL BACKGROUND: An epistle from the Prophet to the Saints regarding baptisms for the dead. This epistle was given September 1, 1842, at Nauvoo, Illinois.

THE STORY: In the July 1838 edition of the *Elders' Journal*, Joseph Smith penned the answers to twenty questions related to Mormonism. Joseph answered question 16 in the following:

"If the Mormon doctrine is true, what has become of all those who have died since the days of the apostles?" The Prophet answered,

"All those who have not had an opportunity of hearing the gospel, *and being administered to by an inspired man in the flesh,* must have it hereafter before they can be finally judged." The Prophet's thought is clear—the dead must have someone in mortality administer the saving ordinances for them to be saved in the kingdom of God. Significantly, the answer given by the Prophet marks his first known statement concerning the doctrine of vicarious work for the dead. However, it was not until more than two years later that the principle was put into practice.

http://www.mormonhistoricsitesfoundation.org/publications/studies_spring2002/MHS3.1Spring2002Baugh.pdf

THE FACT: The following has reference to Alvin Smith's vicarious baptism:

In the early 1840s, Nauvoo had four landing sites—the Upper Stone House Landing, the Kimball Wharf, the Lower Stone House Landing, and the Main Street Dock near Joseph Smith's Homestead and later the Nauvoo House. Each of these locations likely would have provided a suitable place for baptisms to be performed, although the ordinance was conducted at any number of locations near the riverbank. Traditionally, the Main Street Landing has been the site generally believed to be where baptism, both for the living and the dead, was performed most frequently. There is a good possibility that Alvin Smith, Joseph Smith's older brother who died in November 1823, was one of the first deceased persons to have his baptismal work performed. Lucy Mack Smith recalled that just prior to her husband's death, Joseph told his father, "that it was . . . the privilege of the Saints to be baptized for the dead," whereupon Joseph Sr., requested that, "Joseph be baptized for Alvin immediately." Significantly, Joseph Sr. died on 14 September 1840, less than a month after the Prophet first taught the doctrine of baptism for the dead and only two days after Jane Neyman was baptized in behalf of her deceased son. If Joseph and the Smith family were true to their father's request that Alvin's baptism be done "immediately," the likelihood exists that it was performed sometime around mid-September. The record containing the early proxy ordinance information indicates that Hyrum acted as proxy (not Joseph, as Father Smith requested), but does not give any other date than the year 1840. The ordinance was performed for Alvin a second time, again by Hyrum in 1841, and was probably done after the font was completed and dedicated in the basement of the Temple. A friend and contemporary of the Prophet, Aroet Hale, stated that Joseph Smith instructed the Saints, "to have the work done over as quick as the temple was finished, when it could be done more perfect."

http://www.mormonhistoricsitesfoundation.org/publications /studies_spring2002/MHS3.1Spring2002Baugh.pdf

QUESTION:

127. In September 1870, after Martin Harris arrived in Salt Lake City to be with the Saints, he was rebaptized into the Church. What event took place immediately after his baptism?

    a. He received a mission call
    b. He was baptized for dead relatives
    c. He bore his testimony of the Book of Mormon
    d. He spoke on baptism for the dead

SECTION 128

BRIEF HISTORICAL BACKGROUND: An epistle from Joseph Smith to the Church at Nauvoo, Illinois, on September 6, 1842. Joseph gave further teachings on baptism for the dead.

THE STORY: It's obvious that there were some irregularities with the ordinance pertaining to baptisms for the dead in the early Church. It's understandable that there would be a developmental period with this practice from the Nauvoo years to the way we perform the ordinance today. For instance, at the first baptism for the dead in September 1840, a female, Jane Neyman, was baptized for her son, a male. Second, the witness, again a female, Vienna Jacques, was not a priesthood holder. Third, history is silent whether there was a confirmation coupled with the baptism. Finally, records were not always kept. In 1873, Brigham Young taught the following:

> When Joseph received the revelation that we have in our possession concerning the dead, the subject was opened to him, not in full but in part, and he kept on receiving. When he had first received the knowledge by the spirit of revelation how the dead could be officiated for, there are brethren and sisters here, I can see quite a number here who were in Nauvoo, and you recollect that when this doctrine was first revealed and in hurrying in the administration of baptism for the dead, that sisters were baptized for their male friends, were baptized for their fathers, their grandfathers, their mothers and their grandmothers, &c. I just mention this so that you will come to understanding, that as we knew nothing about this matter at first, the old Saints recollect, there was little by little given, and the subject was made plain, but little was given at once. Consequently, in the first place people were baptized for their friends and no record was kept. Joseph afterwards kept a record, &c. Then women were baptized for men and men for women.

http://www.mormonhistoricsitesfoundation.org/publications
/studies_spring2002/MHS3.1Spring2002Baugh.pdf

THE FACT: Quick facts on Nauvoo baptism for the dead:

— There were 6,818 baptisms performed in 1841, the majority in the Mississippi River.
— Nehemiah Brush was the most active proxy, being baptized for more than one hundred deceased relatives
— Sarah M. Cleveland was the most active female proxy being baptized for forty deceased relatives
— Robert Horne records the following:

I saw Elders baptizing for the dead in the Mississippi River. This was something new to meand the beauty of this great principle dawned upon me. I had never heard of such a doctrine then. Orson Pratt was baptizing. Brother Joseph stood on the banks.

— Aroet Hale records the following:

I remembered Joseph Smith performing more than two hundred baptisms in the Mississippi River. Then the apostles and other elders went into the river and continued the same ordinance. Hundreds were baptized there.

— Wilford Woodruff states:

. . . that Joseph Smith "went into the Mississippi River, and so did I, as well as others, and we each baptized a hundred for the dead."

— Even though Joseph Smith performed many baptisms for the dead, there is no record indicating that he was a proxy at a baptism.

Although the Saints were instructed not to perform proxy baptisms outside the temple after the October 1841 conference, a few recorded instances were found showing that there were exceptions to the policy. Charlotte Haven, a non-Latter-day Saint who lived in Nauvoo in 1842–43, wrote a letter to her family in the east describing a baptismal service she observed being performed in behalf of the dead. In the letter, dated 2 May 1843, she wrote:

Last Sunday morning . . . was a balmy spring day, so we took a bee-line for the river, down the street north of our house. Arriving there we rested a while on a log, watching the thin sheets of ice as they slowly came down and floated by. Then we followed the bank toward town, and rounding a little point covered with willows and cottonwoods, we spied quite a crowd of people, and soon perceived there was a baptism. Two elders stood knee-deep in the ice cold water, and immersed one another as fast as they could come down the bank. We soon observed that some of them went in and were plunged several times. We were told that they were baptized for the dead who had not had an opportunity of adopting the doctrines of the Latter Day Saints. So these poor mortals in ice-cold water were releasing their ancestors and relatives from purgatory! We drew a little nearer and heard several names repeated by the elders as the victims were douched, and you can imagine our surprise when the name George Washington was called. So after these fifty years he is out of purgatory and on his way to the "celestial" heaven! It was enough and we continued our walk homeward."

http://www.mormonhistoricsitesfoundation.org/publications
/studies_spring2002/MHS3.1Spring2002Baugh.pdf

QUESTION:

128. On August 15, 1840, Joseph Smith introduced the principle of baptism for the dead at whose funeral?

    a. Joseph Smith Sr.
    b. Lucy Mack Smith
    c. Seymour Brunson
    d. Don Carlos Smith

SECTION 129

BRIEF HISTORICAL BACKGROUND: Instructions given by Joseph Smith on how to distinguish spirits and ministering angels. This teaching was given at Nauvoo, Illinois, on February 9, 1843.

THE STORY: The words of William Taylor, the brother to President Taylor, pay a fitting tribute to this great gift of the Prophet:

> He seemed to be just as familiar with the Spirit World, and as well acquainted with the other side, as he was here.

The Prophet states the following:

> A man came to me in Kirtland, and told me he had seen an angel, and described his dress. I told him he had seen no angel, and that there was no such dress in heaven. He grew mad, and went into the street and commanded fire to come down out of heaven to consume me. I laughed at him, and said, You are one of Baal's prophets; your God does not hear you; jump up and cut yourself: and he commanded fire from heaven to consume my house.

History of the Church, 5:267–68

Why could Joseph state that the man had not seen an angel? It's because he had received numerous visitations of personalities from all dispensations.

THE FACT: The following is a listing of the known appearances to the Prophet Joseph Smith:

PERSONAGES WHO APPEARED TO THE PROPHET JOSEPH SMITH OR WHO WERE SEEN BY HIM IN VISION

List Compiled by H. Donl Peterson

	PERSONAGE	REFERENCES
1.	God the Father	JS–H 1:17; HC 1:5; D&C 76:20
2.	Jesus Christ	JS–H 1:17; HC 1:5–6; D&C 76:20–24; 110:2–10
3.	Moroni (see appendix A)	JS–H 1:30–49; JD 17:374
4.	Elijah	D&C 110:13–16; JD 17:374
5.	John the Baptist	D&C 13; HC 1:39–40
6–8.	Peter, James, John	D&C 27:12; 128:20; HC 1:40–42; JD 18:326
9.	Adam (Michael)	HC 3:388; 2:380; D&C 128:21; JD 18:326
10.	Noah (Gabriel)	D&C 128:21; JD 21:94
11.	Raphael	D&C 128:21
12.	Moses	D&C 110:11; JD 21:65
13.	Elias	D&C 110:12; 27:6; JD 23:48
14.	Joseph, son of Jacob	D&C 27:10

	Personage	References
15.	Abraham	D&C 27:10; JD 21:94
16.	Isaac	D&C 27:10; JD 21:94
17.	Jacob	D&C 27:10; JD 21:94
18.	Enoch	JD 21:65
19–27.	Twelve Jewish Apostles (Peter, James, and John already counted above.) Names are in Matthew 10:1–4 & Luke 6:13–16.	JD 21: 94
28–39.	Twelve Nephite Apostles (Including Three Nephites; names are recorded in 3 Nephi 19:4)	JD 21:94
40.	Nephi	JD 21:161; Orson Pratt Letter Box 3/11/1876 (CHO)
41.	Seth	JD 21:94; HC 3:388; D&C 107:53–57
42.	Methuselah	JD 21:94; HC 3:388; D&C 107:53–57
43.	Enos	JD 21:94; HC 3:388; D&C 107:53–57
44.	Mahalaleel	JD 21:94; HC 3:388; D&C 107:53–57
45.	Jared (Bible)	HC 3:388; D&C 107:53–57
46.	Lamech	JD 18:325
47.	Abel	JD 18:325; HC 3:388
48.	Cainan	HC 3:388; D&C 107:53–57
49.	Zelph the Lamanite	T&S 6:788

	PERSONAGE	REFERENCES
50.	Alvin Smith, Joseph Smith's deceased brother	HC 2:380
51.	Mormon	JD 17:374
52.	Paul	TPJS 180
53.	Eve	Oliver B. Huntington Diary, Part 2, 214, BYU Library
54.	Alma	JD 13:47
55.	Unnamed Angel	D&C 27 (concerning wine in sacrament
56.	Unnamed Angel	Sent to accept dedication of Temple. *Life of Heber C. Kimball*, 106; *Temples of the Most High*, 159
57.	Unnamed Angel	Visited Joseph Smith three different times and commanded him to practice polygamy—Eliza R. Snow, *Biography and Family Records of Lorenzo Snow*, 69–70
58.	"I saw many angels"	Warren Cowdery's Account of the First Vision, Joseph Smith's First Vision, 159
59.	Satan as an angel of light (and his associate)	D&C 128:20; JD 3:229–30

http://rsc.byu.edu/archived/joseph-smith-prophet-man/13-joseph-smith-gifted-learner-master-teacher-prophetic-seer

QUESTION:

129. According to George Q. Cannon, what is better than seeing a ministering angel?

    a. Seeing the gold plates
    b. Serving a mission
    c. Receiving the Holy Ghost
    d. Earning your Duty to God or Young Woman's Recognition Award

SECTION 130

BRIEF HISTORICAL BACKGROUND: Additional instructions given by Joseph Smith to the Saints on April 2, 1843, at Ramus, Illinois.

THE STORY: On a trip to Ramus, Joseph Smith traveled with Orson Hyde and William Clayton. William Clayton joined the Church in England in 1837 and emigrated to Nauvoo by 1840. At this point, he acted as the Prophet's scribe and entrusted to store the most important records of the Church.

THE FACT: What is known about Ramus:

Ramus, Illinois, was originally settled by Revolutionary War veteran Ute Perkins and his family in 1826 and lies approximately 20 miles east of Nauvoo, Illinois. At the time of its initial settlement, Ramus was referred to as the Perkins Settlement, after the Perkins family.

Joel Hills Johnson, a member of the LDS Church, moved to Carthage in early 1839 and commenced preaching the gospel in the surrounding area. Ute Perkins and many members of his family were converted and a branch of The Church of Jesus Christ of Latter-day Saints was organized on April 17, 1839, named the Crooked Creek Branch. As the area grew, the branch was reorganized by Hyrum Smith into a stake with Brother Johnson as stake president. Also around this time, the name of the area was officially changed to Ramus, a latin word meaning branch. When the town was formally incorporated in March 1843, the area was named Macedonia.

Joseph Smith made many trips to Ramus and often stayed with a close friend, Benjamin F. Johnson or one of his sisters, Sophronia or Catherine, both of whom lived in Ramus. Additionally, Joseph Smith received Doctrine and Covenants sections 130 and 131 while in Ramus.

The members of the Church in Macedonia left en masse with the exodus of the Saints who went West in 1846. After the exodus, the name of Macedonia was changed again to its present-day name of Webster.

QUESTION:

130. What did William Clayton name the odometer he invented as the Saints were crossing the plains in 1847?

    a. Mileage counter
    b. Roadometer
    c. Odometer
    d. Wheel counter

SECTION 131

BRIEF HISTORICAL BACKGROUND: Joseph Smith traveled to Ramus again to instruct the Saints. As in the first visit, he stayed at the home of Benjamin Johnson. This instruction is given May 16–17, 1843.

THE STORY: The following is Benjamin Johnson's conversion story:

About this time we began to hear more about the "Golden Bible" that had been found by "Joe Smith" the "money digger," etc., etc. My elder brother, David, having gone to visit Joel H. in Amherst, Ohio, had remained there until the next season, in the spring of which the first elders, going from Kirtland to Missouri, stopped and raised up a large branch of the Church into which both of my brothers were baptized. Previous to this, rumors had come from Ohio of the spread of what was called "Campbellism," a new sect, of which Sidney Rigdon was then the chief apostle, and through fear that my brothers would become deluded by the new doctrines, my mother had written a letter of caution to them, which was soon answered to say that they had both joined the "Mormonites" (then so called), believers in the Prophet Joseph Smith and the Book of Mormon or "Golden Bible." This news came upon us almost as a horror and a disgrace. The first news was soon followed by the Book of Mormon, accompanied by a lengthy explanation, on the receipt of which my mother, brother Seth, sister Nancy, and Lyman R. Sherman, with some of the neighbors, all devoted to religion, would meet together secretly to read the Book of Mormon and accompanying letter, or perhaps to deplore the delusion into which my brothers had fallen. But their reading soon led to marveling at the simplicity and purity of what they read, and at the spirit which accompanied it, bearing witness to its truth. After a few days of secrecy I was permitted to meet with them, to hear it read, being then 13 years of age; and in listening, a feeling of the most intense anxiety came over me to learn more. It seemed as if I must hear it all before I could be satisfied; and the principle of faith began to spring up in my heart to believe it. This was in the early fall of 1831. Now a bright hope began to arise in my heart that there really was a living prophet on the earth, and my greatest fear was that it would not prove true.

Later in the fall my brothers came from Ohio to see us and bear their testimony, and were accompanied by Almon W. Babbitt, then not seventeen years of age. They bore a faithful testimony, but neither of them seemed capable of teaching in a public capacity. As a family we were being converted to the truth, when unexpectedly there came to us Elders James Brackinbury and Jabez Durfee. Elder Brackinbury was a capable man and a great reasoner, and the Spirit of the Lord rested mightily upon him, confirming the words we had already received. My mother, and Lyman R. Sherman, my brother-in-law, were soon baptized, shortly followed by the baptism of all my brothers and sisters who had attained their majority. At this time my father was employed upon job work as a canter in Fredonia and not being inclined to accept the gospel, would not permit us minor children to receive our baptism. My mother, brothers, sisters, brother-in-law and neighbors who were now in the church had always been esteemed among the most eminent in religious society, and the news spreading around, the priests began to howl about Faith, Prophets, and Delusions, and to do all possible to turn us away from the truth, calling publicly for "signs," etc., asking why my sister Nancy, who then walked upon crutches, was not healed? But upon the subject of her being healed I have written more full in "Faith Promoting Series."

http://www.boap.org/LDS/Early-Saints/BFJohnson.html

THE FACT: Benjamin Johnson remembers when he was first taught the principle of plural marriage. The following is from his autobiography:

As I have alluded to the law of plural marriage [D&C 132] I will relate the time and manner in which it was taught to me.

About the first of April, 1843, the Prophet with some of the Twelve and others came to Macedonia to hold a meeting, which was to convene in a large cabinet shop owned by Brother Joseph E. and myself, and as usual he put up at my house. Early on Sunday morning he said, "Come Brother Bennie, let us have a walk." I took his arm and he led the way into a by-place in the edge of the woods surrounded by tall brush and trees. Here, as we sat down upon a log he began to tell me that the Lord had revealed to him that plural or patriarchal marriage was according to His law; and that the Lord had not only revealed it to him but had commanded him to obey it; that he was required to take other wives; and that he wanted my Sister Almira for one of them, and wished me to see and talk to her upon the subject. If a thunderbolt had fallen at my feet I could hardly have been more shocked or amazed. He saw the struggle in my mind and went on to explain. But the shock was too great for me to comprehend anything, and in almost an agony of feeling I looked him squarely in the eye, and said, while my heart gushed up before him, "Brother Joseph, this is all new to me; it may all be true—you know, but I do not. To my education it is all wrong, but I am going, with the help of the Lord to do just what you say, with this promise to you—that if ever I know you do this to degrade my sister I will kill you, as the Lord lives." He looked at me, oh, so calmly, and said, "Brother Benjamin, you will never see that day, but you shall see the day you will know it is true, and you will fulfill the law and greatly rejoice in it." And he said, "At this morning's meeting, I will preach you a sermon that no one but you will understand. And furthermore, I will promise you that when you open your mouth to your sister, it shall be filled."

http://www.boap.org/LDS/Early-Saints/BFJohnson.html

QUESTION:

131. How many members are listed in the branch at Ramus?

    a. 422
    b. 123
    c. 78
    d. 219

SECTION 132

BRIEF HISTORICAL BACKGROUND: Joseph Smith receives revelation at Nauvoo, Illinois, on July 12, 1843, in relation to eternal marriage and the new and everlasting covenant.

THE STORY: Additional information to this section:

Section 132 contains the doctrinal basis of the practice of plural marriage. Although some were distressed by it, others found plural marriage "the most holy and important doctrine ever revealed"

(W. Clayton, in A. Jensen, *Historical Record* 6:226). This revelation was recorded on July 12, 1843, in the brick store in Nauvoo. At the urging of Hyrum Smith so that Emma Smith might be convinced of its truth, the Prophet Joseph Smith dictated it sentence by sentence. Clayton reported that "after the whole was written Joseph asked me to read it through, slowly and carefully, which I did, and he pronounced it correct" (*CHC* 2:106–7). That evening, Bishop Newel K. Whitney received permission to copy the revelation. The next day, his clerk, Joseph C. Kingsbury, copied the document, which Whitney and Kingsbury proofread against the original. This copy was given to Brigham Young in March 1847; it was officially adopted as revelation at a general conference in Salt Lake City in August 1852, and was first published for public review in the *Deseret News* in September 1852.

> http://eom.byu.edu/index.php/Doctrine_and_Covenants#Sections_131-132

THE FACT:

The date in the heading of the Revelation on the Eternity of the Marriage Covenant, including the Plurality of Wives, notes the time at which the revelation was committed to writing, not the time at which the principles set forth in the revelation were first made known to the Prophet. . . . There is indisputable evidence that the revelation making known this marriage law was given to the Prophet as early as 1831. In that year, and thence intermittently up to 1833, the Prophet was engaged in a revision of the English Bible text under the inspiration of God, Sidney Rigdon in the main acting as his scribe. As he began his revision with the Old Testament, he would be dealing with the age of the Patriarchs in 1831. He was doubtless struck with the favor in which the Lord held the several Bible Patriarchs of that period, notwithstanding they had a plurality of wives. What more natural than that he should inquire of the Lord at that time, when his mind must have been impressed with the fact—Why, O Lord, didst Thou justify Thy servants, Abraham, Isaac and Jacob; as also Moses, David, and Solomon, in the matter of their having many wives and concubines (see opening paragraph of the Revelation)? In answer to that inquiry came the revelation, though not then committed to writing.

Corroborative evidences of the fact of the revelation having been given thus early in the Prophet's career are to be found in the early charges against the Church about its belief in "polygamy." For example: When the Book of Doctrine and Covenants was presented to the several quorums of the priesthood of the Church for acceptance in the general assembly of that body, the 17th of August, 1835, an article on "Marriage" was presented by W. W. Phelps, which for many years was published in the Doctrine and Covenants. It was not a revelation, nor was it presented as such to the general assembly of the priesthood. It was an article, however, that represented the views of the assembly on the subject of marriage at that time, unenlightened as they were by the revelation already given to the Prophet on the subject. What the Prophet Joseph's connection was with this article cannot be learned. Whether he approved it or not is uncertain, since he was absent from Kirtland at the time of the general assembly of the priesthood which accepted it, on a visit to the Saints in Michigan (see *History of the Church*, vol. 1, 243–53).

In this article on marriage the following sentence occurs:

"Inasmuch as this Church of Christ has been reproached with the crime of fornication and polygamy, we declare that we believe that one man should have one wife, and one woman but one husband, except in case of death, when either is at liberty to marry again."

From this it is evident that as early at least as 1835 a charge of polygamy was made against the Church. Why was that the case unless the subject of "polygamy" had been mooted within the Church? Is it not evident that some one to whom the Prophet had confided the knowledge of the revelation he had received concerning the rightfulness of plural marriage—under certain circumstances—had unwisely made some statement concerning the matter?

Again, in May, 1836, in Missouri, in a series of questions asked and answered through the Elder's Journal, the following occurs:

"Do the Mormons believe in having more wives than one?"

To which the answer is given:

"No, not at the same time."

This again represents the belief of the Saints at that time, unenlightened as they then were by the revelation received by their Prophet. But again, why this question unless there had been some agitation of the subject? Had some one before the time had come for making known this doctrine to the Church, again unwisely referred to the knowledge which had been revealed to the Prophet some seven years earlier?

All these incidents blend together and make it clearly evident that the revelation on marriage was given long before the 12th of July, 1843. Doubtless as early as 1831.

In addition to these indirect evidences is the direct testimony of the late Elder Orson Pratt, of the council of the Twelve Apostles. In 1878, in company with President Joseph F. Smith, Elder Pratt visited several states east of the Mississippi in the capacity of a missionary; and at Plano, Illinois, at a meeting of the so-called Reorganized Church of the Latter-day Saints, he was invited by the presiding officer, a Mr. Dille, and the meeting, to occupy the time, which he did. In his remarks, according to his own and his companion's report of the meeting—

Elder Pratt gave a plain, simple narration of his early experience in the Church, relating many interesting incidents connected with its rise; explained the circumstances under which several revelations were received by Joseph, the Prophet, and the manner in which he received them, he being present on several occasions of the kind. Declared [that] at such times Joseph used the Seer-stone when inquiring of the Lord, and receiving revelation, but that he was so thoroughly endowed with the inspiration of the Almighty and the spirit of revelation that he often received them without any instrument, or other means than the operation of the spirit upon his mind. Referred to the testimony which he received of the truth of the great latter-day work while yet a boy. Testified that these things were not matters of belief only with him, but of actual knowledge. He explained the circumstances connected with the coming forth of the revelation on plural marriage. Refuted the statement and belief of those present that Brigham Young was the author of that revelation; showed that Joseph Smith the Prophet had not only commenced the practice himself, and taught it to others, before President Young and the Twelve had returned from their mission in Europe, in 1841, but that Joseph actually received revelations upon that principle as early as 1831. Said "Lyman Johnson, who was very familiar with Joseph at this early date, Joseph living at his father's house, and who was also very intimate with me, we having traveled on several missions together, told me himself that Joseph had made known to him as early as 1831, that plural marriage was a correct principle. Joseph declared to Lyman that God had revealed it to him, but that the time had not come to teach or practice it in the Church, but that the time would come." To this statement Elder Pratt bore his testimony. He cited several instances of Joseph having had wives sealed to him, one at least as early as April 5th, 1841, which was some time prior to the return of the Twelve from England. Referred to his own trial in regard to this matter in Nauvoo, and said it was because he got his information from a wicked source, from those disaffected, but as soon as he learned the truth, he was satisfied.

(Signed) Orson Pratt,

(Signed) Joseph F. Smith

History of the Church, 5: xxix–xxxii

QUESTION:

132. Verses 3–6 read, "all those that have this law revealed unto them must obey the same." The Quorum of the Twelve understood this. What did Brigham say when Joseph taught him this principle?

    a. "I won't live it."
    b. "Are you sure?"
    c. "This will be the death of the Church."
    d. "It's the first time in my life I desired the grave."

SECTION 133

BRIEF HISTORICAL BACKGROUND: Revelation given to Joseph Smith at Hiram, Ohio, on November 3, 1831. Various elders inquired their responsibility and Joseph approached the Lord.

THE STORY: This revelation was given at the same conference at the John Johnson farm in Hiram, Ohio, when the ten elders present decided to collect the revelations that the Prophet had received up to this time into the Book of Commandments. It was at this conference that Joseph Smith received what would have been a revelation placed between sections 66 and 67, but instead it was called the preface to the Book of Commandments, and as such, assigned section 1. Section 133 was also received two days later at the same conference, and it was called the appendix to the Book of Commandments. It wasn't until the 1876 edition of the Doctrine and Covenants that Brigham Young assigned it a section number, no longer appearing as an appendix.

THE FACT: As mentioned earlier, the revelations were taken to Independence to be printed into the Book of Commandments. This we know never happened because the press was destroyed. If it weren't for Mary and Caroline Rollins, the revelations would also have been destroyed by the mob. What some people may not realize is that it wasn't only the two girls who helped save the revelations. A young man by the name of John Taylor (not the same John Taylor as the future president of the Church) also risked his life. He reached between the logs of the print shop and retrieved some of the revelations and was fortunate to escape before the mob noticed him and attempted to stone him.

Gerry Avant, "Books History: A tale of Mobs, Heroic Rescues," *Church News,* Dec. 30, 1984, 6

The following from Ann Scott:

[The mob] frequently searched my father's house, and were very insulting in their deportment. They also searched other houses of the Saints, including that of President Joseph Smith, who at the time was confined in Liberty Jail. Joseph's confinement in jail, coupled with the ruthless invasions of the mob, caused his scribe, Elder James Mulholland, to seek a place of safety for important church papers in his possession. Among the papers in Mulholland's keeping was the manuscript of the Inspired Translation of the Bible, the revelation on the rebellion, etc., etc. Brother Mulholland requested me to take charge of the papers, as he thought they would be more secure with me, because I was a woman, and the mob would not be likely to search my person. Immediately on taking possession of the papers, I made two cotton bags of sufficient size to contain them, sewing a band around the top ends of sufficient length to button around my waist; and I carried those papers on my person in the daytime, when the mob was around, and slept with them under my pillow at night. I cannot remember the exact length of time I had those papers in my possession; but I gave them to sister Emma Smith, the prophet's wife, on the evening of her departure for Commerce.

Emma Smith left Far West, en route to Commerce, Illinois, on February 15, 1839, and according to the report, she "wore the bags just as Ann Scott had done."

Robert J. Matthews, *Plainer Translation: Joseph Smith's Translation of the Bible, a History and Commentary* (Provo, Utah: Brigham Young University Press, 1975), 99–100

QUESTION:

133. What language, other than English, was the Doctrine and Covenants first translated into?

  a. Welsh
  b. Spanish
  c. Dutch
  d. Canadian

SECTION 134

BRIEF HISTORICAL BACKGROUND: Church leaders issued a declaration at Kirtland, Ohio, on August 17, 1835, regarding laws and governments.

THE STORY: The Church and the government have had an interesting past. The following quotations shed light on some of the Saints attitude toward the government:

John Taylor said the following:

He stated he would be a free man if he had done what "tens of thousands of others do, live in conditions of illicit love. And then if any child should result from this unsanctified union, why not follow our Christian exemplars, remove the fetal encumbrance, call in some . . . abortionist, male or female, that pollute our land? That would have been . . . genteel, fashionable, respectable, Christian-like, as Christianity goes in this generation."

Bill Harris, A New Zion (San Diego: Thunder Bay Press, 2004), 109

The following is from the autobiography of Joel Johnson:

August 23, 1879. Terrible hot and dry; the sky is a wonderful blue. No prospect of rain. In looking over the newspapers, I find the U.S. government is doing their best to stop the Saints from emigrating to Utah. They accuse all foreign Mormon emigrants of being criminals whose object in coming to the United States is to break her laws. The corruptions of the U.S. Government will soon come to an end. The sword of justice will soon drop. The government cannot bear to have one saint left in the United States. . . . . .

"Selections from Joel H. Johnson, Voice from the Mountains, Being a Testimony of the Truth of the Gospel of Jesus Christ, as Revealed by the Lord to Joseph Smith, Jr." Juvenile Instructor (1881), 3–4, 12–16

Brigham Young said the following in response to Presidents Polk's request for a 500-man battalion:

The first offer we have ever had from the government to benefit us.

James B. Allen and Glen M. Leonard, The Story of the Latter-day Saints. 2d ed. (Salt Lake City: Deseret Book, 1992)

THE FACT: When Joseph Smith decided to run for president of the United States, part of his platform was to eliminate slavery by no later than 1850. How was he going to do this? The politicians at the time were most likely breathing a sigh of relief that Joseph Smith never had the opportunity to run, although I'm sure many of the American people would have been all for his plan. He was determined to buy out every slaveholder by reducing congressional pay from eight dollars to two dollars per day (this in an age when the average man worked for one dollar per day). Joseph Smith was also going to eliminate the number of members in the House of Representatives from 223 to 40. Basically two members for every one million in American population.

Arnold K. Garr, "Joseph Smith: Candidate for President of the United States," *Illinois,* edited by H. Dean Garrett, Regional Studies in Latter-day Saint Church History series (Provo, Utah: Brigham Young University, 1995), 151–68

QUESTION:

134. What one factor listed below is not only consistent with the Saints' persecution in Kirtland, but also in Independence and Nauvoo?

   a. Slavery
   b. The Lamanites
   c. Politics
   d. Polygamy

SECTION 135

BRIEF HISTORICAL BACKGROUND: A document written by John Taylor describing the events surrounding Joseph and Hyrum Smith's martyrdom, on June 27, 1844, at Carthage, Illinois.

THE STORY: Verse 3 states, "Joseph Smith, the Prophet and Seer of the Lord, has done more, save Jesus only, for the salvation of men in this world, than any other man that ever lived in it. . . . He lived great and he died great in the eyes of God and his people."

THE FACT: The testimonies of some of "his people":

President Jesse N. Smith, of Snowflake, Apache County, Arizona, was born in Stockholm, St. Lawrence County, New York, December 2, 1834, and was baptized into the Church between his eighth and ninth year, August 13, 1843. His parents had previously embraced the gospel and had joined the Saints in their first gathering place—Kirtland—in May, 1836. He first saw the Prophet in Kirtland, though he was then but a child. Afterwards he met him at Nauvoo. Of his estimate of the Prophet's character he says: he was "Incomparably the most Godlike man I ever saw." And this is his testimony of him:

I know that by nature he was incapable of lying and deceitfulness, possessing the greatest kindness and nobility of character. I felt when in his presence that he could read me through and through. I know he was all that he claimed to be.

The little incident given below is one which he recollects of the Prophet Joseph:

In 1843, for a short time, I attended a school kept by a Miss Mitchell in Hyrum Smith's brick office. Passing the Prophet's house one morning, he called me to him and asked what book I read in at my school. I replied, "The Book of Mormon." He seemed pleased, and taking me into the house he gave me a copy of the Book of Mormon to read in at school, a gift greatly prized by me.

Sister Louisa Y. Littlefield, was born in the town of Hector, Tompkins County, New York, May 1st, 1822, and was baptized into the Church at Kirtland, Ohio, in 1834. Here she first met the Prophet, of which she says, "I felt an assurance when I first beheld Joseph Smith that he was a Prophet of God." Her testimony of him is:

I can and do herein bear testimony that I knew, in 1834, when a mere child, and that now, in 1891, I still know that Joseph Smith was a Prophet of God, called and chosen to stand at the head, under Christ, of the dispensation of the fullness of times.

Of her recollections of his disposition she gives the following:

I will speak of a prominent trait of his character which was perhaps more marked in his early career than was the case after public cares and responsibilities multiplied upon him from so many sources. I mean his natural fondness for children. In Kirtland, when wagon loads of grown people and children came in from the country to meeting, Joseph would make his way to as many of the wagons as he well could and cordially shake the hand of each person. Every child and young babe in the company were especially noticed by him and tenderly taken by the hand, with his kind words and blessings. He loved innocence and purity, and he seemed to find it in the greatest perfection with the prattling child.

Elder James Worthington Phippen, whose home is in Salt Lake City, was born October 12th, 1819, in Springfield, Clark County, Ohio. He was baptized into the Church on the 3rd of February, 1839, in Fredonia, Chautauqua County, New York. Moving to Commerce, (afterwards Nauvoo) Hancock County, Illinois, with his parents he first met Joseph Smith in company with Brigham Young on the banks of the Mississippi River. Concerning the Prophet's appearance and character he says:

I was favorably impressed with his noble mien, his stately form and his pleasant, smiling face and cheerful conversation.

The testimony he gives of him is:

Before I ever saw Joseph Smith I was satisfied that he was a man inspired of God, and when I beheld him if anything further could have increased my knowledge of him being a Prophet of the Lord, I was confirmed. During my acquaintance with him from 1839 until 1844, his teachings and examples were strong proof to me of his divine calling, without the inspiration of the Lord. I was an attentive listener and observer of the teachings, sayings and example of the Prophet Joseph Smith from the first time I saw him till the month of May, 1844, at which time I left Nauvoo for the state of New York on a mission. And being quite familiar with the history of his life as written, I remember many sayings recorded that I heard him utter. In common with those who were acquainted with his public life and doings in the midst of the Saints in Nauvoo, I had great joy and satisfaction in listening to his teachings.

Elder Lyman O. Littlefield, who resides at Smithfield, Cache County, Utah, joined the Church in Clay County, Missouri, being baptized by Peter Whitmer, in 1834. He first saw the Prophet Joseph in Zion's Camp, in Missouri, that same year. Concerning his appearance he says:

I was a mere boy, between thirteen and fourteen years old, when I first met the Prophet. His appearance as a man won my reverence for him; but his conversation and public teaching—all attended by a power truly Godlike—established me in the faith and knowledge of his prophetic mission which strengthened with the lapse of years until he sealed his testimony with his blood in the jail at Carthage, in 1844.

This testimony he also bears of the Prophet:

The Spirit of the Lord had previously testified to me, in the state of Michigan, that Joseph Smith was a Prophet of God, and when I beheld him at Salt River, where Zion's Camp was resting near Brother Burget's house, the spirit of truth furnished me with an additional evidence of his divine mission. I bear my testimony that he was a Prophet of God.

Elder Thomas Cottam, whose home is in St. George, Washington County, Utah, first met the Prophet Joseph Smith, in April 1842, in Nauvoo, having emigrated there from England, his native country, where he received the gospel February 2nd, 1840. Brother Cottam states that the Prophet's appearance when he first saw him was just what he had previously conceived it to be—that of a noble, fine-looking man.

My testimony of him is that he was a true Prophet of God, raised up in this last dispensation of the fullness of times, and that his sayings and teachings are true and faithful, and that he sealed his testimony with his blood.

Of his recollections concerning this great man, he adds:

There are some things that are, as it were, engraved on my memory. One is particularly so. In Nauvoo I lived near Brother Caspar's on the creek, about a mile and a half from the temple. Accidentally going into the city on that fatal day, the 27th of June, I met Brothers Joseph and Hyrum with others of the brethren and a posse of men on their leaving Nauvoo for Carthage for the last time. His appearance and demeanor conveyed plainly to my mind that he realized he was going as a lamb to the slaughter. I should judge his feelings to be similar to that of the Savior when he uttered these memorable words: "O Jerusalem, Jerusalem, thou that killest the prophets, and stonest them which are sent unto thee, how often would I have gathered thy children together, even as a hen gathereth her chickens under her wings, and ye would not!"

As I was on guard in and around Nauvoo I did not see the bodies of our honored dead after they were brought home, but I recollect the feeling that came upon me when I just heard of their death. "Can it be possible! can it be possible!" I repeated in my mind; "well, I shall have to go back to England." But it was only temporary, for I soon realized that there would be a leader for the people. Even some of the disciples of Jesus thought momentarily that they would have to return again to their fishing.

Elder William Fawcett, now residing in St. George, Washington County, Utah, and whose native town is Malton, Yorkshire, England, where he was born December 13th, 1814, embraced the gospel on January 1st, 1840. He saw the Prophet Joseph for the first time on the 12th of April, 1843, at the steamboat landing in Nauvoo. Speaking of the Prophet's appearance and character, he says:

His appearance was that of a fine, portly gentleman, six feet high, weighing about two hundred pounds. He was pleasant and kind. His character was unimpeachable among the Saints. They loved him and he loved them.

My testimony of Joseph Smith is that he was a Prophet of the living God, and held the keys of the Holy Melchizedek Priesthood, and of the everlasting gospel to this generation; and that he saw God and His Son Jesus Christ, and talked with them, and also holy angels who ordained him to this priesthood, and talked with and called him to establish God's Church upon the earth again in our day. I know these things are true by the testimony of the Spirit given unto me.

My heart has been made glad by the sayings of the Prophet many times, in fact whenever I heard him. When Joseph was kidnapped in Dixon, his brother Hyrum called for volunteers, and I volunteered to go to rescue Joseph. I felt willing to lay down my life for him. I loved him, and have ever believed that that offering of mine was acceptable to the Lord. I recollect Joseph was preaching one day outdoors to a large congregation. When he said, "I understand that a man in the meeting has offered a thousand dollars for my head. I wonder if he will get it!" and then he kept on preaching.

Elder James Leech, who lives in Salt Lake City, relates the following incident in his experience on first meeting with the Prophet Joseph:

I was born on the 2nd of May, 1815, at Pilling Lane, Lancashire, England. About the year 1827, my parents, with their family, moved to Preston. In the year 1835 I remember waking in the night and hearing my mother, who was a very religious and good woman, relating a dream or vision she had just had to my father. In this dream it had been shown to her that the gospel was going to come to the earth again as it was in the days of our Savior.

In 1837 the gospel of Jesus Christ, as it was taught anciently, came to old England, and was first heralded in Preston by President Heber C. Kimball, Brothers Joseph Fielding, Orson Hyde and Willard Richards. My mother's dream was fulfilled to her satisfaction, and she was one of the first to embrace the gospel. My three sisters joined soon after, but my father did not do so for some time.

In the year 1841 Henry Nightingale, my sister's husband, began to prepare to gather with the Saints in Nauvoo, Illinois. My sister asked me if I would like to go with them. I said I would, but did not think I was worthy to be baptized, as I was up to the time of my hearing the gospel what people called an infidel. As my parents were willing, I came to America with them. We sailed in the early part of May, 1841.

After arriving in Nauvoo we were five or six weeks looking for employment, but failed to get any. One morning I said to my brother- in-law, "Let us go and see the Prophet. I feel that he will give us something to do." He considered a short time, then consented to go. On arriving at his house we inquired for the Prophet. We were told he was over the road. So we went over, and found him in a little store selling a lady some goods. This was the first time I had had an opportunity to be near him and get a good look at him. I felt there was a superior spirit in him. He was different to anyone I had ever met before; and I said in my heart, he is truly a Prophet of the most high God.

As I was not a member of the Church I wanted Henry to ask him for work, but he did not do so, so I had to. I said, "Mr. Smith, if you please, have you any employment you could give us both, so we can get some provisions?"

He viewed us with a cheerful countenance, and with such a feeling of kindness said, "Well, boys, what can you do?"

We told him what our employment was before we left our native land.

Said he, "Can you make a ditch?"

I replied we would do the best we could at it.

"That's right, boys," and picking up a tape line he said, "Come along with me."

He took us a few rods from the store, gave me the ring to hold, and stretched all the tape from the reel and marked a line for us to work by.

"Now, boys," said he, "can you make a ditch three feet wide and two and a half feet deep along this line?"

We said we would do our best, and he left us. We went to work, and when it was finished I went and told him it was done.

He came and looked at it and said, "Boys, if I had done it myself it could not have been done better. Now come with me."

He led the way back to his store, and told us to pick the best ham or piece of pork for ourselves. Being rather bashful, I said we would rather he would give us some. So he picked two of the largest and best pieces of meat and a sack of flour for each of us, and asked us if that would do. We told him we would be willing to do more work for it, but he said, "If you are satisfied, boys, I am."

We thanked him kindly, and went on our way home rejoicing in the kindheartedness of the Prophet of our God.

In November of the same year I was baptized into the Church, and from that time until the martyrdom of our Prophet, I often had the privilege of seeing his noble face lit up by the Spirit and power of God, as he taught the Saints the principles of eternal life.

http://www.boap.org/LDS/Early-Saints/REC-JS.html

QUESTION:

135. What did Joseph Smith prophesy to the Saints in Missouri eighteen months before they were forced to leave the state?

    a. They would return to Jackson County
    b. They would build the temple in Jackson County
    c. They would never be pushed from the state
    d. They would be forced from the state

SECTION 136

BRIEF HISTORICAL BACKGROUND: Revelation given to Brigham Young near Council Bluffs, Iowa, on January 14, 1847.

THE STORY: As Saints, we're familiar with such locations as Council Bluffs and Winter Quarters, yet, surprisingly, the Church had been settled in Iowa longer than it had in Nauvoo. The Saints established many communities on or near the Missouri River. For instance, one such community, Cutler's Park, shares this brief history.

> On August 7th or 8th, 1846, the Mormons created Nebraska's first and shortest lived planned community, complete with a governing council, and even a police force. The settlement was three to four miles to the west of present day Florence along what is now known as the Mormon Bridge Road, both east and west sides, and just south of Young Street.
>
> Approximately twenty days later (Aug 25th), about 150 Indian chiefs and braves of the Omaha/Ottawa/Chippewa and Oto/Missouri natives came to collect rent for staying on their land. Brigham Young, the leader of the Mormons (though not President of the Mormon Church at the time) met with the Indians. A war nearly broke out when the Omaha/Ottawa/Chippewa natives were offered the same rent as the Oto/Missouri natives. The Omaha/Ottawa/Chippewa natives had only been in the area since 1843 (three years earlier) but the Oto/Missouri had been in the area since the 1700s. At that point, the Church leaders made an agreement with Big Elk, chief of the Omaha nation, to live on land closer to the Missouri River. Immediately, camp was moved back to the area known now as Florence. By September 11th, 1846 Cutler's Park had been completely vacated
>
> http://winterquarters.byu.edu/pages/Nebraska.aspx#SummerQuarters

THE FACT: Verse 3 reads, "Let the companies be organized with captains of hundreds, captains of fifties, and captains of tens, with a president and his two counselors at their head, under the direction of the Twelve Apostles." According to Edson Whipple, some of these companies were organized in Bethlehem, another small Mormon community south of present-day Omaha:

> Some personal narratives make mention of Bethlehem. "I [Edson Whipple] was called to assist him [Wilford Woodruff] in visiting the saints and help gather them. I had been laboring in Maryland, where I baptized several and organized a branch of 16 members. Visiting Bro. Woodruff in Boston, I was requested to cross the plains in his company in the summer of 1850. I met him at Bethlehem, at the crossing of the Missouri river, where his company was organized with captains of tens, fifties and hundreds. I was appointed captain of fifty." After a long illness he [Russell King Homer] moved west again to a small village called Bethlehem on the east bank of the Missouri River and went into the mercantile business." The Clemens family were part of the company formed by Orson Hyde two miles from the ferry above Bethlehem with *Warren Foote* as captain." [Sophia Goodridge and others] started from Kanesville at 1:00 p.m. for Bethlehem. Rode ten miles and camped at Margarets Creek, a very beautiful shady spot. We heard the wolves howl in the night for the first time. Our horses were frightened. *8th* Saturday. Traveled seven miles, camped three miles from Bethlehem. We enjoyed ourselves very much at the last two places we camped. Had two violins in our ten . . . *14th.* Went three miles, camped at Bethlehem, had a pleasant time, some music and dancing." Subsequently about forty small settlements were founded in the same county, most of which flourished until the general removal of the Saints to Great Salt Lake Valley in 1852. Among these may be mentioned . . . *Bethlehem.*"
>
> http://winterquarters.byu.edu/pages/Mills%20County.aspx#Bethlehem

QUESTION:

136. How many Mormon communities were established close to and along the Missouri River from 1846 to 1853?

    a. 12
    b. 90
    c. 7
    d. 51

SECTION 137

BRIEF HISTORICAL BACKGROUND: Joseph Smith received a vision in the Kirtland Temple on January 21, 1836, in connection with the salvation for the dead.

THE STORY: Just prior to receiving this vision, Joseph Smith was in the upper chambers of the nearly finished Kirtland Temple along with his counselors and other Church leaders. Oil was consecrated, and all present anointed and blessed Joseph Smith Sr. to preside as the Church's patriarch.

History of the Church, 2:379–80

THE FACT: Additional information on the office of Patriarch:

On the occasion of his 100th birthday, Elder Eldred G. Smith, patriarch emeritus, is remarkable not just for being only the second former General Authority in history to attain the century mark (Elder Joseph Anderson, an emeritus General Authority, died in 1992 at age 102), but because he is a living, breathing — and healthy — vestige of a chapter in Church history.

Elder Smith, who turned 100 on Jan. 9, is the last person to have held the position of Patriarch to the Church, one that originated in 1833 with the calling of Joseph Smith Sr., the father of the Prophet Joseph Smith.

Eldred Smith is the eldest son of Hyrum Gibbs Smith, who served as Patriarch to the Church from 1912 until his death in 1932. As such, he is a great-great-grandson of Hyrum Smith.

And so it was that in 1947, when he had just recently returned home from Oak Ridge, Tenn., where he had been involved with the atomic energy project during World War II, he was called in to meet with Church President George Albert Smith. The man who had been serving as Patriarch to the Church, Joseph Fielding Smith (not to be confused with the Church president of the early 1970s) had been released due to ill health; Eldred Smith was being called to fill the position.

http://www.ldschurchnews.com/articles/50015
/Century-long-life-for-patriarch-emeritus.html

QUESTION:

137. Who gave the first patriarchal blessing in this dispensation?
    a. Joseph Smith Sr.
    b. Joseph Smith Jr.
    c. Oliver Cowdery
    d. Sidney Rigdon

SECTION 138

BRIEF HISTORICAL BACKGROUND: In Salt Lake City on October 3, 1918, President Joseph F. Smith received a vision of the Savior visiting those personages in spirit prison.

THE STORY: Additional information on this occurrence:

President Joseph F. Smith was ill during the last six months of his life and spent much of his time confined to his room. His son, Elder Joseph Fielding Smith, spent many days with him taking dictation, tending to chores for him, and taking him for rides (see Smith and Stewart, *Life of Joseph Fielding Smith,* 200). At the October conference of 1918, six weeks before his death, President Smith said:

"As most of you, I suppose, are aware, I have been undergoing a siege of very serious illness for the last five months. It would be impossible for me, on this occasion, to occupy sufficient time to express the desires of my heart and my feelings, as I would desire to express them to you, but I felt that it was my duty, if possible, to be present. . . .

". . . Although somewhat weakened in body, my mind is clear with reference to my duty, and with reference to the duties and responsibilities that rest upon the Latter-day Saints; and I am ever anxious for the progress of the work of the Lord, for the prosperity of the people of the Church of Jesus Christ of Latter-day Saints throughout the world. . . .

"I will not, I dare not, attempt to enter upon many things that are resting upon my mind this morning, and I shall postpone until some future time, the Lord being willing, my attempt to tell you some of the things that are in my mind, and that dwell in my heart. I have not lived alone these five months. I have dwelt in the spirit of prayer, of supplication, of faith and of determination; and I have had my communication with the Spirit of the Lord continuously."

In Conference Report, Oct. 1918, 2

THE FACT:

Two weeks after the general conference, Elder Joseph Fielding Smith wrote down the vision as his father dictated it to him (see Smith and Stewart, *Life of Joseph Fielding Smith,* 201). After it was endorsed by the counselors in the First Presidency and by the Quorum of the Twelve, it was published in the *Improvement Era* (Dec. 1918, 166–70).

During April conference of 1976 it was accepted as scripture and approved for publication in the Pearl of Great Price. In June 1979 the First Presidency announced that it would become section 138 of the Doctrine and Covenants

http://www.ldsces.org/inst_manuals/dc-in/manualindex.asp

QUESTION:

138. Where was Joseph F. Smith born?

    a. Far West, Missouri

    b. Kirtland, Ohio

    c. Nauvoo, Illinois

    d. Adam-ondi-Ahman, Missouri

ANSWERS

SECTION 1: (D) All of the above

SECTION 2: (C) In 1876

Brigham Young asked Elder Orson Pratt to include section 2 in the Doctrine and Covenants.

SECTION 3: (C) Thomas B. Marsh

SECTION 4: (A) 1830

The Church grew from nine (many believe this number was six—nevertheless *History of the Church* 1:77 sets this number at nine) members in 1829, prior to the organization of the Church in 1830, to 280 members at the close of 1830. This is a 3111 percent change. For the last eleven years, the percent growth has been between 2.22 to 2.94 percent, which corresponds to over 300,000 new members each year.

SECTION 5: (C) A Mormon preacher

When most of the Saints moved on—to Missouri, to Nauvoo, and to the West—Martin Harris remained in Kirtland. There he was rebaptized by a visiting missionary in 1842. In 1856 Caroline and their four children took the long journey to Utah, but Martin, then seventy-three years of age, remained on his property in Kirtland. In 1860 he told a census taker that he was a "Mormon preacher," evidence of his continuing loyalty to the restored gospel. Later he would tell a visitor, "I never did leave the Church; the Church left me" (quoted in William H. Homer Jr., "'Publish It Upon the Mountains': The Story of Martin Harris," *Improvement Era,* July 1955, 505), meaning of course that Brigham Young led the Church west and the aging Martin remained in Kirtland.

http://www.lightplanet.com/mormons/conferences/99_apr/oaks_martin.htm

SECTION 6: (D) Lyman Cowdery

About this time, the elder Joseph and Lucy met Oliver Cowdery for the first time. His brother Lyman had applied to teach school in the Manchester district and had spoken first with twenty-eight-year-old Hyrum, a trustee of the district, who called a meeting of the other trustees. They agreed to employ Lyman and settled on the terms. But, as Lucy later recalled, "the next day [Lyman] brought his brother Oliver and requested them to receive him in the place of himself." Whether because of coincidence or providence, Lyman Cowdery was unable to fulfill his obligation; Lucy remembered that business "had arisen" that would oblige him to disappoint them. Whatever this unnamed business was it set Oliver Cowdery's life on a startling new course.

Alexander L. Baugh, *Days Never to be Forgotten*
(Salt Lake City: Deseret Book, 2009), 19–20

SECTION 7: (B) 3.88 billion and 2,233 languages

Five of the books of the Bible were written by John: the Gospel of John, three epistles, and the book of Revelation. The world's most widely distributed book is the Bible, portions of which have been translated into 2,233 languages as of 2000. It has been estimated that between 1815 and 1999 some 3.88 billion Bibles were printed (see *Guinness World Records 2002*, 138). Certainly John's written prophecy has gone forth among the nations.

http://institute.lds.org/manuals/doctrine-and-covenants-institute-student-
manual/dc-in-001-7.asp

SECTION 8: (A) Joseph Knight Sr.

SECTION 9: (B) The Liahona

Attended meeting a discourse from W. W. Phelps. He related a story told him by Hyrum Smith which was as follows: Joseph, Hyrum,

Cowdery & Whitmere went to the hill Cormorah. As they were walking up the hill, a door opened and they walked into a room about 16 ft square. In that room was an angel and a trunk. On that trunk lay a book of Mormon & gold plates, Laban's sword, Aaron's brestplate.

http://maxwellinstitute.byu.edu/publications/jbms/?vol=13&num=1&id=338

SECTION 10: (C) Immediately after section 3

In 1921, B. H. Roberts and the committee responsible for publication of the 1921 edition of the Doctrine and Covenants recognized that section 10 had been misdated in previous editions, and reckoned the actual date to have been sometime in the summer of 1828, a conclusion based on *History of the Church*. The numerical order of the revelations in the Doctrine and Covenants, however, was not changed at that time. Thus, section 10 is presently out of its proper chronological order, which would place it immediately after section 3. The reader is encouraged for the sake of continuity and perspective to read the sections in that order: 3, 10, 4.

http://www.lds.net/forums/scripture-study-forum
/33286-july-09-1828-d-c-10-received.html

SECTION 11: (D) Presiding Bishop

SECTION 12: (B) 20

http://www.lds.org/ensign/1989/01/the-knight-family
-ever-faithful-to-the-prophet?lang=eng

SECTION 13: (D) 3 Nephi 11:22–26

SECTION 14: (D) All of the above

The Prophet and Oliver Cowdery arrived first, then Emma. The severe alteration of household patterns burdened Mary with more work, but David told Orson Pratt and Joseph F. Smith of a special confirmation that she received. Mary, on her way to milk the cows, met a special messenger, who said: "You have been very faithful and diligent in your labors, but you are tried because of the increase of your toil; it is proper therefore that you should receive a witness that your faith may be strengthened."

He showed her the plates and, David related, she never felt to complain at her increased labors after that. John C. Whitmer, Jacob's son, was twenty-one when his grandmother died, and heard Mary's story first-hand on "several occasions." He gave many more details; the "kind, friendly tone" of the messenger's address; her "inexpressible joy and satisfaction" on hearing his explanations; her view of the engravings as the leaves of the plates were turned one by one before her eyes. He added: "I knew my grandmother to be a good, noble and truthful woman, and I have not the least doubt of her statement in regard to seeing the plates being strictly true. She was a strong believer in the Book of Mormon until the day of her death."

Richard Lloyd Anderson, "The Whitmers: A Family That Nourished the Church," *Ensign,* August 1979, 35

SECTION 15: (A) The Book of Commandments

SECTION 16: (C) Serve as a bodyguard for Oliver Cowdery

[Early 1830] A revelation came to Joseph commanding him to see that Oliver transcribed the whole work a second time and never take both transcripts to the office . . . so that in case one was destroyed the other would be left furthermore Peter Whitmer was commanded to remain at our house to assist in guarding the writings and also to accompany Oliver to the Office and back when no other person could be spared . . .

http://saintswithouthalos.com/b/whitmer_p_jr.phtml

SECTION 17: (A) Oliver Cowdery

Oliver Cowdery returned to the Church in 1848 after having been absent from membership for ten years. He visited the Saints in Kanesville, where he was rebaptized. He hoped to travel west with the Saints, but his health failed him and he died in 1850 in Richmond, Missouri. The monument is located over his gravesite. The monument was erected in 1911 under the direction of Junius F. Wells. A metal casket within a concrete base was placed under the monument which contained copies of the History of the Church, Volume 1, the Book of Mormon, the Doctrine & Covenants, the

Pearl of Great Price, the Cowdery Family Genealogy, the Contributor, Volume 5 containing George Reynolds' "History of the Book of Mormon," and engraved portraits of Oliver Cowdery, Martin Harris, and David Whitmer. The dedication of the monument occurred on November 22, 1911 and was performed by Elder Heber J. Grant.

http://www.mormonhistoricsitesfoundation.org/USA
/missouri/richmond/threeWitnesses/complete.pdf

SECTION 18: (D) Martin Harris

SECTION 19: (A) First Sergeant

During the War of 1812, Harris enlisted and was eventually promoted to First Sergeant in the Thirty-ninth New York Militia. He was known as an honored veteran when he returned to his home.

http://www.mormonwiki.com/Martin_Harris

SECTION 20: (B) Native Americans

However, there are isolated examples of later communities finding healing through baptism; for example, Native Americans in the Great Lakes region viewed baptism by Jesuit missionaries as a healing ritual.

http://papers.ssrn.com/sol3/papers.cfm?abstract_id=1664180

SECTION 21: (B) For Joseph and Oliver to be ordained to the office of an elder in the Melchizedek Priesthood.

When Joseph and Oliver first received the Melchizedek Priesthood under the hands of Peter James, and John in June of 1829, they were not ordained to a specific office in the Priesthood. This was to be reserved for the day that the Church was organized.

http://eom.byu.edu/index.php/Organization_of_the_Church,_1830

SECTION 22: (A) The River Ribble in Preston, England

The record for the most people attending a baptism could very well be Sunday July 23, 1837, when Elder Heber C. Kimball baptized nine individuals in the River Ribble in Preston, England, in the presence of 8,000 curious bystanders.

Dan Barker, *Mormon History 101* (Springville, Utah: Cedar Fort Inc., 20110, 34; *Truth Will Prevail: The Rise of The Church of Jesus Christ of Latter-day Saints in the British Isles, 1837–1987*, edited by V. Ben Bloxham, James R. Moss, and Larry C. Porter, eds. (Cambridge: Cambridge University Press, 1987)

SECTION 23: (C) 5

When this revelation was first published in the Book of Commandments, it was divided into five parts comprising chapters 17 through 21. In all later editions, however, they were combined into one section.

http://www.ldsces.org/inst_manuals/dc-in/dc-in-021.htm

SECTION 24: (D) The mob looked right at them but did not recognize them. The following from Newell Knight's journal:

Knowing it was their duty to visit us, they called upon our Heavenly Father in mighty prayer, that he would grant them an opportunity of meeting us; that he would blind the eyes of their enemies that they might not see, and that on this occasion they might return unmolested. Their prayers were not in vain. A little distance from my house they encountered a large company of men at work upon the public road, among whom were found some of our most bitter enemies, who looked earnestly at the brethren, but not knowing them, the brethren passed on unmolested. That evening the Saints assembled and were confirmed, and partook of the sacrament. We had a happy meeting, having much reason to rejoice in the God of our salvation, and sing hosannas to His holy name.

Brian and Petrea Kelly, *Illustrated History of the Church* (American Fork, Utah: Covenant Communications Inc, 2008), 57

SECTION 25: (A) Adam-ondi-Ahman

SECTION 26: (B) 190 times

Dan Barker, *Mormon History 101* (Springville, Utah: Cedar Fort Inc., 2011), 155; David Daniell, *The Bible in English: Its History and Influence* (New Haven and London: Yale University Press, 2003)

SECTION 27: (C) Joseph and Oliver escaping court with the help of their lawyer

[Joseph Smith] said that at Colesville, New York, in 1829, he and Oliver were under arrest on a charge of deceiving the people. When they were at the justice's house for trial in the evening, all were waiting for Mr. Reid, Joseph's lawyer. While waiting, the justice asked Joseph some questions, among which was this: "What was the first miracle Jesus performed?"

Joseph replied, "He made this world, and what followed we are not told."

Mr. Reid came in and said he wanted to speak to his clients in private and that the law allowed him that privilege, he believed. The judge pointed to a door to a room in the back part of the house and told them to step in there. As soon as they got into the room, the lawyer said there was a mob outside in front of the house. "If they get hold of you they will perhaps do you bodily injury; and I think the best way for you to get out of this is to get right out there," pointing to the window and hoisting it.

They got into the woods in going a few rods from the house. It was night and they traveled through brush and water and mud, fell over logs, etc., until Oliver was exhausted. Then Joseph helped him along through the mud and water, almost carrying him.

They traveled all night, and just at the break of day Oliver gave out entirely and exclaimed, "Oh, Lord! Brother Joseph, how long have we got to endure this thing?"

They sat down on a log to rest, and Joseph said that at that very time Peter, James and John came to them and ordained them to the apostleship.

They had sixteen or seventeen miles to go to get back to Mr. Hale's, his father-in-law's, but Oliver did not complain any more of fatigue.

Hyrum L. Andrus and Helen Mae Andrus, comps., *They Knew the Prophet* (Salt Lake City: Bookcraft, 1974), 15

SECTION 28: (B) Wore it around his neck

SECTION 29: (A) Moroni 8:12

SECTION 30: (D) Frederick G. Williams

SECTION 31: (D) Quietist

> I remained in Boston several years engaged in the type foundry. During this period I became acquainted with several friends whose opinions concerning religion were like my own. We kept aloof from sectarians, and were called by them Quietists, because we resembled so much a sect in France known by that name professing to be led by the Spirit.
>
> http://saintswithouthalos.com/b/marsh_tbh.phtml

SECTION 32: (D) Lilburn W. Boggs

SECTION 33: (A) First

> I think the first church attempted to be established in opposition to "Mormonism" was that established by Wycam Clark, in Kirtland. He was baptized about the same time as Sidney Rigdon, and, in company with Northrop Sweet and four others, seceded from this Church, and said they could carry the whole world with them by preaching "Mormon" principles. They had two or three meetings; but the society would never have been known in the world, had not a few of us remembered the circumstance and told of it.
>
> http://www.gospeldoctrine.com/DoctrineandCovenants/DC%2033.htm

SECTION 34: (C) 19

The Church News, June 13, 1948

SECTION 35: (B) To Kirtland, to watch over the branch

> Before continuing their mission to the West, Oliver Cowdery and his companions sent word to Joseph Smith, "desiring him to send an elder to preside over the branch which they had raised up" in

Kirtland. The Prophet sent John Whitmer, who arrived in mid-January 1831. Upon his arrival, he found a congregation of about three hundred, more than double that previously reported. Reacting to this growth, John Whitmer wrote a letter to Joseph, "desiring his immediate assistance in Kirtland in regulating the affairs of the Church there."

https://ojs.lib.byu.edu/spc/index.php/RelEd/article/viewFile/2367/2204

SECTION 36: (A) To his relatives in Massachusetts

SECTION 37: (C) Sidney Rigdon and Edward Partridge

SECTION 38: (D) Conduct group songs and prayers

Fortunately, the specific threat concerning Joseph Smith Sr. and Hyrum Smith never materialized. However, members leaving New York encountered opposition, especially in Buffalo. When a group of Saints led by Lucy Mack Smith arrived in the town, the Colesville Saints who had preceded them warned them not to mention that they were Mormons, "for if you do, you will not get a boat nor a house." Specifically, Thomas Marsh warned her, "Now, Mother Smith, if you do sing and have prayers and acknowledge that you are Mormons here in this place, as you have done all along, you will be mobbed before morning." Nothing materialized with the mobs, in spite of Lucy's determination to "sing and attend to prayers before sunset, mob or no mob"; however, one wonders if these perceived threats in Buffalo were not based, at least in some part, on fact. The Prophet himself certainly felt that some danger lay in wait for him and his family there.

https://ojs.lib.byu.edu/spc/index.php/RelEd/article/viewFile/2367/2204

SECTION 39 & 40: (B) 5

After the dedication of the Kirtland Temple, the shout was given formally on only five occasions during the lifetime of Joseph Smith. The first was the 6 April 1837 solemn assembly at Kirtland. The second came when the cornerstones of the Far West Temple were laid on 4 July 1838, following Sidney Rigdon's fiery and politically imprudent "Salt Sermon." Elder Parley P. Pratt said: "This declaration was received with shouts of hosannah to God and the Lamb with many long cheers by the assembled thousands, who were determined to yield their rights no more, unless compelled by superior power."

The next two occurrences of the shout came in connection with the mission of the Twelve to England. Joseph Smith was not present on either occasion. The first was the anointing of John Taylor in November 1839, and the second came when Brigham Young "landed on the shore [and] gave a loud shout of hosannah." He had been confined to his berth with seasickness for the entire trip but had promised such a shout before leaving Illinois.

The last time Joseph Smith participated in a hosanna shout was 11 April 1844, two days after his last and perhaps greatest general conference where he delivered his famous King Follet sermon. Meeting with the recently organized Council of Fifty, Joseph Smith said: "had a very interesting time. The Spirit of the Lord was with us, and we closed the council with loud shouts of Hosanna!"

During the 150 years of Mormon hosanna shouts, some differences in its performance have been recorded. In the Kirtland Temple, participants gave the shout with uplifted hands, most likely with upward gestures on each word or phrase (HC 2:386-87; Woodruff 1:132-33). At the reorganization of the First Presidency in 1847, according to Norton Jacob's journal, participants struck the right fist into the palm of the left hand on each word or phrase. At the 1862 general conference, participants clapped their hands together (*Deseret News*, 15 Oct. 1862). Beginning in 1892, with the capstone laying at the Salt Lake Temple, participants waved handkerchiefs with each word or phrase (*Millennial Star* [11 July 1892]: 435; *Salt Lake Tribune*, 7 April 1892). The tradition of waving handkerchiefs has continued to the present.

http://www.dialoguejournal.com/wp-content
/uploads/sbi/articles/Dialogue_V19N03_117.pdf

SECTION 41: (C) Nathanael

D&C 41:11 And this because his heart is pure before me, for he is like unto Nathanael of old, in whom there is no guile.

SECTION 42: (A) Symonds Ryder

SECTION 43: (C) The Law of Christ

SECTION 44: (B) 1953

SECTION 45: (B) It would become the greatest power the world has ever known

"If Mormonism is able to endure, unmodified, until it reaches the third and fourth generation, it is destined to become the greatest power the world [has] ever known."

The Church News, November 16, 1991

SECTION 46: (D) 3 Nephi 18:22

"And behold, ye shall meet together oft; and ye shall not forbid any man from coming unto you when ye shall meet together, but suffer them that they may come unto you and forbid them not."

SECTION 47: (C) Book of John Whitmer

SECTION 48: (C) Kirtland, Ohio

It appears that many of the Saints in 1831 thought that the command to move to Ohio was an indication that the New Jerusalem would be there. John Whitmer spoke of this feeling when he wrote: "The time drew near for the brethren from the state of New York to arrive at Kirtland, Ohio. And some had supposed that it was the place of gathering, even the place of the New Jerusalem spoken of in the Book of Mormon, according to the visions and revelations received in the last days." ("Church History," *Journal of History,* Jan. 1908, 53.)

http://institute.lds.org/manuals/Doctrine-and-Covenants
-institute-student-Manual/dc-in-041-48.asp

SECTION 49: (B) Return the favor by serving a mission to the Mormons.

The Shakers decide to "give him union." Ashbel goes to Thompson and speaks to a meeting "in the dooryard, among the Mormons; but few of them attended. They appeared to be struck with terror and fear lest some of them might get converted."

http://saintswithouthalos.com/b/copley_l.phtml

SECTION 50: (D) John Smith

(September 1832) ordains Uncle John Smith (brother of Joseph Smith Sr.) an elder. September 10, 1832 baptizes George A. Smith (son of Uncle John) at Potsdam, New York.

SECTION 51: (A) The Columbus Ohio Temple lot

Ownership of the temple site has ties to Julia Clapp Murdock, a devoted member who lived at the time of Joseph Smith in Kirtland. On April 30, 1831, the day that Emma's twins were born and died, Julia passed away after giving birth to twins herself. Julia's husband asked the Prophet and Emma to care for the twins feeling he was unable, which somewhat softened Emma's sorrow. Julia's father, Orris, was a member of Sidney Rigdon's congregation, who eventually became embittered toward the Church and left New York for Ohio accompanied by his brother, Abner Clapp. Upon their arrival, Abner purchased the land where the temple now stands [the Columbus Temple]. Records indicate he was the land's first owner, and as far as can be ascertained, he did not share his brother's animosity toward the Church.

http://www.ldschurchtemples.com/columbus/

SECTION 52: (A) The Nauvoo School

Another indicator is the old Nauvoo School located in Deerfield. When the log schoolhouse, which had been built in 1832, became outdated, residents replaced it with a new brick school in 1879 and named it the Nauvoo School.

Laureen Gaunt, "Research and Perspective: The Pioneer Saints of Winchester, Indiana," *Ensign*, October 1992, 56.

SECTION 53: (A) Ignore a mission call from the Prophet

He lacked confidence in his ability to preach, however, and, according to some reports, he said he "would rather die than go forth to preach the Gospel to the Gentiles" (*History of the Church*, 2:118). Ironically, he later contracted cholera and died. Heber C. Kimball recorded in his journal that "the Lord took him at his word." Elder B. H. Roberts wrote of Brother Gilbert, "The remarks in the body of the history, and this expression from Elder Kimball's journal are liable to create a misunderstanding concerning Brother Algernon Sidney Gilbert, than whom the Lord has had few more devoted servants in this dispensation" (*History of the Church,* 2:118n).

http://institute.lds.org/manuals/Doctrine-and-Covenants-institute-student-Manual/dc-in-051-53.asp

SECTION 54: (B) Over 200

We usually hear of the United Order at work in Orderville, Utah; nevertheless it might surprise you when you read that there were actually over two hundred united orders established in Latter-day Saint settlements, including settlements in Idaho, Nevada, and Arizona. In the larger communities of Ogden, Provo, and Logan, more than one order was set up, with each one specializing in different production projects. Salt Lake City had a separate order for each of its twenty wards.

The Church of Jesus Christ of Latter-day Saints, *Church History In The Fulness of Times* (Salt Lake City: Published by the Church of Jesus Christ of Latter-day Saints), 404

SECTION 55: (D) Member of the High Council in Kirtland

SECTION 56: (B) A compilation of early revelations received by the Prophet

Through careful study, Joseph Smith Papers Project scholars have determined that the "Book of Commandments and Revelations" served as the principal source for the 1833 publication of a Book of Commandments and that both the "Book of Commandments and Revelations" and the "Kirtland Revelation Book" became the basis for the first edition of the Doctrine and Covenants in 1835.

http://www.lds.org/ensign/2009/07/the-joseph-smith-papers
-the-manuscript-revelation-books?lang=eng

SECTION 57: (A) Lilburn W. Boggs

Governor over the State of Missouri at the time he issued the infamous extermination order for the expulsion of the Saints.

SECTION 58: (B) William W. Phelps

The first Sabbath after our arrival in Jackson county, Brother W. W. Phelps preached to a western audience over the boundary of the United States, wherein were present specimens of all the families of the earth; Shem, Ham and Japheth; several of the Lamanites or Indians—representative of Shem; quite a respectable number of negroes—descendants of Ham; and the balance was made up of citizens of the surrounding country, and fully represented themselves as pioneers of the West. At this meeting two were baptized, who had previously believed in the fulness of the Gospel.

History of the Church, 1:190–91.

SECTION 59: (D) 20 acres

Twenty acres were purchased in 1904. A chapel, visitor center, [and now a mission home] have been built on this property.

Church Educational System, *Church History and the Fulness of Times* (Salt Lake City: The Church of Jesus Christ of Latter-day Saints, 1993), 476

SECTION 60: (C) Cain

On the sad character Cain, an interesting story comes to us from Lycurgus A. Wilson's book on the life of David W. Patten. From the book I quote an extract from a letter by Abraham O. Smoot giving his recollection of David Patten's account of meeting "a very remarkable person who had represented himself as being Cain." As I was riding along the road on my mule I suddenly noticed a very strange personage walking beside me. . . . His head was about even with my shoulders as I sat in my saddle. He wore no clothing, but was covered with hair. His skin was very dark. I asked him where he dwelt and he replied that he had no home, that he was a wanderer in the earth and traveled to and fro. He said he was a very miserable creature, that he had earnestly sought death during his sojourn upon the earth, but that he could not die, and his mission was to destroy the souls of men. About the time he expressed himself thus, I rebuked him in the name of the Lord Jesus Christ and by virtue of the Holy Priesthood, and commanded him to go hence, and he immediately departed out of my sight.

Spencer W. Kimball, *The Miracle of Forgiveness*
(Salt Lake City: Bookcraft, 1969), 127–128

SECTION 61: (D) 550

Considering the dangers facing these relatively small ships as they crossed the oceans, it is a remarkable thing to note that between 1840 and 1890, not a single vessel carrying Mormon emigrants across the Atlantic Ocean was lost at sea—not one went down in 550 voyages. This is in sharp contrast to the fact that at least 59 non-Latter-day Saint immigrant ships were lost at sea while crossing the Atlantic just between the years of 1847–53, alone.

Susan Arrington Madsen and Fred E. Woods,
I Sailed to Zion (Salt Lake City: Deseret Book, 2000), 6

SECTION 62: (C) Most likely the first man baptized in the Independence area

The elders to the Lamanites were told that they had to leave the Indian lands. They then concentrate their missionary efforts on the white settlers in the Independence area. They baptized seven individuals, including four women, Joshua Lewis, and his wife.

Parley P. Pratt, *Autobiography of Parley P. Pratt,* 4th edition
(Salt Lake City: Deseret Book, 1950), 57–58, 60

SECTION 63: (A) The Detroit Michigan Temple

Chad S. Hawkins, *The First One Hundred Temples*
(Salt Lake City: Eagle Gate, 2001), 173

SECTION 64: (C) Her servant

One of the best-known pioneer Blacks in the early Church was Green Flake, a slave of James and Agnes Flake who joined the Church in North Carolina in the winter of 1843–44. After migrating to Nauvoo, the Flakes joined the exodus west. Their servant, (the Flake slaves had been offered their freedom but three chose to stay with the family) Green Flake, was selected to accompany the Pioneer Party to the valley in 1847. When his owner died in 1850, his wife joined a group of settlers to San Bernadino. Before leaving Utah, however, she wanted to settle her tithing account and offered Green as tithing. Brigham and Heber Kimball made brief use of his labor before he moved to Union as a free man and loyal Saint.

http://www.500littleknownfacts.com/archives/448

SECTION 65: (B) When Joseph Smith stretched out her arm, perspiration began to flow, causing the cords in her arm to loosen.

When Joseph came to Kirtland his fame spread far and wide. There was a woman living in the town of Hiram, forty miles from Kirtland, who had a crooked arm, which she had not been able to use for a long period. She persuaded her husband, whose name was [John] Johnson, to take her to Kirtland to get her arm healed.

I saw them as they passed my house on their way. She went to Joseph and requested him to heal her. Joseph asked her if she believed the Lord was able to make him an instrument in healing her arm. She said she believed the Lord was able to heal her arm.

Joseph put her off till the next morning, when he met her at Brother Whitney's house. There were eight persons present, one a Methodist preacher [Ezra Booth], and one a doctor. Joseph took her by the hand, prayed in silence a moment, pronounced her arm whole, in the name of Jesus Christ, and turned and left the room.

The preacher asked her if her arm was whole, and she straightened it out and replied: "It is as good as the other." The question was then asked if it would remain whole. Joseph hearing this, answered and said: "It is as good as the other, and as liable to accident as the other."

The doctor who witnessed this miracle came to my house the next morning and related the circumstance to me. He attempted to account for it by his false philosophy, saying that Joseph took her by the hand, and seemed to be in prayer, and pronounced her arm whole in the name of Jesus Christ, which excited her arm and started perspiration, and that relaxed the cords of her arm.

Philo Dibble, in "Early Scenes in Church History,"
Four Faith Promoting Classics, (Salt Lake City: Bookcraft, 1968), 74–96

SECTION 66: (A) Deacon

Joseph Smith, *Manuscript History of the Church, Volume A-1*
See Smith, Joseph, *History, 1839–1856, Volume A–1*

SECTION 67: (A) The signing of a statement to appear at the back of the Book of Commandments that the revelations are true

Kurt Elieson, *Historical Context Of The Doctrine and Covenants*
(Dallas, Texas: Kurt Elieson, Self Published, 2011), 347–48

SECTION 68: (A) Joseph Smith Sr.

At the time when Luke Johnson was no longer a member of the Church, but a constable in the Kirtland area, he arrested Joseph Smith Sr. for what he felt was an illegal marriage. The Prophet's father appeared before a court and ordered to pay $3000 dollars or go to the penitentiary. Luke Johnson took Joseph Smith Sr. and Hyrum Smith to a back room in the building where the court session was being held and told Hyrum to get him and his dad out the window and to freedom.

Scot Facer Proctor and Maurine Jensen Proctor, ed., *The Revised and Enhanced History of Joseph Smith By His Mother* (Salt Lake City: Bookcraft, 1996), 350-52

SECTION 69: (D) $2694.70

It's possible that Oliver Cowdery and John Whitmer were carrying a major chunk of this money, or possibly all of it. Maybe now we can understand the Lord's concern that John Whitmer travel with Oliver Cowdery to safeguard the revelations and the money.

Church Educational System, *Church History in the Fulness of Times*
(Salt Lake City: The Church of Jesus Christ of Latter-day Saints, 1993), 109

SECTION 70: (C) The capstone

Conference Report, Apr. 1987, 105, 108

SECTION 71: (A) Ezra Booth

http://institute.lds.org/manuals/doctrine-and
-covenants-institute-student-manual/dc-in-071-71.asp

SECTION 72: (B) Bury them

http://www.boap.org/LDS/Early-Saints/clayton-diaries

SECTION 73: (D) The Gulf of Mexico

Wilford Woodruff's journal
    30 March 1873
    (Altar of Adam at Adam-ondi-Ahman)
    Again President Young said Joseph the Prophet told me that the garden of Eden was in Jackson Co., Missouri, & when Adam was driven out of the garden of Eden He went about 40 miles to the Place which we Named Adam Ondi Ahman, & there built an Altar of Stone & offered Sacrifice. That Altar remains to this day. I saw it as Adam left it as did many others, & through all the revolutions of the world that Altar has not been disturbed.
    Joseph also said that when the City of Enoch fled & was translated it was whare the gulf of Mexico now is. It left that gulf a body of water.

http://emp.byui.edu/marrottr/Zion-Enoch-Gulf%20of%20Mex.pdf

SECTION 74: (B) Read a chapter from the Bible and prayed

In a period of trial and persecution in 1831, he wrote of the Lord's "watchful care and loving kindness . . . day by day" and of making it a rule "wherever there was an opportunity, to read a chapter in the Bible, and pray; and these seasons of worship gave . . . great consolation."

https://www.lds.org/ensign/1997/08/
the-joseph-smith-translation-plain-and-precious-things-restored?lang=eng

SECTION 75: (C) He didn't have any at this time

http://byustudies.byu.edu/PDFLibrary
/23.4QuinnJesse-98bb9ecb-9ec1-4fe7-913e-09eefbb387c7.pdf

SECTION 76: (C) A transcript from the records of the eternal world

History of the Church 1:252–53

SECTION 77: (D) John the Baptist

  Henry Bigler heard the Prophet Joseph Smith teach the following: I heard him say to some elders going on missions, "Make short prayers and short sermons, and let mysteries alone. Preach nothing but repentance and baptism for the remission of sins, for that was all John the Baptist preached."

http://www.boap.org/LDS/Early-Saints/REC-JS.html

SECTION 78: (A) There was no longer a need to protect these individuals since all have passed on, including the persecutors

SECTION 79: (B) 95

Jared Carter, Journal, quoted in Woodford, "The Historical Development of the Doctrine and Covenants," 1006; holograph in the LDS Church History Library.

SECTION 80: (B) New Hampshire

An extract from a letter by Levi B. Wilder of Dalton, New Hampshire, states, "A small church was formed in this place in the July of 1833, consisting of 15 members: brother Stephen Burnet was the first one that sounded the glad tidings of the everlasting gospel in this place."

Susan Easton Black, *Who's Who in the Doctrine and Covenants* (Salt Lake City: Bookcraft, 1997), 39–41

SECTION 81: (D) Methodist

Robert J. Woodford, "Jesse Gause, Counselor to the Prophet," *BYU Studies,* Spring 1975, 362–64

SECTION 82: (B) Firm

http://www.splendidsun.com/wp/wp-content/uploads/2010/12/78-84.pdf

SECTION 83: (C) 18

SECTION 84: (D) Patrol Nauvoo City streets at night

> Elder Richards and I attended the deacon's meeting. The deacons have become very efficient looking after the welfare of the Saints; every part of the city is watched with the strictest care, and whatever time of night the streets are traveled, at the corner of every block a deacon is found attending to his duty.
>
> *History of the Church,* 7:399

SECTION 85: (A) Order of Enoch

> http://speeches.byu.edu/reader/reader.php?id=6126

SECTION 86: (D) Orson Pratt

> *The Church News,* June 13, 1948

SECTION 87: (C) They would experience the same devastation they handed the Saints

> Elder B. H. Roberts published a reported prophecy of Joseph Smith to Alexander Doniphan, his lawyer in Missouri. According to Doniphan's brother-in-law, writing the incident over seventy years after it occurred, Joseph Smith warned Doniphan that "'God's wrath hangs over Jackson County . . . and you will live to see the day when it will be visited by fire and sword. The fields and farms and houses will be destroyed, and only the chimneys will be left to mark the desolation.'
>
> "General Doniphan said to me," his brother-in-law continued, "that the devastation of Jackson county [during the Civil War] forcibly reminded him of this remarkable prediction." Elder Roberts cites additional descriptions of Jackson County's role during the Civil War as fulfillment of this prophecy.
>
> *History of the Church,* 1:538–59

SECTION 88: (B) Joseph Smith

The Prophet Joseph Smith started up the School of the Prophets in Kirtland, Ohio, which was the first organized school for adult education in America.

> Leonard J. Arrington, *Great Basin Kingdom: An Economic History of the Latter-day Saints, 1830–1900* (Cambridge: Harvard University Press), 245–51

SECTION 89: (A) The early 1920s

> http://fairmormon.org/Word_of_Wisdom/History_and_implementation

SECTION 90: (D) The School of the Prophets in Kirtland, Ohio

D&C 90:7–8

SECTION 91: (D) The Spirit

D&C 91:4–6

SECTION 92: (C) Sermon writer for Joseph Smith

> http://saintswithouthalos.com/b/williams_fg.phtml

SECTION 93: (A) Snoring

Horace Eldridge records: About 11 o'clock in the Evening the curiosity of the Guard was excited by some unusual noise suposed to be a mule choked. I was called up by O. P. Rockwell and Luke Johnson, and upon examination we found it to be bishop Whitney a snoring somewhat to the annoyance of some of the camp. No harm done but ended in a little sport.

> Horace Sunderlin Eldridge, Journal, March 10, 1847, Church Archives

SECTION 94: (B) A woman trying to clean his house accidentally burned them.

> http://byustudies.byu.edu/PDFLibrary
> /42.1StakerThou-a8f4b834-fa8f-4e84-87c2-f6acbd2e735b.pdf

SECTION 95: (B) James Garfield

As a boy, he became acquainted with prominent Mormon leaders Sidney Rigdon and Parley P. Pratt, had Mormon neighbors, and had LDS relatives, including Cousin John F. Boynton, who was one of the original Twelve Apostles. Later, Garfield attended functions at the Western Reserve Teachers Seminary and Kirtland Institute, which was housed in the Kirtland Temple.

Dan Barker, *Unique Stories and Facts From LDS History*
(Springville, UT: Cedar Fort, Inc., 2010), 160

SECTION 96: (C) The organization of the Relief Society

As part of the united order, in March and April 1833 the Church purchased from Peter French a farm and two businesses being operated on it. The land would be used for the temple and home sites. One of the businesses, the Peter French Tavern, served as a public house and hotel. This was the place where the Church's first printing operation in Kirtland began in December 1833. At this site, the first patriarchal blessing was given, the first Patriarch to the Church was called, and the mummies of Michael Chandler were displayed, and from it the Twelve Apostles left on their first mission. When the united order was disbanded, the building was given to John Johnson and became known as the Johnson Inn.

SECTION 97: (B) Forced to sign an agreement to leave the county

See heading to section 97

SECTION 98: (B) Lieutenant Governor Lilburn W. Boggs

My father rented a log room of Lilburn W. Boggs, the same that was afterwards governor and took an active part in driving the Saints from their homes.

http://www.boap.org/LDS/Early-Saints/EmPart.html

SECTION 99: (D) The first martyr for the gospel

http://www.gospeldoctrine.com/DoctrineandCovenants/DC%2099.htm

SECTION 100: (A) I will welcome them for your sake, but I would much rather have a nest of vipers turned loose on us.

One day in October, 1833, a wagonload of people stopped at the door of Freeman Nickerson's home. They had with them two strange men—Joseph Smith and Sidney Rigdon. Although so remote from the States, rumors of a new prophet and a "golden bible" had reached Mount Pleasant, Brunt County, Ontario, Canada, and had been wondered over and commented upon.

Freeman had been told that his parents had joined the new church, and he was rather disgusted with the news. His father was indeed full of the gospel he had embraced, and was so anxious for the eternal welfare of his sons in Canada that he had hitched up his carriage, gone on a visit to Kirtland, Ohio, and prevailed upon the Prophet Joseph Smith and Elder Sidney Rigdon to accompany him on a visit to his sons, Moses and Freeman, in Mount Pleasant.

"Well, Father," said Freeman, when told who the two strangers were, "I will welcome them for your sake. But I would just about as soon you had brought a nest of vipers and turned them loose upon us."

Moses and Freeman were wealthy merchants and men of influence in Mount Pleasant. On the evening of the arrival, after the bustle of welcome and a warm supper were over, everyone was too tired to talk, so all retired to rest.

Next morning many were the curious glances that I cast at this strange man who dared to call himself a prophet. I saw a tall, well-built form, with the carriage of an Apollo; brown hair, handsome blue eyes, which seemed to dive down to the innermost thoughts with their sharp, penetrating gaze; a striking countenance, and with manners at once majestic yet gentle, dignified yet exceedingly pleasant.

Elder Rigdon was a middle-aged man of medium height, stout and quite good-looking, but without the noble grandeur that was so distinguishing a mark of the Prophet.

The Elders were very wise. They said nothing about their views or doctrines, but waited patiently until some one should express an interest.

As evening drew near, Mr. Nickerson became anxious to hear something of the newcomer's faith.

"Oh," said he to his wife, "just let him talk; I'll silence him, if he undertakes to talk about the Bible. I guess I know as much about the scriptures as he does."

As soon as supper was over, he invited his visitors and family to go upstairs to the parlor, where he said they would have some talk. "Now Mr. Smith," he said, "I wish you and Mr. Rigdon to speak freely. Say what you wish and tell us what you believe. We will listen."

Turning to his wife, he whispered, "Now you'll see how I shall shut him up."

The Prophet commenced by relating the scenes of his early life. He told how the angel visited him, of his finding the plates and the translation of them, and gave a short account of the matter contained in the Book of Mormon.

As the speaker continued his wonderful narrative, I was listening and watching him intently. I saw his face become white and a shining glow seemed to beam from every feature.

As his story progressed, he would often allude to passages of scripture. Then Mr. Nickerson would speak up and endeavor to confound him. But the attempt was soon acknowledged even by himself to be futile.

The Prophet bore a faithful testimony that the priesthood was again restored to the earth, and that God and His Son had conferred upon him the keys of the Aaronic and Melchizedek Priesthoods. He stated that the last dispensation had come, and the words of Jesus were now in force: "Go ye into all the world and preach the gospel to every creature. He that believeth and is baptized shall be saved; but he that believeth not shall be damned."

Elder Rigdon spoke after the Prophet ceased. He related some of his early experiences, and told those present that he had received a testimony for himself of the truth of what Joseph had said. "God," said Elder Rigdon, "is no respecter of persons, but will give to all that ask of Him a knowledge of the things Joseph Smith has declared unto you, whether they are true or false, of God or of man."

After both men were through speaking, many questions were asked by all present, for information. The listeners were honest-hearted people, and when truth is told to such they are constrained to accept and believe.

"And is this, then," said Mr. Nickerson, "the curious religion the newspapers tell so much about? Why, if what you have said is not good sound sense, then I don't know what sense is."

A feeling of agreeable disappointment was felt by Mr. Nickerson and family, that these strange men were so different from the various representations of them.

Next day, notice was sent out that there would be public preaching in the Nickerson Brothers' new store-house. A large and attentive audience was present. Elder Sidney Rigdon spoke to the people with great clarity on the first principles of the gospel, and closed with a strong testimony to the truth of so-called "Mormonism."

The Prophet then arose and poured forth a golden stream of words, many of which were verily pearls without price, setting forth the restoration of the gospel and the great work that had commenced on the earth. With power he exhorted everyone who was present to seek for the truth of his and his companion's words from the source of all light, all truth, and all religion, and a knowledge of the truth of the same should surely follow.

Great was the excitement among the peaceful dwellers in Mount Pleasant.

The day following, a meeting was again held, and after it was over the Prophet baptized twelve persons, including myself, Mr. Nickerson and all of his household.

http://josephsmith.net/josephsmith/v/index.jsp?vgnextoid=6c8fd2efbece4010VgnV
CM1000004d82620aRCRD&exhibit=a81808961ece401008961ece401059340c0a_____

SECTION: 101: (C) The Battle above the Blue

http://www.mormonhistoricsitesfoundation.org/publications/studies_2007/2-
MHS_2007_Prairie-Branch-Jackson-County.pdf

SECTION 102: (D) Luke Johnson

D&C 102:3

SECTION 103: (C) Richard W. Young, nephew of Brigham Young on April 16, 1918

Richard Neitzel Holzapfel et al, *On This Day in the Church*
(Salt Lake City: Eagle Gate, 2000), 75

See also: Willard Young, son of Brigham Young, attended West Point Academy at the age of seventeen, became a commissioned officer in the US Army, and, with time, fought in the Spanish-American War.

Douglas F. Tobler and Nelson B. Wadsworth, *The History of the Mormons in Photographs and Text: 1830 to the Present* (New York: St. Martins Press, 1987), 31.

Section 104: (A) 420,000 pounds

The church helped make a house-by-house survey of unemployment in the Salt Lake district and then contributed over $12,000 in cash plus some 420,000 pounds of fruits and vegetables to be delivered to the needy in Salt Lake City during the winter of 1930.

Bruce D. Blumell, "'Remember the Poor': A History of welfare in the Church of Jesus Christ of Latter-day Saints, 1830–1980," 88, typescript, Library of the Joseph Fielding Smith Institute of Church History, Brigham Young University, Provo, Utah; *New Views of Mormon History,* edited by Davis Bitton and Maureen Ursenbach Beecher (Salt Lake City, University of Utah Press, 1987), 249

Section 105: (B) 207

Depending where you read, this number is generally between 200 and 207.

Section 106: (C) 1 and 2 Nephi

Apparently, the Prophet Joseph Smith also used proof sheets to spread the work in Harmony. Pomeroy Tucker recorded such an instance, remarking, "The first and second books of 'Nephi,' and some other portions of the forthcoming revelation were printed in sheets;—and armed with a copy of these, Smith commenced other preparations for a mission to Pennsylvania, where he had some relatives residing.

Section 107: (D) 2

Only twice did the Quorum of the Twelve Apostles undertake a quorum mission under the direction of JS. Their success in the British Isles in 1840–1841 is well known. Less well known is their first quorum mission to the eastern states in the spring and summer of 1835, shortly after the quorum was organized. The "record of the transactions of the Twelve apostles" contains the official account of that mission.

http://josephsmithpapers.org/paperSummary/record-of-the-twelve-14-february%E2%80%9328-august-1835

SECTION 108: (A) To thwart the apostates' plans of using the printing office to spread their slander toward the Prophet and the Church

> After the Prophet's flight to Missouri in early 1838, dissenters in Kirtland sought to use the printing office and materials to "bolster up a church organization opposed to the Prophet." In an attempt to curtail such action, the printing office was set on fire and destroyed. While Church leaders in Missouri presumed this act of arson to have been perpetrated by the "Parrish party," it was Lyman Sherman who started the fire to thwart Joseph's enemies.
>
> http://byustudies.byu.edu/PDFLibrary/19.1CookLyman -d25407a7-adc6-4656-962f-bf64c724b7e9.pdf

SECTION 109: (A) The Lord's House

> The early Saints referred to the Kirtland Temple as simply the "Lord's House," as the term *temple* was not in general use at the time.
>
> http://www.ldschurchtemples.com/kirtland/

SECTION 110: (D) The Jewish Passover

> On Easter Sunday, April 3, 1836, during the Jewish Passover, the Lord appeared to Joseph Smith and Oliver Cowdery in the Kirtland Temple, accepting His house. Priesthood keys were then restored through three ancient prophets: Moses, the keys to the gathering of Israel; Elias, the dispensation of the gospel of Abraham; and Elijah, the sealing keys.
>
> http://www.ldschurchtemples.com/kirtland/

SECTION 111: (A) $13,000

> http://www.gospeldoctrine.com/DoctrineandCovenants/DCindex.htm

SECTION 112: (A) The first day the gospel was preached on English soil in the first England mission

> See heading to section 112.

Section 113: (B) Calvin Coolidge

Reed Smoot related the following: The last time I visited him was shortly before his death. I sat by his bedside. We talked over conditions existing in our country, and when I was about to leave, the President said to me; "Senator, there is some plan in your Church, isn't there, where men administer to the sick and pray for them?" I said, "Yes, Mr. President. We call that administering to the sick." He said, "Can anyone in the Church administer to anyone outside of the Church?" I told him "Yes." He said, "Reed, I wish you would administer to me." I did so, and I want to say to you, my brothers and sisters, I never felt happier in my life than when I laid my hands upon him and asked God to bless him.

Reed Smoot, in Conference Report, Apr. 1939, 56.

Section 114: (C) He wasn't certain of his birth date

On February 14, 1835, Patten was chosen as one of the Twelve Apostles and was ordained the following day by Oliver Cowdery. On May 22, 1835, the Prophet Joseph Smith directed that the seniority of the Twelve be determined according to the members' ages. Patten was uncertain of his exact birth date, and Thomas B. Marsh (born 1800) was mistakenly adjudged to be the older of the two, and thus was made the President of the Quorum. [Whoever made the decision to place David second in seniority, rather than first, made the correct call. Thomas B. Marsh was born Nov. 1, 1799, whereas David Patten was born Nov. 14, 1799.]

http://eom.byu.edu/index.php/Patten,_David_W

Section 115: (D) John Whitmer

http://www.ldschurchtemples.com/farwest/

Section 116: (C) Spring Hill

See section heading to section 116.

Section 117: (D) His name has been canonized in scripture (section 117)

Critics of the LDS Church have said that the Prophet Joseph Smith gave a false prophecy in the verse quoted above because the average member of the church today has not heard of Oliver Granger. The key in understanding this scripture is to determine who is speaking and thus, who is to do the remembering. The Lord said he will remember Oliver Granger forever and ever. A secondary key is to note that Oliver Granger will be remembered "from generation to generation, forever and ever." This is the type of time frame the Lord uses to refer to dealings with him, not dealings of man. This scripture does not promise Oliver Granger he will be remembered BY generation to generation, but FROM. This key point signifies a time length, which length is the length the Lord deals with things. It never promises that the Church or even any earthly person will have a particular remembrance. This prophecy, which in my opinion is more of a statement than a foretelling, is completely fulfilled, no doubt about it. It is interesting to note, but it does not even matter, that Oliver Granger is canonized in modern LDS scripture in the verse, making it so that every member of the LDS church who reads his scriptures reads the name of Oliver Granger.

http://www.olivergranger.com/prophecy%20fullfiled.htm

SECTION 118: (B) Winston Churchill

During 1910 to 1914, the Church was severely persecuted in Great Britain, and of course received bad press. Many people in England believed that the Church was still practicing polygamy and that the Mormon elders were in their country to recruit young girls to send to Utah. It was at this time that England was on the verge of expelling all Latter-day Saints from English soil. Young Winston Churchill, displaying great courage, helped the Church's cause by invoking the right to religious freedom. No expulsions took place.

Church History in the Fulness of Times (Salt Lake City: The Church of Jesus Christ of Latter-day Saints, 1993), 471–72

SECTION 119: (B) Donation

March 15, 1887: Attended Theological class. Restoration was spoken upon. Bishop gave us to understand that no more tithing would be received. The name must be changed to donations. Wondered if the changing of the name would affect many.

This next entry may explain why the bishop wanted to change the name:

> January 29, 1888: Pres. Smoot and counselor spoke to us today. Bros. S. said that no more than 25% of the tithing was paid. We will eventually rule the nations if but 12 men remain true.

Excerpts from the journal of Douglas M. Todd Sr.

SECTION 120: (C) Honeybees

I took a tour in company with Elisha H. Groves and Francis Case on Grand River some 60 miles north, bee hunting. We were from home six weeks and got about five barrels of beautiful honey. Though it rained about one week while we were out, the richest tree we found contained 11 1/4 gallons, though I heard of 20 gallons being taken from one tree.

http://www.boap.org/LDS/Early-Saints/DOsborn.html

SECTION 121: (D) The "Prison-temple"

http://lds.org/library/display/0,4945,538-1-4543-1,00.html

SECTION 122: (A) 52

Joseph Smith Jr. ranks 52nd and Brigham Young at 74th on America's most influential personality list. This list appears in the December 2006 issue of the *Atlantic Monthly* who polled ten prominent historians to compile the inventory.

David Roberts, *Devils Gate—Brigham Young and The Great Mormon Handcart Tragedy* (New York City: Simon and Schuster, 2008), 32.

SECTION 123: (C) The Trail of Tears

In 1833, the year Jackson County citizens drove the Mormons out, Georgia officials forced the Cherokee from their lands. In 1836, sixteen thousand Cherokee walked to Oklahoma from Georgia along the Trail of Tears, their eviction enforced by seven thousand federal troops.

From 1837–38, the Chickasaw were forcibly removed from

Mississippi and Alabama. Government-enforced tribal relocations continued during the next decade

http://mormonhistoricsitesfoundation.org/publications/studies_spring_01/
MHS2.1Hartley.pdf

SECTION 124: (B) Jesus Christ

It was sent April 6, 1845.

SECTION 125: (A) The conference in which Brigham Young appeared and sounded like the Prophet Joseph Smith

Amidst the many trials the Saints faced many miracles occurred in and near Zarahemla like the Miracle of the Quail; Healings of July 22, 1839; and the prophecy of the Rocky Mountains in connection with the Saints. Even though trials had brought them there, miracles seemed to lighten their heavy loads.

http://winterquarters.byu.edu/pages/Other.aspx

SECTION 126: (D) Peritonitis, the affects of a rupture appendix

http://unicomm.byu.edu/about/brigham.aspx?content=brigham7

SECTION 127: (B) He was baptized for dead relatives

One example of this is the case of Martin Harris, one of the Three Witnesses to the Book of Mormon. On 29 August 1870, Harris arrived in Utah. During the first week of September he met with several Church leaders who instructed him concerning some of the doctrines that had been revealed since his disaffection from the Church in late 1837, including the principle of baptism for the dead. Following his own rebaptism by Edward Stevenson and reconfirmation by Orson Pratt, "he returned into the font and was baptized for several of his dead friends—fathers, grandfathers, etc. . . . [and] his sister also was baptized for the female relatives, and they were confirmed for and in behalf of those whom they were baptized for, by . . . Jos. F. Smith being mouth.

http://www.mormonhistoricsitesfoundation.org/publications/studies_
spring2002/MHS3.1Spring2002Baugh.pdf

SECTION 128: (C) Seymour Brunson

http://www.ldsces.org/inst_manuals/chrchhstryinst32502000
/chapters/chrchhstryinst32502000_23.pdf

SECTION 129: (C) Receiving the Holy Ghost

Some people think, "If I had only the ministration of an angel, it would satisfy me." Do you know that when you receive the Holy Ghost you receive something that is greater than an angel? . . . The ministering of an angel appeals to our outer senses. We see with our eyes. But we may be deceived, for Satan, it is said, is able to transform himself almost like an angel of light. But not so with the Holy Ghost. When that descends upon a man, he knows it, and the testimony which it gives cannot be taken away.

George Q. Cannon, *Gospel Truth: Discourses and Writings of President George Q. Cannon*, selected, arranged, and edited by Jerreld L. Newquist (Salt Lake City: Deseret Book., 1987), 266

SECTION 130: (B) Roadometer

An odometer called the roadometer was invented in 1847 by the Mormon pioneers crossing the plains from Missouri to Utah. The roadometer attached to a wagon wheel and counted the revolutions of the wheel as the wagon traveled. It was designed by William Clayton and Orson Pratt, and built by carpenter Appleton Milo Harmon.

Clayton had determined that 360 revolutions of a wagon wheel made a mile, [and] he then tied a red rag to the wheel and counted the revolutions to keep an accurate record of the mileage travelled. After seven days, this method became tiresome and Clayton went on to invent the roadometer, first used on the morning of May 12, 1847. William Clayton is also known for his writing of the pioneer hymn "Come, Come, Ye Saints."

"I walked some this afternoon in company with Orson Pratt and suggested to him the idea of fixing a set of wooden cog wheels to the hub of a wagon wheel, in such order as to tell the exact number of miles we travel each day. He seemed to agree with me that it could be easily done at a trifling expense."

"Brother Appleton Harmon is working at the machinery for the wagon to tell the distance we travel and expects to have it in operation tomorrow, which will save me the trouble of counting, as I have done, during the last four days."

"About noon today Brother Appleton Harmon completed the machinery on the wagon called a 'roadometer' by adding a wheel to revolve once in ten miles, showing each mile and also each quarter mile we travel, and then casing the whole over so as to secure it from the weather."—From William Clayton's Journal

http://inventors.about.com/library/inventors/bl_Odometer.htm

SECTION 131: (A) 422

http://carto.byu.edu/mormonplaces/index.php/Ramus_Branch_(IL)

SECTION 132: (D) It's the first time in my life I desired the grave

Those to whom the Prophet Joseph Smith revealed this doctrine were morally obligated to live the law. The Twelve understood this all too well—hence Brigham Young's response to the doctrine, "it was the first time in my life that I had desired the grave, and I could hardly get over it for a long time."

History of the Church, 2:103

SECTION 133: (A) Welsh

The Church has also published the Doctrine and Covenants in many languages other than English. Beginning in 1851 with the Welsh edition, the Doctrine and Covenants has been translated and published in its entirety in a score or more languages and selections from it in many others.

http://www.lightplanet.com/mormons/basic/scripture/editions.html

SECTION 134: (C) Politics

The Ohio newspapers of the early 1830s painted the "Mormonite" sect as a misdirected gaggle of idiots, lacking any reason or common sense. The fantastic religious claims of angels, revelation, and golden plates were regularly ridiculed. By 1835, however, the Mormon settlement in Kirtland had become a large well-established force at the polls. This made many nervous. If these people could believe in angels, what could be expected from them politically?

These religious impostors'. . . object is to acquire political power as fast as they can, without any regard to the means they made use of. They are ready to harness in with any party that is willing to degrade themselves by asking their assistance. They now carry nearly a majority of this township, and every man votes as directed by the prophet and his elders. Previous to the recent township elections here, it was generally understood that the Mormons and Jacksonians had agreed to share the 'spoils' equally, in consequence of which the other citizens thought it useless to attend the polls. This brought out an entire Mormon ticket which they calculated to smuggle in, independent of the "*democrats*" *n*ot under the orders of the prophet. This caused the citizens to rally and make an effort, which, by a small majority, saved the township from being governed by *revelation* for the year to come." (Ohio, *Painesville Telegraph*, Friday, April 17, 1835 from http://www.sidneyrigdon.com/dbroadhu/OH/paintel4.htm)

http://www.gospeldoctrine.com/DoctrineandCovenants/DCindex.htm

SECTION 135: (D) They would be forced from the state

On another occasion he preached and chastised the rich, or those who had money, for buying land at government price and selling it in small lots to their poor brethren at a high price. He said the Lord was not pleased with their conduct. "You say I am a Prophet. Well, then, I will prophesy, and when you go home write it down and remember it. You think you have been badly treated by your enemies; but if you don't do better than you are now doing, I prophesy that the state of Missouri will not hold you. Your sufferings have hardly commenced."

I think about eighteen months after this we all left the state.

http://www.boap.org/LDS/Early-Saints/REC-JS.html

SECTION 136: (B) 90

http://winterquarters.byu.edu/pages/settlements.htm

SECTION 137: (B) Joseph Smith Jr.

The Prophet Joseph gave the first patriarchal blessings in this dispensation. Quoting from Essentials in Church History, page 168: "While the elders were assembled in the printing office on this occasion [December 18, 1833 in Kirtland, Ohio], the Prophet [Joseph Smith] gave the first patriarchal blessings in this dispensation. It was his privilege to do this, for he held the keys of all the authority in the church, and was spoken of as the first patriarch in the Church because of this fact." Those who received blessings at this time were Oliver Cowdery, Joseph Smith Sr., Lucy Mack Smith, Hyrum Smith, Samuel Smith, and William Smith. Oliver Cowdery, who held the keys of the priesthood with Joseph, also pronounced some patriarchal blessings.

http://www.ldsfacts.net/didyou12.htm

SECTION 138: (A) Far West, Missouri

http://lds.org/churchhistory/presidents/controllers
/potcController.jsp?topic=facts&leader=6